MUSLIM-NON-MUSLIM
Marriage

The **Institute of Southeast Asian Studies (ISEAS)** was established as an autonomous organization in 1968. It is a regional centre dedicated to the study of socio-political, security and economic trends and developments in Southeast Asia and its wider geostrategic and economic environment. The Institute's research programmes are the Regional Economic Studies (RES, including ASEAN and APEC), Regional Strategic and Political Studies (RSPS), and Regional Social and Cultural Studies (RSCS).

ISEAS Publishing, an established academic press, has issued almost 2,000 books and journals. It is the largest scholarly publisher of research about Southeast Asia from within the region. ISEAS Publishing works with many other academic and trade publishers and distributors to disseminate important research and analyses from and about Southeast Asia to the rest of the world.

MUSLIM-NON-MUSLIM

Marriage

Political and Cultural Contestations in Southeast Asia

Edited by
Gavin W. Jones,
Chee Heng Leng and
Maznah Mohamad

ISEAS

INSTITUTE OF SOUTHEAST ASIAN STUDIES
SINGAPORE

First published in Singapore in 2009 by ISEAS Publishing
Institute of Southeast Asian Studies
30 Heng Mui Keng Terrace
Pasir Panjang
Singapore 119614

E-mail: publish@iseas.edu.sg
Website: <http://bookshop.iseas.edu.sg>

The responsibility for facts and opinions in this publication rests exclusively with the contributors and their interpretations do not necessarily reflect the views or the policy of the publisher or its supporters.

ISEAS Library Cataloguing-in-Publication Data

Muslim-non-Muslim marriage: political and cultural contestations in Southeast Asia / edited by Gavin Jones, Chee Heng Leng, Maznah Mohamad.

1. Interfaith marriage—Southeast Asia.
2. Marriage law—Southeast Asia.
3. Marriage—Religious aspects—Islam.
I. Jones, Gavin W.
II. Chee, Heng Leng.
III. Maznah Mohamad.
HQ1031 M98   2009

ISBN 978-981-230-874-0 (hard cover)
ISBN 978-981-230-822-1 (PDF)

Typeset by Superskill Graphics Pte Ltd
Printed in Singapore by Mainland Press Pte Ltd

CONTENTS

Preface   *vii*

The Contributors   *ix*

Glossary   *xv*

Introduction

Chapter 1   Muslim-non-Muslim Marriage,
                 Rights and the State in Southeast Asia   1
                 Chee Heng Leng, Gavin W. Jones and
                 Maznah Mohamad

SECTION I
Political and Legal Contestations

Chapter 2   Trapped between Legal Unification
                 and Pluralism: The Indonesian Supreme
                 Court's Decision on Interfaith Marriage   33
                 Ratno Lukito

Chapter 3   Private Lives, Public Contention:
                 Muslim-non-Muslim Family Disputes
                 in Malaysia   59
                 Maznah Mohamad, Zarizana Aziz and
                 Chin Oy Sim

Chapter 4   Legal Aspects of Muslim-non-Muslim
                 Marriage in Indonesia   102
                 Mark Cammack

Chapter 5   The Politico-Religious Contestation:
                 Hardening of the Islamic Law
                 on Muslim-non-Muslim Marriage
                 in Indonesia   139
                 Suhadi Cholil

                              SECTION II
                            Lived Realities

Chapter 6   "Not Muslim, not Minangkabau":
                 Interreligious Marriage and its
                 Cultural Impact in Minangkabau Society   161
                 Mina Elfira

Chapter 7   Khao Khaek: Interfaith Marriage
                 between Muslims and Buddhists in
                 Southern Thailand   190
                 Amporn Marddent

Chapter 8   Interethnic Marriages and Conversion
                 to Islam in Kota Bharu   219
                 Jolanda Lindenberg

                              SECTION III
                            Perspectives

Chapter 9   Promoting Gender Equity through
                 Interreligious Marriage: Empowering
                 Indonesian Women   255
                 Siti Musdah Mulia

Chapter 10   Muslim-non-Muslim Marriage
                 in Singapore   283
                 Noor Aisha Abdul Rahman

Index   319

PREFACE

Among the many changes sweeping Southeast Asia, trends in marriage are prominent. These include delayed marriage and increased non-marriage, and new developments in marriage across boundaries of various kinds — including the boundaries of nation states, of ethnic groups and of different religions. In September 2006, the research cluster on the changing family in Asia of the Asia Research Institute, National University of Singapore held a conference on "International Marriage, Rights and the State in Southeast and East Asia", followed by a one-day workshop on "Muslim-non-Muslim Marriage, Rights and the State in Southeast Asia". This workshop brought together researchers working on Indonesia, Malaysia, Thailand and Singapore to examine various legal, political and cultural aspects of marriage across religious boundaries — specifically marriages between Muslims and non-Muslims. In order to bring the papers from this workshop to a wider audience, revised versions of a selection of papers, supplemented by one additional paper, were prepared for publication in this book.

Although the book covers a good deal of ground, it is far from comprehensive. For example, there is no separate chapter on the Philippines. However, it is our hope that the book will open up this rather sensitive topic for wider discussion. Wider discussion is much needed, because it is clear that in a globalizing world, the frequency of cases where Muslims and non-Muslims wish to marry is likely to increase, whereas the legal situation relating to such marriages in Southeast Asia is confused and unsatisfactory.

Our thanks go to the chapter authors, who have been cooperative in following up our requests for revision. We would also like to thank Saharah Abubakar, who has provided excellent assistance in the editing of the manuscript. Finally, our thanks go to the Institute of Southeast Asian Studies, especially Mrs Triena Ong, Head of the Publications Unit, for accepting the manuscript and seeing it through to timely publication.

Gavin W. Jones
Chee Heng Leng
Maznah Mohamad

Singapore
September 2008

THE CONTRIBUTORS

Amporn Marddent is a lecturer in the Cultural Studies Programme at the Institute of Liberal Arts, Walailak University in Nakhon Si Thammarat, Thailand. She earned a Master's degree in Comparative Religion at Mahidol University in Bangkok in 2001, where she conducted research on a range of gender and sexuality research projects at the Centre for Health Policy Studies (CHPS). Amporn is currently a Ph.D. student at the department of Southeast Asian Studies at the University of Passau (Germany). Her recent publication is *Sexual Culture among Young Migrant Muslims in Bangkok* (2007).

Chee Heng Leng (Ph.D.) is Senior Research Fellow with the Changing Family in Asia Research Cluster, at the Asia Research Institute, National University of Singapore. Although her primary research area has been in the political economy of health and health care, she has maintained an interest in issues related to women and gender studies. She is now beginning to work in a research project on marriage migration.

Chin Oy Sim is currently the Executive Officer for the Malaysian Bar Council's Human Rights Committee. Until December 2007 she was a Programme Officer at Women's Aid Organization (WAO), where her work focused on the impact of civil and syariah laws on women in multi-ethnic and multi-religious Malaysia, particularly the laws that affect the rights of a wife and children when a husband converts to Islam. Her work is also related to the rights guaranteed in Malaysia's Federal Constitution, especially the freedom of belief, and the increasing trend of "Islamization" in Malaysia. She is a lawyer by training.

Gavin W. Jones is a demographer in the Asia Research Institute, National University of Singapore, where he is professor and research team leader on the Changing Family in Asia Cluster. He was formerly with the Demography and Sociology Programme at the Australian National University for twenty-eight years, serving as head of programme for an eight-year period, and conducting research mainly on Southeast Asia. His published books include *Marriage and Divorce in Islamic Southeast Asia* (1994) and a volume edited with Mehtab Karim, *Islam, the State and Population* (2005). His recent research has focused on determinants of marriage and fertility, issues of ageing, cross-boundary marriage, and urbanization.

Jolanda Lindenberg is currently a Ph.D. candidate working on identity dynamics in Belgium at the Max Planck Institute for Social Anthropology in Halle (Saale), Germany. Her M.A. thesis on interethnic marriages in Malaysia was completed at the Radboud University in Nijmegen, the Netherlands.

Mark Cammack is Professor of Law at Southwestern Law School, specializing in comparative law. He is editor with R. Michael Feener of *Islamic Law in Contemporary Indonesia: Ideas and Institutions* (2007). His articles on Islamic law in Indonesia and the Indonesian legal system have appeared in, inter alia, *The International and Comparative Law Quarterly*, *The American Journal of Comparative Law*, and *Indonesia*.

Maznah Mohamad (Ph.D.) is currently holding a joint appointment as Senior Visiting Fellow at the Asia Research Institute and the Southeast Asian Studies Programme of the National University of Singapore. She was formerly Associate Professor of Social Sciences at the University of Science, Malaysia. Among her publications are *Feminism: Malaysian Experience and Critique* (1994); *The Malay Handloom Weavers: A Study of the Rise and Decline of Traditional Manufacture* (1996); *Risking Malaysia: Culture, Politics and Identity* (co-editor, 2001) and *Feminism and the Womenís Movement in Malaysia* (co-author, 2006). Her present research is on the State and Changing Malay Marriage and Family, and the Politics of Ethnicity and Religion in Malaysia.

Mina Elfira is Associate Professor at the Faculty of Humanities, University of Indonesia. She received her M.A. from the Faculty of Arts, University of Melbourne, Australia, where she is finishing her Ph.D. programme on Gender Studies. Some of her related publications are *"Bundo Kanduang*: A Powerful or Powerless Queen? A literary analysis of *Kaba Cinduo Mato (Hikayat Nan Muda Tuanku Pagaruyung)"*, in *Jurnal Makara* 11, no. 1 (June 2007), and "Gender and Kinship, Descent Systems and Islam: In East Asia, Southeast Asia, Australia and the Pacific", in *Encyclopedia of Women and Islamic Cultures*, Volume 2, edited by Suad Joseph et al. (2005).

Noor Aisha Abdul Rahman (Ph.D.) is currently Assistant Professor at the Department of Malay Studies, National University of Singapore. Her research areas include Malay legal history and institutions, Muslim law and its administration in Singapore and Malaysia, and sociology of religion (Islam and Malay religious orientations). She authored *Colonial Image of Malay Adat Laws* (2005) and co-edited *Secularism and Spirituality: Striving for Integrated Knowledge and Success in Madrasah Education in Singapore* (2005). She has also written several articles, including

"Traditionalism and its Impact on the Administration of Justice: the Case of the *Syariah* Court of Singapore", in *Inter-Asia Cultural Studies* 5, no. 3 (December 2004), and "Changing Roles, Unchanging Perceptions and Institutions: Traditionalism and its Impact on Women and Globalization in Muslim Societies in Asia", in *The Muslim World* 97, no. 3 (July 2007): 479–507. She is currently a member of the Board of Trustees of ISEAS, and the National Heritage Board.

Ratno Lukito received his DCL (Doctor of Civil Law) from the Faculty of Law, McGill University, Montreal, in 2006, and is currently an associate professor at the State Islamic University Sunan Kalijaga, Yogyakarta, Indonesia. He is also an Indonesian director of the International Institute for Quranic Studies (IIQS), LibforAll Foundation Indonesia. His writings include "Shariah and the Politics of Pluralism in Indonesia: Understanding State Rational Choice in Legal Pluralism", *Studia Islamika* (December 2007); *Interpersonal Law in Modern Indonesia: Trapped between Pluralism and Uniformism* (Center for the Study of Law and Social Change, Yogyakarta, 2007); *Hukum Sakral dan Hukum Sekuler: Konflik dan Resolusi dalam Sistem Hukum Indonesia* (2008) and *Tradisi Hukum Indonesia* (2008).

Siti Musdah Mulia (Ph.D.) is Research Professor of The Indonesian Institute of Sciences (LIPI), and a lecturer on Islamic Political Thought in the School of Graduate Studies of Syarif Hidayatullah State Islamic University, Jakarta, Indonesia. She is the Chairperson of the Indonesian Conference on Religion for Peace, an NGO which actively promotes interfaith dialogues, pluralism and democracy for peace. She was a Senior Advisor of the Minister for Religious Affairs, and through that institution, in her capacity as the coordinator of the Team for Gender

Mainstreaming, she launched The Counter Legal Draft of the Compilation of Islamic Law. She also headed the Research Division of The Council of Indonesian Ulema (MUI) (2000–05).

Suhadi Cholil is a lecturer at the Center for Religious and Cross-cultural Studies (CRCS), Gadjah Mada University, Indonesia. He obtained his Bachelor's degree in Islamic Family Law from the State Institute for Islamic Studies (IAIN) Sunan Kalijaga Yogyakarta and his M.A. degree in interdisciplinary religious studies from Gadjah Mada University. Suhadi is currently also a Ph.D. student at Radboud University Nijmegen, Netherlands and author of *Kawin Lintas Agama Perspektif Kritik Nalar Islam* (Inter-religious Marriage in Islamic Critical Perspective, 2006).

Zarizana Abdul Aziz is a practising lawyer in Penang, Malaysia. She is actively involved in numerous human rights and women's rights activities nationally and internationally. Her primary areas of interest and expertise include issues revolving around law reform, and incorporation of international human rights standards into domestic laws. Zarizana is a director of Women Living Under Muslims Laws (WLUML), former President of the Women's Centre for Change, Malaysia, and is deputy chairperson of the Human Rights Committee of the Malaysian Bar Council.

GLOSSARY

ahl al-kitab (kitabiyah)	"People of the Book"; term used in the Qur'an to refer to Jews and Christians who, like Muslims, have scriptures recognized as having been revealed by God.
akad nikah	Sacred legal contract of marriage
faraid	Injunction, statutory portion, lawful share; action made obligatory on Muslims by Allah
fatwa	Ruling on a point of law or dogma given by a scholar who has the authority to do so
fiqh	Islamic jurisprudence
ijma	Social consensus
ijtihad	Independent judgment, based on recognized sources of Islam, on a legal or theological question (in contrast to *taqlid*, judgment based on tradition or convention)
kadi	A judge of the religious court
kafir	Infidel, non-Muslim
kaum muda	Islamic modernist movement originating in West Sumatra in the early 1900s

khalifah fi al-ardh	The vice regent of God on earth
khao khaek	Become a Muslim, in southern Thai usage
mahar	A gift, mandatory in Islam, given by the groom to the bride
mufti	In the Singapore context, the mufti is the highest religious official appointed by the President of Singapore, and chairs the Legal Committee of the Muslim Religious Council of Singapore.
musyrik	Generally refers to those who believe in more than one God
nikah	Marry; or unite; legal union of a man and woman as husband and wife
sufi	A Muslim mystic
syariah	Divine guidance as given by the Qur'an and Sunnah and includes all aspects of Islamic beliefs and practices
tasawuf	Mysticism
ulama	Islamic scholars
wali	Guardian
zauj	To pair; used in the Qur'an, along with the term nikah, as meaning to marry

Chapter 1

MUSLIM-NON-MUSLIM MARRIAGE, RIGHTS AND THE STATE IN SOUTHEAST ASIA

Chee Heng Leng, Gavin W. Jones
and Maznah Mohamad

INTRODUCTION

Marriage has never just been between two people. The academic literature on how and why this is so is voluminous. In various societies, at various times, marriages have been made to cement bonds between families, as part of business relationships, and in the case of the ruling classes, to establish diplomatic ties between countries. Levi-Strauss's classic work on marriage as constituting an exchange of women as bearers of social value in society has, of course, been variously examined, built upon, and challenged. Recent studies on international marriages in Asia, for example, are challenging the perspective that women are passive objects of exchange, positing instead that women's agency often plays a strong and decisive role in the contracting of such marriages (Constable 2005).

1

It is often the case, therefore, that marriage becomes a site of contestation — between and among individuals, families, communities, and states. In this part of the world, the example that comes easily to mind is the case of Maria Hertogh, a Dutch girl whose Catholic parents left her with a Muslim woman, Aminah Mohammed, in the chaotic circumstances of the Japanese invasion of Java in 1942. When the war ended, the Dutch parents who had returned to Holland after losing trace of Maria, searched for and found her in the Malay peninsula in late 1949, being brought up as a Muslim by Aminah. The events that ensued in Singapore witnessed the progression of a legal wrangle over adoption to full-scale riots in December 1950.[1]

The issues were complicated, notably, by the fact that Maria, at the age of thirteen, had married Mansoor Adabi, a Muslim from the state of Kelantan, under Muslim law on 1 August 1950, three days after the first set of legal actions failed to return Maria to her parents. Nevertheless, the second set of legal actions instituted by her parents, challenging the validity of the marriage while claiming custody and parental rights, was successful. The merits of the legal judgement notwithstanding, the local Malay population widely perceived it to be a dismissal of Islamic marriage law, and the issues, as cast by the Malay nationalist movement, became inextricably entangled with those of religious confrontation, Malay nationalism, and anti-colonialism (Hussin 2005).

More than half a century on, controversies surrounding religion and rights have again erupted in the region, and marriage is once again one of the intertwining variables. In Malaysia, where there is a stark division of jurisdiction in family law between civil and syariah courts, non-Muslims can only marry Muslims after conversion to Islam. This effectively means that issues of marriage and divorce are intricately mixed with issues of religious conversion.

In Indonesia, marriage between Muslims and non-Muslims used to be easy and fairly common, especially in Central Java and Yogyakarta, where local registries frequently find ways to accommodate dual religious couples wishing to marry. Even in recent times, a leading Muslim scholar of more liberal bent, Nurcholish Majid, took pride in his accommodation of interfaith marriages, solemnized in both Muslim and Christian ceremonies on the campus of his Islamic University of Paramadina. Nevertheless, the situation appears to have hardened in recent decades.

Issues of marriages between Muslims and non-Muslims, therefore, cause considerable controversy in Malaysia and Indonesia, and provide a battleground between conservative and liberal forces within Islam. The resolution of these issues in these two Muslim-majority countries are of interest to other nations, not least because Indonesia is the country with the largest Muslim population, and both are seen as potentially providing the leadership for a "moderate" Islam that could reconcile with other faiths in peaceful coexistence in these turbulent times.

Nevertheless, other countries in Southeast Asia — Singapore, Thailand, the Philippines — have significant Muslim minorities. In fact, it may be argued that the southern parts of Thailand and Philippines together with Indonesia, Malaysia, and Brunei form a coterminous Muslim-majority region that has been divided up in the course of colonial history. As they are today parts of different post-colonial nation states, cross-country comparisons of the different legal structures and social conditions within which interreligious marriages occur will provide important insights.

HISTORICAL PERSPECTIVE

In *Southeast Asia in the Age of Commerce: 1450–1680*, Anthony Reid writes of a time in Southeast Asia when people were relatively relaxed about sex, marriage, and religion. Premarital sexual relations were not prohibited, and marriages were characterized by monogamy, fidelity, and easy dissolution. Noting that religion was not a barrier to marriage, he quotes two observations of the time:

> ... in Melaka 'the infidel marries Muslim women while the Muslim takes pagans to wife' (Ibn Majid 1462, p. 206, cf. Pires 1515, p. 268); in Makassar 'Christian Men kept Mahometan women and Mahometan Men, Christian women' (Navarrete 1676, pp. 122–23) (Reid 1988, p. 155).

This began to change during the sixteenth century, however, as Christianity and Islam gained adherence, although even so, the application of the syariah was for a long time limited to the urban elites in the cities (Reid 1988, pp. 151–58).

It is not possible to trace the path by which Islamic law came to be embedded in the region in this short piece, but particularly relevant were the movements of Islamic reform beginning in the early nineteenth century, one aspect of which were efforts to establish the syariah as the foundations of polities. In Southeast Asia, the influence from this movement was increasingly felt during the late nineteenth century (Roff 1970; Milner 1981). By that time, and into the early twentieth century, a second wave of modernist reform was spreading in the Islamic world.

The late nineteenth century also saw the "forward movements" of the European colonial regimes in Southeast Asia. From their trading centres and ports, the European colonial powers expanded their scope of power and jurisdiction into the hinterlands. In many polities, they set up state bureaucracies and institutions, including colonial laws and courts, which, in many cases, added further complexity to the legal plurality that already existed. Islamic family law, however, was perpetuated, resulting in the parallel existence of the Islamic and civil laws in many states.

In the Malay peninsula, for example, the British played a major role in institutionalizing the dual legal system of civil and Islamic laws that now exists in the country. From the 1870s, the British Forward Movement progressively extended colonial rule over the Malay states. In the process of negotiation and struggle, agreements were drawn up to leave the matter of Islam and Malay customs exclusively in the hands of the Malay rulers, while all other areas of governance had to be effected in consultation with the British. As the scope of their powers decreased in all other areas, the Malay rulers increasingly turned their attention to the religious sphere to exercise their power, solidifying in each state a religious bureaucracy that is staffed by traditional religious leaders, the *ulama*.

At the turn of the twentieth century when pilgrims and students returned from the Middle East carrying with them modernist reform ideas, there was already in place an established Islamic administration and bureaucracy. The Kaum Muda, as the reformists are called, criticized the *ulama* and attacked the colonial order, but the state structures controlled by the traditional religious elites remained intact. Nevertheless, the reformers merged Islamic reform into the Malay nationalist movement, and although theirs was not the movement that ultimately held sway, their ideas continued to influence the politics of the new nation.

POST-INDEPENDENCE DEVELOPMENTS IN MALAYSIA

Although it has been argued that Islamic law was integrated into the early laws of the Malay states, in particular, the later versions of the Melaka Laws, it is also recognized that as a separate legal code, the Islamic family laws were only enacted from the very late nineteenth century onward (Badriyah 2000). As the sultan of each state is the head of the Islamic state institution, Islamic law was enacted by the sultans at different times for the different states. The Islamic family laws that were enacted were administered in an *ad hoc* manner, and to different extents, whether it was in the Straits Settlements, the Federated Malay States, or the unfederated states, by the court systems set up by the British. It was only in the 1950s and 1960s that syariah courts were set up under the jurisdiction of the religious departments in each state to administer the Islamic laws.

During the period when the new nation was being formed (the Federation of Malaya became independent in 1957 and Malaysia was formed in 1963), many states had just established syariah courts and passed various enactments for the administration of Islamic family law. The country ended up therefore having fourteen sets of Islamic family law, one each for the thirteen states, and a separate set for the Federal Territories, each administered by a separate syariah court. There have been attempts to make these fourteen sets of legislation more uniform, but to date, the effort is still continuing.

The differences in state Islamic family laws notwithstanding, contradictions arose from the parallel jurisdiction of the syariah court system at the state level and the civil court system at the federal level. There were cases in which Muslims brought marital and divorce cases for appeal to the federal court, sometimes in addition to having had their cases ruled by the syariah court; and the federal court had proceeded to judge these cases, resulting in contention over areas of jurisdiction (Noraida 2000). To address this, Article 121 of the Constitution was amended in 1988 with the intention to exclude the civil court system from having any jurisdiction over matters that are considered to be within the province of the syariah courts.

The amendment (Article 121 Clause 1A), however, does not fully resolve the contradictions, as a spate of legal cases since then testifies (Noraida 2000). Problems arise primarily when a person in an existing civil marriage converts to Islam, often for reasons such as to force a separation from the spouse, or to contract another marriage; or the other way around, when a person converts to Islam in order to contract a marriage which subsequently dissolves, and the person then wishes to leave the Islamic faith. A current controversy revolves around a woman, born a Muslim, who has petitioned to the federal court system to leave Islam. Although this case does not seem to involve marriage or divorce, the petitioner is anxious for a ruling because she wishes to contract a civil marriage with a non-Muslim. (See Maznah et al., Chapter 3 in this volume.) In Malaysia, therefore, issues of marriage, divorce, and the freedom of religious belief seem as entangled as ever (Othman 2005).

HARDENING OF ATTITUDES IN INDONESIA

After independence from Dutch colonialism, the new Indonesian government gave high priority to the replacement of the colonial legal structure (which had different legal systems for three different groups — Europeans, "foreign" orientals, and indigenous Indonesians). Marriage law reform was considered very important (Lev 1972), but proved difficult to bring about, one reason being disagreement over whether there should be a unified law or separate statutes for different ethnic or religious communities.

The draft marriage law introduced into the Indonesian legislature in 1973 was a unified marriage law in which religious affiliation was not relevant to matrimonial law. Article 11(2) stipulated that religious differences were not an obstacle to marriage. This, along with a number of other articles in the draft law, met with strong opposition from Muslim groups who wished to see state enforcement of religious doctrine. The Marriage Law finally adopted in 1974 was a compromise between those seeking reforms to prevent marriage at a very young age, arbitrary divorce, and polygamy (all of which were achieved to an extent), and those who wanted religious law to have effect (whose aims were also achieved through their insistence that these restrictions operate within a framework acknowledging standard interpretations of Islamic doctrine) (Katz and Katz 1975; Azra 2003).

The 1974 Marriage Law stated that marriage is religious in character, specifically (Elucidation, Article 2) "There is no marriage outside of the laws of the respective religions and beliefs". There have been conflicting legal interpretations of what this means (Bowen 2003, p. 183). In 1980, the Soeharto-appointed Majelis Ulama Indonesia (MUI) or Indonesian Ulama Council issued a *fatwa* against interreligious marriages. (A *fatwa* is a ruling on a point of law or dogma given by a scholar who has the authority to do so.) The *fatwa* even forbade marriage between a Muslim man and a woman of the *ahl al-kitab* ("People of the Book"), a marriage that is interpreted as being permitted in the Qur'an 5:5 and in Shafie law (Bowen 2003, p. 235).

Over time, there has been an ongoing process of judicial interpretation and executive and legislative revision and clarification. One important step was the promulgation of the Compilation of Islamic Law (CIL) as a guide for Indonesia's Islamic courts in 1991. The CIL was not enacted by the legislature, but was implemented through a Presidential Instruction. The aim of the CIL was to achieve more uniformity in the decisions of the Islamic courts. In so doing, however, the influence of conservative defenders of traditional marriage doctrines was dominant.

In 2001, the Ministry for the Empowerment of Women argued that some of the provisions of the CIL reinforced social attitudes that contribute to violence against women, particularly domestic violence. It was also claimed to be in conflict with many domestic and international laws and conventions, including the 1948 Universal Declaration on the Rights of Man and the 1990 Cairo Declaration on Human Rights in Islam. Therefore, in 2001, the Minister for Religious Affairs appointed a "Working Group for Gender Mainstreaming" to review the CIL.

The Counter Legal Draft (CLD) prepared by this Working Group, stressing as it did autonomy and choice in marriage, and the equality of men and women within marriage, was met with intense and sharply differing responses from the Muslim community. Its most important feature in the context of the present book is the authorization of marriage of Muslims and non-Muslims, based on principles of mutual respect and esteem for the right of free exercise of religion and belief. This feature, along with its constraints on polygamy, was also one that stirred the greatest controversy (Musdah Mulia 2007). Some Muslim paramilitary groups threatened acts of violence if the CLD was adopted, claiming that some of its principles are forms of secularism and liberalism (both of them highly derogatory terms in conservative Indonesian Islamic parlance). Because of concern over the polarization of Islamic opinion over the draft, the Minister for Religious Affairs announced in February 2005 that the CLD was being withdrawn from consideration.

THE PHILIPPINES AND THAILAND

There is very little written about marriage and family issues among the Muslims of the Philippines and Thailand, or on Muslim-non-Muslim marriages in the majority Muslim areas of these two countries.[2] Since 1977, Presidential Decree 1083 has provided for the application of Islamic family law to the Muslim population of the Philippines, which is an important minority, notably in the Autonomous Region of Muslim Mindanao (ARMM), where nine in ten of the 2.4 million population in 2000 were Muslims (Hooker 1984, Chapter 6). However, the application of Islamic family law must always conform to the Philippine Constitution, which is the fundamental law of the state, and the Supreme Court has the constitutional power to review on appeal the decisions of the Shari'ah District Court (Ali 2007). According to Lacar (1980, p. 20), a Maguindanao Muslim woman marrying a non-Muslim man (an action which is forbidden in syariah law) finds herself subjected to all kinds of pressures from her own kin group and by the community, although it is not possible to prevent such marriages through legal means (see also Maruhom 2003).

In southern Thailand, the accepted practice requires one partner to convert into the other's religion before marriage, though this does not always happen (see Marddent, Chapter 7 in this volume). Nishii (2007, pp. 302–03) reports that demographic, political, and economic conditions affect the incidence of intermarriage between Muslims and non-Muslims. In the west coast provinces of southern Thailand and in the city of Bangkok, where Muslims are a minority, Muslim-non-Muslim marriages occur far more frequently, and religious conversion can be in either direction. On the east coast provinces of southern Thailand where Muslims are in the majority, however, such intermarriages are infrequent, and the non-Muslim usually converts to Islam.

MARRIAGE AND CONVERSION

In both the Muslim-majority countries of Indonesia and Malaysia, the contentious issue in interreligious marriage between a Muslim and a non-Muslim revolves around the question of religious conversion. In Indonesia, the issue debated is whether or not such marriages should be allowed; in Malaysia, where they are not allowed, the primary contestation is over issues related to conversion out of Islam (the issues of freedom of the individual, and which court has jurisdiction). In Thailand and the Philippines, the main issues of the Muslim regions are those relating to poverty, marginalization, identity, autonomy, and separation. Nevertheless, insofar as Muslim and non-Muslim marriages are separately registered and recognized, the issue of religious conversion will no doubt be an important aspect of interreligious marriages at the individual level.

For a couple from different religious backgrounds contemplating marriage, the options are: one spouse can convert to the religion of the other, both can maintain separate religions, both can convert to another religion, or one or both can drop out of religious involvement. Actually, it could be that neither had much religious involvement in the first place, but the realistic options that are opened to the couple will depend very much on the legal and social context in which they are placed.

The legal requirements placed on Muslims to marry according to syariah regulations in effect imposes an asymmetrical condition — that the non-Muslim partner converts, rather than the other way around; and leads to many "conversions of convenience" by non-Muslims, as the only way to marry the person they love. This leads to complications if the marriage does not work out and the spouse who had converted wishes to leave the religion after the dissolution of the marriage.

Although the issue of religious conversion is actually independent of marriage issues, the reality is that these two sets of issues are linked for persons who wish to contract marriages across the Muslim-non-Muslim divide. There is also a gender dimension layered onto these issues. It has been observed, for example, that in Thailand, even though women play a central role in daily religious observances, they also convert out of their religion for marriage more frequently than men do (Nishii 2007, p. 303). In the case of Islam, even where the interpretation allows for interreligious marriage, it is Muslim men who can marry certain categories of non-Muslim women (the *ahl al-kitab* noted above), and not the reverse. The condition underlying this allowance is for the Muslim male head of the family to bring his wife to his religion, while it is assumed that it just cannot happen the other way around.

ONE WAY OUT?

The case of marriage laws in India is instructive. In the personal laws that govern marriages for specific religious communities, that is, Muslim, Hindu, and Christian, religious identity is treated as the paramount and primary marker of individual identity. There are no means by which parties of different religions can keep their own religious identities while being married under any particular personal law. In other words, a Hindu or Muslim marriage cannot recognize the parties as separately Hindu and Muslim (An-Na'im 2005, pp. 69, 146).

There is, however, a legal way out, for cases in which the parties to the marriage wish to retain their separate religious identities, through the Special Marriage Act 1954. This "provides a special form of marriage which can be taken advantage of by any person in India and all Indian nationals in foreign countries irrespective of the faith which either party to the marriage may profess. The parties may observe any ceremony for the solemnisation of their marriage, but certain formalities are prescribed before the marriage can be registered by the Marriage Officers" (An-Na'im 2005, p. 71).

An-Na'im notes that the Special Marriage Act has to be understood in the context of the discourse on secularism in the independent Indian state. Some thinkers in India argue that, given the importance of religious identity for the vast majority of Indians, secularism is a derivative discourse from Western political theory and both alien and inadequate to the Indian context. Others see secularism as a value that is not necessarily antithetical to expressions of religious identity. In any event, the Special Marriage Act, while enabling interreligious marriage, causes disadvantages to some taking part in such marriages; for example, Muslims married under the Special Marriage Act and their descendants cannot benefit from the Islamic Law of Succession (An-Na'im 2005, p. 71).

The provisions for Muslim and non-Muslim marriages in Singapore bear a resemblance to the Indian case. In Singapore's dual family law system, Muslims, who are a significant minority, come under the jurisdiction of the syariah court, which does not recognize marriage between a Muslim and a non-Muslim. Nonetheless, such marriages can occur under the civil law. Unlike in India, however, two Muslims cannot choose to contract a civil marriage under Singapore's laws. The civil marriage between a Muslim and a non-Muslim will not be recognized by the Syariah Court, which has its attendant consequences upon marriage dissolution or death. This could mean, for example, difficulties in resolving issues related to custody of children, alimony payments, inheritance, and burial rights.

Needless to say, this way of resolving the inherent potential conflict of a dual family law system is only open to a state that is avowedly secular. For example, in Turkey, an overwhelmingly Muslim country which has been a secular nation state since the Republican period began in 1920, the New Turkish Civil Code does not prohibit a Muslim woman from marrying a non-Muslim man, although custom strongly urges the bridegroom's prior conversion to Islam (Levy 1965). States that declare themselves Islamic, or those with a strong Islamist faction, or even governments that have to engage with strong Islamist lobbies will need to rationalize their policies according to the Islamic law that is dominant in their countries.

STATE, IDEOLOGY, AND RELIGIOUS RIGHTS

In the range of interpretations of Islamic law with regard to interreligious marriage, one may discern a position at one extreme end that absolutely forbids a Muslim from marrying a non-Muslim, and at the same time prevents Muslims from leaving the faith. Although apostasy carries with it a death sentence in a few countries, such a position is increasingly untenable in today's globalized world. To modern sensitivities, it seems extremely harsh and inhumane to restrict an individual's freedom to such an extent; even more so when the apostate is a divorced individual who had converted for the sake of marriage in the first instance. On the other hand, others argue that converts at least had a choice, but not so those born into the religion.

The argument in direct opposition to this view would be a perspective set within the framework of individual human rights. Proponents often call upon the authority of the 1948 Universal Declaration on Human Rights (UDHR), which includes the right of an individual to "freedom of thought, conscience and religion", including the "freedom to change religion or belief" (Article 18), as well as the right to enter into marriage freely (Article 16). Many Muslim countries had at one time endorsed this declaration. In recent decades, however, misgivings have been expressed that it is not compatible with Islamic law. As part of this response, the Organization of the Islamic Conference in 1990 adopted the Cairo Declaration of Human Rights in Islam which is based on the tenets of the syariah (Cairo Declaration 1990). One provision of this declaration is that "Men and women have the right to marriage, and no restrictions stemming from race, colour or nationality shall prevent them from exercising this right". Religion is notably missing from this list.

It is clear from the Cairo Declaration that the position which privileges an individual's right to freedom of religious belief over and above all else is not one that can be realistically adopted in many of the Muslim countries in current times (Kazemi 2002). From this other perspective, the human rights framed by the UDHR are individualistic and ride roughshod over the interests of the Islamic community.

In any case, aside from the question of Islam, there are basic restrictions on the freedom of religious belief both in Indonesia and Malaysia, in the sense that everyone is expected to have a religion. In both countries, state ideology on religion is clearly enunciated based on a belief in God. The Indonesian *Pancasila*, or five underlying principles, includes belief in God, and it is not only mandatory to have a religion in Indonesia, indeed it must be one of the six recognized religions: Islam, Catholicism, Christianity (by which is meant Protestantism), Hinduism, Buddhism, or Confucianism.[3] After the 1965 coup and the massacre of Communists and Communist sympathizers, anyone not claiming a religion was in danger of being branded a Communist. There was, therefore, a rush to claim one of the recognized religions on the part of those previously not espousing one, and those who were holding beliefs or practising rituals not accepted as belonging to one of the recognized religions.

In Malaysia, the national ideology is in the *Rukunegara*, a pledge of allegiance containing five principles, the first of which is belief in God. While the *Pancasila* was set forth in the preamble of the Indonesian Constitution at the time of Independence in

1945, the Malaysian *Rukunegara* only came into being after the 1969 racial riots, and is not framed in a context that is enforceable.

Nevertheless, the compulsion for an individual to declare a religion is not a subject of contestation; rather the debates that are currently taking place in both countries are centred on the question of whether the state is or should be Islamic, and what it means for the country to be Islamic. The issue has a different twist in Malaysia, because a Malay, who is accorded special privileges by virtue of ethnicity, is also defined by being Muslim. Thus for Malays to openly declare that they are not Muslim is tantamount to forsaking not only their religion, but also their ethnic identity and the privileges to which they are entitled. This double bind has its origins in the formulation of the Constitution, in which is contained the definition of a Malay (Article 160), the specification of special privileges for the Malays (Article 153), as well as the declaration that "Islam is the religion of the Federation ..." (Article 3), leading subsequently to contestation over what all these mean in totality (Fernando 2006; Puthucheary 2008).

Historians have observed that Islam as lived and practised in Southeast Asia has historically been more heterodox than either in Middle East or in South Asia (Hefner 2006). Hefner, in carving a distinction between a normative Islam as defined by its scriptures and normative commentaries, and Islam as a set of lived cultures, also points out that the Islamic resurgence in recent times has given rise to a trend towards greater orthodoxy and conformity with religious text and law in Southeast Asian countries.

In Indonesia, moves in the 1970s to recognize *aliran kebatinan* as a religion met with strong opposition from Muslim groups, as such recognition would have markedly reduced the number of Javanese officially considered to be Muslim. At that time, it was not uncommon for Indonesians to refer to themselves jokingly as *"Islam statistik"* (Muslims for census purposes) and to others as *"Islam fanatik"*, expressions which have disappeared from common parlance today with the increasing assertiveness of those who see themselves as "purifying" Indonesian Islam. Since 1997, decentralization has also led to greater autonomy for local governments, some of which have adopted Islamic laws.

In Malaysia, Islam is considered the province of state governments, and under the authority of the sultans. But since the early 1980s, the federal Islamic bureaucracy has been expanded at an accelerated pace with a federal level committee set up to upgrade and systematize the Islamic judicial and legal system (Othman et al. 2005).

It has been pointed out that the state plays a central role in the administration of Islamic law, and throughout colonial history, wherever the state allowed Islamic law to be enforced, it had always been under state supervision and had always been in parallel with secular jurisdiction (An-Na'im 2002, p. 16). In contemporary times, Islamic family law is enforced by the state, and is legally binding by virtue of state action.

On the other hand, Islamic family law is only one small part of the syariah, which encompasses a much broader set of principles and norms than purely legal matters in the modern sense. During the colonial period of the late nineteenth and early twentieth centuries, Islamic family law was removed from the broader context of syariah and applied in a large number of Muslim countries. This continued after independence, with the Islamic family law being applied and enforced within the constitutional and legal framework of the modern nation state, while its normative authority continues to be maintained on the basis of a pre-modern system. According to An-Na'im (2002, pp. 1–2), it

is the application of Islamic family law outside the broader context
of the syariah that is the source of many problems today.

MARRIAGE AND BOUNDARIES

The workshop on "Muslim-non-Muslim Marriage, Rights and the
State in Southeast Asia", which provided the genesis of this book,
was convened in Singapore in September 2006, immediately
after a two-day conference on international marriage. We had
originally problematized both Muslim-non-Muslim marriage and
international marriage in relation to boundaries, in particular,
boundaries maintained by nation states.

One may argue that marriage has always involved crossing
boundaries. Family boundaries, for example, prevented Romeo
from marrying Juliet, or Uda from marrying Dara. Some Southeast
Asian Chinese families used to make it difficult for their members
to marry across dialect groups. Marriages across ethnic boundaries
used to be, and in many instances, still are, difficult to contract.

In modern nation states, marriages that cross the boundaries
of citizenship and religion face particular difficulties. In Malaysia
and Singapore, studies on ethnic intermarriage have shown
that such marriage typically occurs within the same religious
groups: thus, Indian Muslims marrying Malays, and Chinese
and Indians marrying if they are both Christians (Hassan 1971;
Kuo and Tong 1990). The prospects for a further contraction of
the already rare interreligious marriage in Malaysia seem high,
given the basic tendency toward marital homogamy ("like
marries like"), the tendency towards stricter imposition of
exclusionary religious norms, and the hardening of attitudes
within Islam towards apostasy.

Aside from the academic challenges that these issues pose,
one may ask what other reasons we may have to desire their

resolution, considering that they are relatively infrequent. First, it should be pointed out that one reason these marriages are infrequent could be the restrictions that are placed on them. Nevertheless, apart from the anguish faced by many of those wishing to marry across religious boundaries, another reason all this matters is that intermarriage between different groups in society can be an effective way to bring greater understanding between these groups. In current times, interreligious marriage tends to be seen as a threat to religious harmony, but in Yogyakarta and Central Java, the prevalence of families with both Muslim and Christian members appears to have facilitated easy and harmonious relations between adherents of different religions and the breaking down of religious boundaries.[4] It has been argued that the region with the highest intermarriage rates also remained peaceful during the civil war in the former Yugoslavia (Varshney 2002, p. 298).

Although for those seeking to maintain the purity and transcendence of their religion, interreligious marriages may be anathema unless the other party converts, from the point of view of ethnic and religious harmony, intermarriage may be seen in a generally positive light. As we have seen, interreligious marriage is a multifaceted phenomenon which cannot be understood from a purely legalistic or human rights approach. In trying to seek resolution, we need to understand the history, culture, and politics of religions and societies.

Intermarriage then is located in the broader context of intergroup relations, and tests social boundaries; for many, religion is a crucial component in personal and group identity. Although marriage is from one perspective a private matter, it also involves society as a whole, through matters such as rights, children's welfare, property matters, and taxation. Society has erected various barriers through social, cultural, and legal institutions. Through

addressing why these barriers are there and how they are
implemented, we may find that some of them can well be
removed. This will be increasingly important where the
international migration of people is leading to societies becoming
more multicultural. Many of the controversies surrounding
marriage and religious conversion are now stuck in a quagmire,
and it would be valuable indeed if scholarly study and exchange
could somehow propel us forward in thinking around the issues.

STRUCTURE OF THE BOOK

The subsequent chapters are arranged into three sections. The
first deals with the political and legal contestations in Indonesia
and Malaysia over marriages between Muslims and non-Muslims,
the second with lived realities of interreligious marriages in three
different Southeast Asian settings, while the third provides a
platform for the exposition of two perspectives on Muslim-non-
Muslim marriage.

Political and Legal Contestations

The issue of marriages between Muslims and non-Muslims in
Indonesia and Malaysia has been a site of political and legal
contestation over many decades. The major portion of the book
is devoted to an examination of these contestations, emphasizing
the historical context, the ways these contestations have evolved,
and the roles of the different players. In both countries, issues
arise from the tension between the claims of Islamic political
parties and other groups such as the Majelis Ulama Indonesia
(MUI) in Indonesia, on the one hand, and the rights of
individuals as enshrined in the constitution of both countries,
on the other hand.

Chapter 2 focuses on the problem that the Marriage Law in
Indonesia lacks clarity on the issue of interfaith marriage, and

hence leaves unresolved issues for the state in dealing with interfaith marriage. To add to the complexity, the attitude and opinions of legal scholars on the issue show considerable diversity. While some think the Marriage Law leaves a legal vacuum on the issue, others argue that it actually forbids interfaith marriage by speaking only of marriage between adherents of the same religion. The confusion permeates into the state bureaucracy. Cases of interfaith marriage are left to be resolved through local government regulations or adjudication methods in the court. The issues are illustrated by focusing on a prominent case of interfaith marriage: Andi Vony v. State. Although it took the Supreme Court almost three years to issue a judgement on this case, the essence of the judgement was that as long as the two parties wishing to marry had the same nationality, it was the responsibility of the state to protect their basic human right to marry any other Indonesian citizen.

Legal reform in Malaysia is currently characterized by a move to accommodate the interests of the Islamic lobby in the judicial system. One of the main aspects of this move is to expand the adoption of syariah principles and infuse Islamic norms within both religious and civil courts. As discussed in Chapter 3, this, together with an environment of embedded ethnic politics, has limited the ability of the judicial system to resolve interreligious family disputes. Recent legal tussles involving interreligious relationships and Muslim-non-Muslim marriages have shown the inability of these emerging legal mechanisms to resolve inter-ethnic tensions and acrimony which have arisen out of these litigations. As will be shown in the chapter, complete resolution of the family cases described is highly improbable given that they have been left in a state of legal and political limbo. It is argued that the impairment of ethnic peace, human liberty, and private happiness has been one of the collateral damages of these ongoing contests over law reforms.

Chapter 4 returns to the debates in Indonesia, and elaborates on a number of the issues raised in Chapter 2. It discusses the heated arguments over the provisions of the 1974 Marriage Law, and notes that the failure to provide a clear direction on the issue of interreligious marriage in the Marriage Law was not a result of oversight, but reflects an impasse over the issue, and the determination of the government not to allow this impasse to prevent the law being approved. As noted above, confusion over the correct interpretation of the Marriage Law in relation to interreligious marriage led to the Andi Vony case reaching the Supreme Court. Though the judgement in this case might seem to represent a clear victory for the principle that the state's role is to protect the freedom of choice of a marriage partner, in terms of facilitating the registration of such marriages it was, in fact, a spectacular failure. The Civil Registry's role in performing interreligious marriages came under intense criticism, and in 1989, the Ministry of Home Affairs in a circular letter to provincial governors, stated that only religious marriages would receive legal recognition, and that registration by the Civil Registry must be preceded by a religious ceremony performed by appropriate religious authorities. Nevertheless, some interreligious marriages do still manage to be registered by the Civil Registry, and possibly others by the KUA, which registers all marriages based on Islamic law. This chapter concludes that although the current status with regard to interreligious marriage has the full approval of almost no one, the prospects for meaningful change are probably remote.

The hard line taken by Islamic groups on the issue of interreligious marriage is placed in context in Chapter 5, which examines the stance taken by Muhammadiyah, NU, and the MUI, and sets these in the context of the perceived "Christianization" threat in Indonesia. More recently, the chapter argues, there has been increasing debate over the issue between conservative and moderate Islamic groups, resulting from changing ideas about Islam and human rights within the last two decades.

Lived Realities

The section of the book entitled "Lived Realities" moves from political and legal contestations to a focus on the lives of those involved in interreligious marriages and those with whom they interact. The section begins with a chapter on the Minangkabau in Indonesia (Chapter 6). This chapter argues that matriliny and Islam are two key defining aspects of Minangkabau identity, although the position of Islam in relation to *adat* (localized traditional law and custom) has changed several times. Using a qualitative approach, this chapter focuses on issues facing Minangkabau women who have entered into marriages with non-Muslim men (which causes greater concern in Minangkabau society than cases of Minangkabau men marrying non-Muslim women). Aside from the opposition to such marriages common in any Islamic society, in the case of the Minangkabau there is the additional belief that such marriages may seriously impact the future of Minangkabau society. Sanctions imposed on those whose marriages were carried out according to another religion can be social, such as being excluded from the community, or material, such as loss of inheritance rights, or both. In general, leaving Islam is perceived as losing Minangkabau identity.

Chapter 7 is the one chapter dealing with southern Thailand. This chapter discusses the issues faced by the individuals and the communities concerned when religious intermarriage takes place, usually between Muslims and Buddhists. A differentiation is drawn between the "deep south" provinces of Pattani, Narathiwat, and Yala, where Malay Muslims form the majority and identity is bound up in the Malay language and customs, and the mid-southern region (provinces such as Nakhon Si Thammarat and Phuket), which provide a very different ethnic and socio-political context. Interfaith marriage seems to be on the increase throughout the south. Normally it involves the conversion of one partner, usually the non-Muslim partner. But the process of integration into the community has many elements beyond the act of conversion. The chapter discusses the many implications of becoming a *khaek* (the term used to refer to Muslims) in the southern Thai context.

The third chapter in this section (Chapter 8) explores the lived experiences of non-Muslims converting to Islam for inter-ethnic marriage in Kota Bharu, Kelantan. The experiences of these Chinese converts, and the strategies the couples employ to maintain relationships with both the Chinese and Malay families of origin, are discussed, based on a number of case studies. Many faced quite hostile reactions from family and community, requiring subtle negotiation strategies to maintain relationships with the Chinese family and community, and gain acceptance into the Muslim community. The coming of children into the marriage tends to facilitate these relationships. The chapter concludes with an ironical insight that "religion seems to connect believers across ethnic boundaries, but simultaneously, it paradoxically divides neighbours and relatives".

Perspectives

The common feature of the two chapters in this section is that they each propound a particular viewpoint of Muslim-non-Muslim marriage, and the argumentation for it. The first of these is by Dr Siti Musdah Mulia, head of the "working group for gender mainstreaming" which prepared the Counter Legal Draft for the

Ministry of Religious Affairs in Indonesia, referred to above. This draft enunciated the principles lying behind its recommendations on nineteen crucial issues, one of which was interreligious marriage. In Chapter 9, Dr Musdah Mulia gives her views on the appropriate Islamic stance on interreligious marriage, based on the need for Islam to be promoted as a humane religion. She notes that there are three Islamic positions on Muslim-non-Muslim marriage: first, that it should be forbidden, second, that it should be allowed if the non-Muslim woman is a *kitabiyah* (Jewish or Christian woman), and third, that Muslims, both men and women, should be allowed to marry non-Muslims. She presents the case for the third of these positions, which she argues is a logical consequence of the application of the noble and idealistic values of Islam in the pluralistic society of Indonesia.

Chapter 10 examines interreligious marriage involving Muslims in Singapore using a conceptual framework drawn from Mannheim's concept of styles of thought. According to the author, it is the dominance of the traditionalist style of thought within the domain of Muslim personal law in Singapore that influences attitudes towards interreligious marriage. For example, a 1991 *fatwa* enunciated by MUIS declared that relationships arising from civil marriages in which one party is a Muslim are adulterous, although alternative perceptions of marriage as a contract bound by conditions and principles exist in Muslim juristic thought. This traditionalist style of thought lacks systematic and rational justifications for the position upheld on the basis of clear principles and values of Islam. It must be conceded, though, that traditionalists have been willing to tamper with the harsh effects of these laws (for example, in putting in question the status of the child born to civil law marriages) in cases that come before them. The author discusses possible ways of curtailing some of the unwarranted effects of traditionalism, including the transfer of disputes pertaining to the status of a marriage and those ancillary to divorce, from the Syariah Court to the civil court in cases where conversion or apostasy is involved, and allowing Muslims the option of registering their marriage under the Women's Charter even in cases where both partners are Muslims.

* * * * *

With chapters ranging from the philosophical to political analysis and to empirically-based ethnographical works, this book covers a good deal of ground, but is far from comprehensive. Our hope is that by providing a dispassionate discussion of issues which frequently stir emotional responses, it will facilitate further research into the legal, theological, and personal issues that arise from the desire of individuals to marry across religious boundaries. What is certain is that in a globalizing world, the frequency of cases where Muslims and non-Muslims wish to marry are only likely to increase, and the present legal situation relating to such marriages in Southeast Asia is confused and unsatisfactory.

Notes

1. An account of this can be found in Hughes (1980). This event has also been referred to as the Nadra Tragedy (Maideen 2000), named after Maria's Muslim name.
2. An important caveat that goes with this claim is that the authors of this article only surveyed English language sources.
3. The fate of Confucianism in the panoply of Indonesian religions has been a chequered one, mirroring changing attitudes towards Chinese Indonesians; after previously being recognized, it was "de-recognized" in 1979, and re-recognized under the Abdurahman Wahid presidency (1999–2001).
4. This statement is based, not on any published evidence, but on observation and discussions over time with a number of keen

observers of social relationships in these areas (Gavin Jones' note). The long-lasting relationships created between and within families contribute to social tolerance at the grassroots level that transcends religious boundaries. One key issue is whether Muslim-Christian marriages tend to be more successful when both parties are not particularly devout, or *vice versa*.

References

Ali, Anshari P. "The Legal Impediments to the Application of Islamic Family Law in the Philippines". *Journal of Muslim Minority Affairs* 27, no. 1 (2007): 93–115.

An-Na'im, Abdullahi A., ed. *Islamic Family Law in a Changing World: A Global Resource Book*. London: Zed Books, 2002.

———. *Inter-religious Marriages among Muslims: Negotiating Religious and Social Identity in Family and Community*. New Delhi: Global Media Publications, 2005.

Azra, Azyumardi. "The Indonesian Marriage Law of 1974: An Institutionalization of the Shari'a for Social Changes". In *Shari'a and Politics in Modern Indonesia*, edited by Arskal Salim and Azyumardi Azra. Singapore: Institute of Southeast Asian Studies, 2003.

Badriyah Haji Salleh. "A History of Pre-syariah Enactments in Malaysia". In *Muslim Women and Access to Justice: Historical, Legal and Social Experience in Malaysia*, edited by Maznah Mohamad. Penang, Malaysia: Women's Crisis Centre, 2000.

Bowen, John R. *Islam, Law and Equality in Indonesia: An Anthropology of Public Reasoning*. Cambridge: Cambridge University Press, 2003.

Cairo Declaration on Human Rights in Islam, 5 August 1990, U.N. GAOR, World Conference on Human Rights, 4th Session, Agenda Item 5, U.N. Doc. A/CONF. 157/PC/62/Add.18 (1993) [English translation].

Constable, N. "Introduction: Cross-border Marriages, Gendered Mobility and Global Hypergamy". In *Cross-Border Marriages: Gender and Mobility in Transnational Asia*, edited by Nicole Constable. University of Pennsylvania: Penn Press, 2005.

Fernando, Joseph M. "The Position of Islam in the Constitution of Malaysia". *Journal of Southeast Asian Studies* 37, no. 2 (June 2006): 249–57.

Hassan, R. "Interethnic Marriage in Singapore: A Sociological Analysis". *Sociology and Social Research* 55 (1971): 305–23.

Hefner, Robert W. *Asian and Middle Eastern Islam*. Paper presented at the Conference on Islam, Islamism, and Democratic Values, organized by Foreign Policy Research Institute (FPRI), Philadelphia, the United States, History Institute, 6–7 May 2006.

Hooker, M.B. *Islamic Law in South-East Asia*. Singapore: Oxford University Press, 1984.

Hughes, T.E. *Tangled Worlds: The Story of Maria Hertogh*. Singapore: Institute of Southeast Asian Studies, 1980.

Hussin, Nordin. "Malay Press and Malay Politics: The Hertogh Riots in Singapore". *Asia Europe Journal* 3, no. 4 (2005): 561–75.

Ibn Majid, Shihab al-Din Ahmad (1462). "Al-Mal'aqiya". In *A Study of the Arabic Texts Containing Material of South-east Asia*, translated by G.R. Tibbets. Leiden and London: E.J. Brill, 1979. [As cited in Reid, A. *Southeast Asia in the Age of Commerce 1450–1680*, Volume One: "The Lands below the Winds". New Haven: Yale University Press, 1988.]

Katz, Ronald and June Katz. "The New Indonesian Marriage Law: A Mirror of Indonesia's Political, Cultural and Legal System". *American Journal of Comparative Law* 23 (1975).

Kazemi, Farouh. "Perspectives on Islam and Civil Society". In *Islamic Political Ethics: Civil Society, Pluralism and Conflict*, edited by Sohail H. Hashmi. Princeton: Princeton University Press, 2002.

Kuo, E. and C. Tong. *Religion in Singapore*. Census Monograph No. 2, Singapore, 1990.

Lacar, Luis Q. *Muslim-Christian Marriages in the Philippines*. Humanities Publication Series No. 2, Silliman University, 1980.

Lev, Daniel S. *Islamic Courts in Indonesia*. Berkeley: University of California Press, 1972.

Levy, Reuben. *The Social Structure of Islam*. London: Oxford University Press, 1965.

Maideen, Haja. *The Nadra Tragedy: The Maria Hertogh Controversy*. Petaling Jaya, Malaysia: Pelanduk Publications, 2000.

Maruhom, Norma. "Marriage: The Philippines". In *Islamic Family Law and Justice for Muslim Women*, edited by Nik Noriani Nik Badlishah. Petaling Jaya, Malaysia: Sisters in Islam, 2003.

Milner, A.C. "Islam and Malay Kingship". *Journal of the Royal Asiatic Society of Great Britain and Ireland*, no. 1 (1981): 46–70.

Musdah Mulia, Siti with Mark E. Cammack. "Toward a Just Marriage Law: Empowering Indonesian Women through a Counter Legal Draft to the Indonesian Compilation of Islamic Law". In *Islamic Law in Contemporary Indonesia: Ideas and Institutions*, edited by Michael R. Feener and M.E. Cammack. Cambridge: Harvard Law School, Islamic Legal Studies Programme, 2007.

Navarrete, Domingo (1676). *The Travels and Controversies of Friar Domingo Navarrete, 1618–1686*, translated by J. S. Cummins in two volumes. Cambridge: Hakluyt Society, 1962. [As cited in Reid, A. *Southeast Asia in the Age of Commerce 1450–1680*, Volume One: "The Lands below the Winds". New Haven: Yale University Press, 1988.]

Nishii, Ryoko. "Southeast Asia". In the section on "Religious Practices: Conversion". In *Encyclopedia of Women and Islamic Cultures, volume 5*, edited by Suad Joseph. Leiden: Brill Academic Publishers, 2007.

Noraida Endut. "Malaysia's Plural Legal System and Its Impact on Women". In *Muslim Women and Access to Justice: Historical, Legal and Social Experience in Malaysia*, edited by Maznah Mohamad. Penang, Malaysia: Women's Crisis Centre, 2000.

Othman, Norani. *Muslim Women and the Challenge of Islamic Extremism*. Kuala Lumpur: Sisters in Islam, 2005.

Pires, Tomé (1515). *The Suma Oriental of Tomé Pires*, translated by A. Cortesão in two volumes (paginated as one). London: Hakluyt Society, 1944. [As cited in A. Reid, 1988.]

Puthucheary, Mavis. "Malaysia's 'Social Contract': The Invention and Historical Evolution of an Idea". In *Sharing the Nation: Faith, Difference, Power and the State 50 years after Merdeka*, edited by N. Othman, M.C. Puthucheary, C. Kessler. Petaling Jaya: Strategic Information and Research Development Centre, 2008.

Reid, Anthony. *Southeast Asia in the Age of Commerce 1450–1680*, Volume One: "The Lands below the Winds". New Haven: Yale University Press, 1988.

Roff, William R. "Southeast Asian Islam in the Nineteenth Century". In *The Cambridge History of Islam 2*, edited by P. M. Holt et al. Cambridge: Cambridge University Press, 1970.

Varshney, Ashutosh. *Ethnic Conflict and Civic Life: Hindus and Muslims in India*. New Haven: Yale University Press, 2002.

SECTION I

POLITICAL AND
LEGAL CONTESTATIONS

Chapter 2

TRAPPED BETWEEN LEGAL UNIFICATION AND PLURALISM
The Indonesian Supreme Court's Decision on Interfaith Marriage

Ratno Lukito

INTRODUCTION

The goal of legal uniformity in Indonesia threatened to sweep away the plurality of laws that people living in this multicultural and multireligious society were familiar with. This at least appeared to be the case on paper, when the new Marriage Law (Law No. 1 of 1974) appeared to ignore a number of issues related to interpersonal relations that concerned people of different religious backgrounds. Thus, although on the basis of the constitution, religions and their values were recognized as valuable sources of family law, in practice, the Marriage Law failed to do just this. It is perhaps ironic that the state's recognition of religious pluralism did not lead to more explicit rules on how to deal with plurality in the domain of personal law. It was as if the state could only conceive of the multireligious nature of its citizens in theory, but not in practice.

One of the biggest issues in this respect was the complicated problem of interfaith marriage. This involves a marriage between two persons having different religious affiliations. For this chapter, the focus will be on marriages between Muslims and non-Muslims. This is because our interest is primarily in identifying the state's attitude towards non-state normative orderings and especially the teachings of Islamic law, given their influence on the majority Muslim population. It is also by analysing such cases of interfaith marriage that we can see how the state has been able to resolve instances of conflict among the different marital traditions.

For this reason, the discussion will be focused on seeing the arguments of the Supreme Court's judges in the conflicts of interfaith marriage brought to the court. The well known case of *Andi Vony vs. State* at the end of the 1980s will be presented specifically as one case study of interfaith marriage in society and how the state, through its justice institutions, gives its response. The background to the legal problems of that case will also be explained in order to show the real nature of the conflict in Indonesia, especially within the framework of the state's programme of legal nationalization.

THE ENIGMA OF THE NATIONAL MARRIAGE LAW

According to the Marriage Law, marriage must reflect the religious values of each party. Espousing some sort of religious belief seems even to be a *conditio sine qua non* for entering into a marital relationship. Article 2(1) of the Law clearly states that a marriage is valid only if done in accordance with the religious laws and beliefs of the parties. Marriage is thus not a mere secular, private business between two persons, but an institution confirming divine values. With its recognition of the important place of religion in the marital relationship, the state confirms the role of religious law in the institution of the family. Validating a marriage on the basis of the couple's religious beliefs is, however, complicated by the fact that the partners in a marriage are not always from the same religious background. Men and women with different religious affiliations quite often fall in love with each other and decide to build a family. Hence, a literal interpretation of the sentence in Article 2(1) that a marriage is valid "if done according to the law of religion and belief of each party" can be taken as a formal prohibition of a marital relationship between two parties of different religion or belief. The Muslim law of marriage, for instance, contains elements that are foreign to Christian tradition, and *vice versa*: thus intermarriage contradicts the law. And since the marital relationship in Indonesia is understood as a contract between two persons from the same religion only, interfaith marriage is thus formally excluded.

On the other hand, it may be unduly restrictive to understand Article 2(1) of the Marriage Law as a prohibition of interfaith marriage, because the Law itself does not explicitly forbid marriage between parties with different religious affiliations. This is supported by the fact that the articles dealing with marriage restrictions are silent as to whether differences in religious affiliations can be a hindrance to a marriage contract (see Article 8 to Article 28 of the Law). It is thus unacceptable, at least in the view of some scholars, that Article 2(1) should be interpreted as a law that prohibits the practice of interfaith marriage in the country. It only states (they argue) that the parties should undertake the marriage contract according to the religious law. Hence, if according to the religious law, there is no hindrance to the marriage, the marriage can be carried out. In other words, banning interfaith marriage solely on the basis of Article 2(1) is not convincing.

This is not to say that interreligious marriage is a problem-free issue ever since the promulgation of the Marriage Law in 1974. Indeed, with the unification of the Marriage Law, the several different laws that governed citizens with varied backgrounds and cultures were abolished,[1] obligating all Indonesians to comply with the new national marriage law. The unification did not, however, resolve the legal problems that arose as a result of interpersonal relationships between people of different religions, since the Marriage Law itself seems to have overlooked the complexity of the problem.

It is also a fact that, from the beginning, the drafters of the Marriage Law came under pressure from the proponents of religious law, especially proponents of Islamic law, so much so that the religious aspects of marriage were made explicit therein. Thus, the Law states very clearly that marriage is a religion-based legal activity, in which the state's role is solely that of ensuring that marriage conforms to the religious law of the parties involved and to other state laws. This is why some early articles of the Law (1 and 2) are very plain in stating the role of religion in the marriage contract. Again, however, the problem is that the Law seems to recognize only marriages contracted between persons from the same religion: the case of interfaith marriage is neglected as though it never happens in society. Hence, due to the fact that the Marriage Law itself has nothing to say about the problem of interfaith marriage, it is not surprising that some legal experts in the country maintain that the state cannot, in fact, proscribe the practice. In addition, this gap in the Law only renders the practice of interfaith marriage more problematic for the two parties as well as for any offspring of the marriage.

Although interfaith marriage is a long-standing practice in Indonesia, it can be said that it was made more complex by the New Order's efforts at unifying the laws of marriage in the country. This is because the silence of the Marriage Law on the problem of interfaith marriage has led to a situation where a legal vacuum on the specific issue has emerged. This silence may even have been deliberate, for the state itself has always stood aloof from the problems of legal pluralism that arose as a result of a number of interpersonal law cases.[2] To make matters worse, the state's accommodation of religious legal principles in the national marriage law appears to have resulted in the removal of the legal solutions needed for the legal problems arising from interfaith marriage.[3] This is shown by the fact that the term "mixed marriage" defined in Article 57 of the Marriage Law refers to marriage contracts between parties of different citizenships, such as Indonesian and non-Indonesian, and to the problems arising from a conflict of the laws to which each has to adhere.[4] The Law thus excludes the case of interfaith marriage from its definition of mixed marriage. Given that interfaith marriage is not a rare phenomenon in the country, this failure to address the phenomenon is peculiar. Even the Dutch government had, as early as 1896, defined mixed marriage as comprising all marriage contracts undertaken between peoples living under different laws or regulations. Interfaith marriage was thus, at that time, incorporated in this definition, and resolved under the explicit rule emanating from Dutch law.[5]

Thus, the uncertainty over interfaith marriage in Indonesia is the result of legal imprecision.[6] The question is: if the Marriage Law is silent on the issue, how should the state deal with the many cases of interfaith marriage taking place in the society? Should all such marriages be hitherto considered as illegal? Such unanswerable questions have posed a considerable problem for the state in the wake of the promulgation of the Marriage Law. Short on answers, the government has left the debate in the hands of legal scholars whose attitudes and opinions on the issue of interfaith marriage can basically be divided into four groups:[7] the first group are a number of scholars, mostly belonging to various religious groups, who state the opinion that interfaith marriage is completely outlawed in the country. Whatever the reason for such a marriage, it is illegal and any offspring resulting from it is illegitimate. It is thus the responsibility of every individual in the country to avoid making such an outlawed contract. The second group is a more pragmatic group of scholars who think that basically interfaith marriage is forbidden on the basis of the Marriage Law, and that one of the parties in the marriage should change his/her religion before the contract is made so that an interfaith marriage could be avoided. It is also the view of this group that if the party does not want to convert, the old principle of the Dutch mixed marriage rule, which requires the wife to comply with the law of the husband's religion, can be applied. The third group, quite similarly, believes that interfaith marriage should be allowed in Indonesia, as long as there is a pre-nuptial agreement between the two parties on the religion of the offspring, whether they should follow the religion of the husband or the wife. On the other hand, the fourth group, consisting of more current scholars, tends to view the case from the perspective of human rights. Interfaith marriage in their view is basically a human right entitled to every person in the country. The government cannot thus make any law or regulation outlawing interfaith marriage because it is a human right that every state should recognize. Also, in line with the Universal Declaration of Human Rights, difference in religious affiliations should not be a hindrance to marriage,[8] and therefore, the Indonesian government cannot simply outlaw interfaith marriages, as this would transgress human rights principles recognized by people throughout the world.

Looking at the arguments made by these scholars, we can see that the perplexity over interfaith marriages in Indonesia can be traced to the different interpretations of the Marriage Law as to whether the Law clearly regulates interfaith marriage. Those who think that the Law is silent on the issue will tend to believe that such marriage is possible in principle, since there is a legal vacuum on the issue, and that this allows for the contract of interfaith marriage to prevail according to the laws and regulations promulgated before the Marriage Law. To the opposers of this view, however, the Marriage Law is clear in forbidding interfaith marriage by virtue of the fact that it speaks only of marriage between parties of the same religion. Thus, there is no legal vacuum on this issue, and the previous colonial laws regulating marriage cannot be applied, especially since those laws were based on different principles and values than those of the national marriage law.[9]

The confusion permeates into the government bureaucracy itself. One example is the differences between the provincial government of the Special Region of Jakarta and the Ministry of Religious Affairs over the licence of the Civil Registration Office (Kantor Catatan Sipil, KCS) and the Office of Religious Affairs (Kantor Urusan Agama, KUA) to register interfaith marriages. Due to many cases of interfaith marriage occurring in the Jakarta region, the Governor of Jakarta in 1986, through his letter No. 2185/-1.755.2/CS/1986, decided to accept such marriages under the following conditions: (1) that interfaith marriage is, in general, to be done under the auspices of the Office of Civil Registration; (2) marriage between a Muslim man and non-Muslim woman should be registered at the Office of Religious Affairs (KUA); (3) marriage between a Muslim woman and non-Muslim man should be registered at the Office of Civil Registration (KCS) after acquiring permission from the Primary Court. The problem was not, however, solved with the issuance of that letter, since less than one month afterwards, the Minister for Religious Affairs, through the Director of the Establishment of Religious Courts, issued letter No. EV/HK.03.4/2803/86, effectively forbidding the registration of interfaith marriage under the terms explained in the Governor's letter. In the opinion of the Ministry of Religion, interfaith marriage is absolutely in opposition to the teachings of Islamic religious law as well as the text and spirit of the Marriage Law. Registering such unions in the Civil Registration Office not only transgresses the state laws (Law No. 1 of 1974, Government Regulation No. 9 of 1975 and Presidential Decision No. 12 of 1983), but also challenges the Islamic proscription of interfaith marriage — as understood from the Qur'an 2:221; 5:5; 60:10, as well as the consensus (*ijma'*) of the *ulama*. The decision of the Governor of Jakarta to allow interfaith marriage was thus to be annulled. Two weeks later, however, the Governor of Jakarta again gave his answer to the Ministry in his letter No. 2009/-1.755.2, in which he asserted the position he had taken in his previous letter. He thus reaffirmed that interfaith marriage was allowed in the Jakarta region, where it could be registered at the offices of either the KUA or the KCS.[10] This shows the bureaucratic complexity of the issue of interfaith marriage throughout the 1980s, an issue that could not in fact be solved through administrative regulations. The disagreement between the two levels of government points to a common uncertainty over the handling of the issue.

LEGAL CIRCUMVENTION AND SIMPLIFIED MANAGEMENT

Interestingly, this uncertainty over the attitude of the Marriage Law towards the issue of interfaith marriage has never meant that the practice has been discontinued in the society. New cases of marriage between people of different religions, in fact, emerge quite often, even though the legal complexities arising from such unions are not easy to resolve. It is due to the complexities resulting therefrom that persons involved in interfaith marriage usually try to find ways to circumvent the Marriage Law. The methods employed to circumvent the law vary, depending on the motivations and intentions of the couple involved in the marriage. The most common method of building agreement between the two aspirants to a marriage is for one of them to convert to the religion of the other before the contract is agreed. Thus when the contract is actually finalized, the marriage would not be an interfaith marriage, since the couple would share the same religious affiliation. After the contract, the person who converted would revert to his/her previous religion. In this way an intra-faith marriage becomes an interfaith one without violating the letter of the law. It is clear that circumvention has been made in order for the two parties to enter into a marriage contract in compliance with the explicit regulations stated in the Marriage Law, particularly the law in Article 2, even though the marital relationship is essentially one between persons of different faiths. This, of course, ignores the subsequent legal problems that might arise from such an undertaking, such as disagreements over the religion of the children or other issues involving one of the two parties or even their families.[11] All in all, the only concern in such instances is that the marriage should be conducted according to the letter of the Marriage Law, regardless of the fact that it might transgress it in spirit.

There seems to have been a number of reasons behind the decision to resort to such a legal circumvention. The most obvious one is the inadequate legal response of the state to the reality of interfaith marriage — a frequent occurrence in Indonesian society. The situation is made worse by the fact that the administrative apparatus of marriage registration has been set up simply to segregate between Muslims and non-Muslims. For Muslims the registration of marriage must be done through the state Office of

Religious Affairs (KUA), while non-Muslims must do so in a Civil Registration Office (KCS),[12] and marriage between Muslims and non-Muslims is thus eliminated as a bureaucratic possibility. This policy of effectively segregating religious groups in the country when it comes to the administration of marriage presents at least two further problems: firstly, it contradicts the government's own strategy of legal pluralism; and secondly, simplifying religious pluralism by separating its administration between Muslims and non-Muslims will certainly not solve the problems arising from interfaith marriage. In short, by distinguishing only between Muslim and non-Muslim groups, the Marriage Law can be said to ignore the existence of the four other officially recognized religious groups besides Muslims; the Catholics, Protestants, Buddhists, and Hindus. With such a limited division, the issue of interfaith marriage is basically restricted to marriage between Muslims and non-Muslims, when, in fact, interfaith marriage could occur between non-Muslims belonging to different religious groups, such as between a Christian man and a Buddhist woman. The regulations are thus predisposed to making the practice of interfaith marriage an "under-the-table" contract.

This strategy of silence on the part of the government is, in fact, not an unprecedented approach to dealing with pluralism. Since early independence, the government has tended to use the same strategy when faced with the complexity of religious pluralism in the framework of national law building. Certainly, religious law could never be entirely marginalized in the national law-making process, but it must always be remembered that its application should not endanger the ideals of legal unification. This meant that as far as the national goal of the country was concerned, the practice of religious law posed no danger to the national ideal of legal unification and uniformity. Thus, the plurality of religious law could be accepted as enriching the national law as long as it does not transgress the basic value of law as a tool for uniting the country. This in itself certainly sounds absurd, since the varied religious laws existing in the country sometimes stand directly in contradiction to the uniformity framed in the national law. The only possible way out is to accept the rules derived from religious law that, as much as possible, run in parallel with the state's legal principles. It is through this method that the acceptance of the religious law will not adversely affect the national law, nor destroy the divine framework attached to the religious law.

It is thus understandable that the Marriage Law is silent, or at least unclear, on the issue of interfaith marriage. The Law is in perfect accord with the prohibition of interfaith marriage prescribed by the nation's religions.[13] It also conforms to the principles of legal unification, whereby the law regulating marriage is the law promulgated only by the government (Law No. 1 of 1974). Hence, the framework of mixed marriage as embodied in the teachings of Dutch law no longer makes sense, inasmuch as the classification of people on the basis of their cultures or religions, as was done by the colonial government, no longer applies in a state composed of citizens. Since all Indonesians are deemed to live under one national law, mixed marriage can only be understood as a marital contract between people of different nationalities, that is, Indonesian and non-Indonesian; a marriage contract between people from different religious affiliations simply falls outside the scope of the law.

Thus, the Marriage Law can be said to be at least consistent with the principles of uniformity developed in the national era of Indonesia. By remaining silent, however, the law effectively abdicates any responsibility for interfaith marriage which is so common in Indonesian society. The consequence is that, by leaving the problem, legally speaking, unresolved in the realm of the state code, the government seems to prefer to allow cases of interfaith marriage to be resolved through local government regulations[14] or on adjudicative methods in the court. That is why we find, particularly in the latter case, that the role of the judge is crucial when people involved in a complex problem of interfaith marriage bring their cases to court.[15]

The Case of Andi Vony v. State

The case presented here is a well known case of interfaith marriage that occurred in 1986 involving a Christian man by the name of Adrianus Petrus Hendrik Nelwan, and a Muslim woman named Andi Vony Gani Parengi. This was one of the most significant cases of interfaith marriage brought before the courts during the entire 1980s. Many viewed *Andi Vony v. the State* as the supreme test of the judge's authority in cases of interfaith marriage. Although this was only one of many such cases, the legal complexities surrounding it and the fact that it was brought before the Supreme Court for its final legal resolution make it a landmark case in the phenomenon of interfaith marriage playing a role in the process of national legal development of the state.

The story began in 1986 when Andi Vony and Adrianus first brought their case to the general court in order to get official approval of their relationship, despite their different religious affiliations: the bride was a Muslim while the groom was a Protestant. They put forth their request to the judge for authorization to get married as their efforts to gain such permission from both the Office of Religious Affairs (KUA) and the Civil Registration Office (KCS) had failed.[16] As a Muslim, Andi Vony had beforehand submitted her application to the KUA so that the marriage could be performed in accordance with Islamic law. Unfortunately, the office rejected her application on account of the fact that the groom was not a Muslim. Similarly, the KCS also rejected their application for a registered marriage because the bride was a Muslim and the groom a Christian.[17] Following these rejections the couple approached the judges in the Primary Court to annul the decision of both offices and permit them to perform their marriage at the KCS office.

It was unfortunate that the judges too rejected their application based on the legal argument that:[18] firstly, the Basic Marriage Law (Law No. 1 of 1974) does not regulate marriages between people of different religions; secondly, in the judges' view, the rejections by both KUA and KCS were not erroneous, based on the regulations promulgated on marriage; and thirdly, there is basically a hindrance to conducting an interfaith marriage in Indonesia on the basis of Article 2 of the Law No. 1 of 1974 and its implementation described in Article 8 of the Government Regulation No. 9 of 1975. The judges' understanding of Islamic law also convinced them that interfaith marriage also transgressed Islamic legal principles, as the Qur'an in verse 2:221 states that a Muslim woman is prohibited from entering into a marriage contract with a non-Muslim. Furthermore, from the judges' understanding of Christian teaching, interfaith marriage is similarly disallowed in the New Testament (2 Corinthians 6:14). According to the judges, therefore, the interfaith marital relationship sought by Andi Vony and Adrianus was in reality unfeasible since both civil and religious law clearly outlawed such a union. The judges believed that Article 2 of the Marriage Law should be understood as a prohibition of interfaith marriage and that such a marriage basically had no place in the country. Thus, they confirmed the decisions of the KUA and KCS offices.[19]

Setting aside feelings of discouragement due to the decision of the judges in the Primary Court, Andi Vony managed to submit this judgement to the Supreme Court on appeal. She herself pleaded before the appellate court, explaining her disagreement with the judges' opinion in the lower court that there was a legal obstruction to interfaith marriage. In her opinion, the Marriage Law does not clearly prohibit interfaith marriage and the negative response of the judge to her proposal was thus not strong enough as it was not adequately supported by legal arguments regarding the basic regulation of marriage. In addition, she argued, her intention to marry Adrianus was perfectly legitimate as it was based on feelings of mutual love, notwithstanding the fact that they were followers of different religions. Both their parents were supportive of their marriage, and based on her knowledge of Islamic law, this strengthened her case and her intention to marry him. It was with these arguments that Vony herself was very determined to marry Adrianus, asking the judge in the Supreme Court to rescind the decision of the lower court and authorize her interfaith marriage. What is interesting to note here is that Vony did not hesitate to reject the judges' interpretation of the Marriage Law, as she felt that since there is no prohibition of interfaith marriage according to the Law, the argument offered by the judges in the lower court was therefore invalid.

Interestingly, although it took about three years for the Supreme Court to issue a judgement, it accepted almost all the arguments advanced by Vony.[20] In their decision, the judges in the Supreme Court agreed to revoke the decision made by the Primary Court as well as to rescind the letter of the Civil Registration Office (KCS) refusing to register the marriage between Vony and Adrianus. This decision in favour of the appellant was essentially based on the following arguments: firstly, the Supreme Court acknowledged that the two parties loved each other and although each belonged to a different religious tradition, their relationship was founded on the basis of mutual affection. Also, the parents of both parties did not oppose the intention of the parties to get married. These indicated that religion was not an issue to them when they embarked on marriage plans. Secondly, in the opinion of the court, Law No. 1 of 1974 does not regulate the case of interfaith marriage. But this cannot, in fact, be outlawed since its prohibition would only transgress the Constitutional Law of the country, particularly Article 27 of the Basic Constitution of 1945.[21] It was understood from that article that all citizens have an equal right to enter into a marital relationship, regardless of whether the parties belong to the same religion. Thirdly, under national law principles, the previous colonial regulations on mixed marriage were no longer valid for cases of interfaith marriage. The court agreed that in essence there was a legal vacuum, so making a clear decision on the case of interfaith marriage was impossible. The court considered the fact that interfaith marriage was a common occurrence in the society and ruled that interfaith marriage was, therefore, possible. Since the only state institution that could accept the marriage would be the Civil Registration Office (KCS), it was ordered to accept the interfaith marriage of Vony and Adrianus.[22]

ANALYSIS: THE HUMAN RIGHTS ARGUMENT

Looking at the Supreme Court's arguments, one can see that no single element was enough to justify the decision favouring Vony. The fact that there was a legal vacuum on the issue of interfaith marriage appears to have been the main reason the court was determined to clarify its legal position in the case. On the one hand, the previous Dutch laws relating to the issue were no longer valid; on the other hand, the national marriage law was not clear in its position. Yet this vacuum might not have been as significant if there were only rare cases of interfaith marriage in the society. It is interesting to see that in view of the legal vacuum on interfaith marriage, the judge relied heavily on the constitution as a solution. Article 27 of the 1945 Constitution indeed states that every citizen has the same and equal right before the law; this was exploited by the judge to indicate the constitutional right of all persons in the country to build a marital relationship, regardless of tribal, customary, or religious distinctions that might exist between them. Their identity as Indonesian nationals seemed thus to be the main point of consideration here.

It can be understood from this proposition that the supreme judges saw Article 2(1) of the Marriage Law as a rule designed for people with the same religion only when both parties to the marriage regarded themselves, from the beginning, as bound by the marriage law of their religion. Yet, this does not mean that the article is designed to prohibit interfaith marriage. On the contrary, the Supreme Court judges seemed to interpret interfaith marriage not as a problem of religion, but more as one of human rights. This consequently led to the decision that marriage could be undertaken regardless of any primordial differences that might distinguish the parties. As long as the two parties had the same nationality, it was the responsibility of the state to protect their basic human right to marry any other Indonesian citizen.

Related to the human rights argument above was the judges' willingness to see this case of interfaith marriage in light of the parties' personal motivation. The judges recognized the marital intentions of Vony and Adrianus as being based purely on the motivation to realize a love relationship that had developed over a long period of time. It thus seemed to the judges unreasonable to sever such a relationship merely on the basis of their different religious affiliation. It appears here that the judges were also convinced of Vony's strong affections for Adrianus by virtue of her high motivation to bring the case before the Supreme Court. Such determination to marry cannot exist without genuine feelings of love for each other and breaking up their relationship would, therefore, only have a bad impact on the parties. It is clear from this that the judges saw the basis of the marital relationship as in essence being the feeling of affection experienced equally by the bride and the groom. Different religious beliefs were not themselves a valid reason for preventing a union. In short, the feeling of affection for someone is essentially the basic right of every person, and so the state is responsible for its protection.

Above all, it is interesting to analyse why the judges in the Supreme Court accepted the proposition of a legal vacuum on interfaith marriage as a starting point for making such a judgement.[23] The acceptance of the legal vacuum would only mean that the judges agreed from the beginning that the Marriage Law did not provide a legal basis for resolving the problem of interfaith marriage in the court. The Supreme Court on its part thought that a sufficient legal resolution was only possible if the judges chose to rule on the basis of the main intention of the marriage. There were at least two considerations here: firstly, as the purpose of the marriage was to be basically the main consideration, it was thus valid to make a decision grounded on the fact that the two parties did indeed love each other. The marital relationship was, therefore, believed to derive in essence from such a reciprocal affection. This could be reinforced by the support of the parents despite the fact that the parties profess different religions. As a result this would indicate to the judges that, basically, the two parties no longer subscribed to the tenets of their religion; or if they did, they had chosen not to comply with the principles of religious law that disapproved of interfaith marriage. Thus, in the view of the judges, Vony, though a Muslim, would be declaring herself no longer bound by the teachings of Islamic law proscribing interfaith marriage. Accordingly, the judges might see Vony as having released herself from compliance to

Islamic law in order to form a marital relationship with Adrianus. If so, it would be legitimate for the judges not to use the principle of Islamic law as the basis for their verdict, although the claimant herself was a Muslim. It can be said, therefore, that the judges were, without acknowledging it, basing themselves on the Dutch-rooted principle of "voluntary acceptance" (*vrijwillige onderwerping*) by the claimant in order to find a resolution. By disregarding the regulations of Islamic law forbidding interfaith marriage, Vony was regarded as having freely rejected Islamic law as a legal tool to decide her case.

Secondly, the judges seemed to have concluded immediately that one of the best legal references for making a judgement was the basic constitutional law. This is why Article 27 of the 1945 Constitution was cited by the judges in support of their decision. The principle of legal equality for all citizens referred to in the Article — though it could be said to have no direct correlation with the specific case of interfaith marriage — was used as a rational basis for allowing the marriage. The right to marriage is essentially a human right, recognized in the Constitution: differences of tribe, skin colour, or even religious backgrounds should not thus pose a hindrance. On the basis of such an interpretation, the general legal proposition contained in Article 27 of the Constitution can be taken as grounds for approving the specific case of interfaith marriage. One might argue that such an interpretation is, in fact, too weak to support a favourable judgement, but in conjunction with others, it provides considerable weight.

Moreover, given the legal vacuum surrounding the issue of interfaith marriage, this constitutional support gains added significance. Without even one specific regulation that could be used to decide the case, Article 27 seemed an ideal basis for the judgement. It also served the ideal of national legal uniformity, according to which the local or cultural differences of people living in the country should not constitute obstructions to the making of any legal contract. In other words, it is a principle of Indonesian nationality that all persons have the right to enter into a marriage contract with anyone, regardless of their backgrounds of custom or religion. The state has thus basically no right to prohibit marriage between citizens of different religions since constitutional law itself secures the human rights of each person, especially since the principles of national law do not recognize differences of background among citizens, beyond the variable of nationality itself.

CONCLUSION

In considering the arguments forwarded by the Supreme Court's judges, one may come to the realization that the case of *Vony v. the State* represented far more than the legal problem of marriage. Beyond the question of how to resolve the fact of legal vacuum on the issue, Vony's case was also a good illustration of the judges' efforts to apply the principles of national law in the process of making a judgement. This is because, theoretically, the judge's duty is believed to involve not only solving cases based on existing normative regulations, but also interpreting how the national legal principles built by the state can be implemented in each case brought to the court. The two factors are in fact inseparable. That is why Supreme Court judges have for so long been lenient on accepting interfaith marriage, even though from the perspective of the religion of the claimant, the marriage is absolutely forbidden.[24] It was thus in consideration of these facts that the judges in the Supreme Court found it impossible to decide the Vony case to the contrary. As a state apparatus, the judge has the main responsibility of deciding the case before him in conjunction with the legal philosophy followed by the state itself. Judging the case so as to outlaw interfaith marriage would, however, have meant contravening the general principles of national law. In that sense, using the Marriage Law, especially Article 2, as a legal basis for proscribing interfaith marriage is diametrically in contradiction with the development of a national legal philosophy. It is thus safer and more sound for the Supreme Court judges to interpret the case as much as possible in keeping with the state's mission to develop further the national law system, which ideally treats all citizens equally, regardless of their primordial background. Nevertheless, a consequence of such a decision is that it might lead to inconsistency with non-state normative orderings.

In turn, the judges' acceptance of Vony's interfaith marriage can also be taken as an indication of their predilection for state law principles over non-state normative orderings such as Islamic law. As stated earlier, such a preference reminds us of the fact that the judge is in essence an active agent in the process of national law development. A judge's decision in cases brought before the court can serve to impart universal values to citizens, whatever their background. As far as Vony's case was concerned, the judges' decision to accept her intention of interfaith marriage, mainly on the basis of her basic right as an Indonesian citizen, reflected their disregard for Vony's religious background when measured against the more general legal principles enshrined in the 1945 Constitution. It could be said that, when there is a conflict between legal principles derived from state law and those of non-state normative orderings, the former should be adhered to. The decision of the judges in the Supreme Court to annul the decision of the lower court was basically a reflection of the judges' compliance with national legal values, regardless of the fact that such compliance might have a negative impact on Islamic legal teachings. In the face of legal uncertainty over the problem of interfaith marriage, the Supreme Court's decision to allow such an undertaking between Vony and Adrianus was a clear statement of the court's priorities. Differently put, the resolution of the Supreme Court judges in accepting interfaith marriage, based on general principles enshrined in the Constitution, was ample proof that the teachings of Islamic law would have to make way when these conflicted with state law. Seen from the broader perspective of the encounter between state and non-state laws, the Vony case was but one of many in which national legal principles have prevailed over non-state normative orderings.

Notes

1. See Article 66 of Law No. 1/1974. Some laws on marriage before the promulgation of the Marriage Law in 1974 are as follows: (1) for indigenous, non-Muslim people, marriage was basically regulated by the *adat* law; (2) for Muslims, the law used for regulating their marriage was Islamic marriage law; (3) for the Indigenous Christian people living in Java, Minahasa, and Ambon, the law used was the *Huwelijks Ordonantie Christen Indonesiers* (HOCI) as explained in S. 1933 No. 74 and S. 1936 No. 607; and (4) for non-indigenous people (such as Chinese and Europeans and their descendants), their marriage law was derived from *Burgelijk Wetboek voor Nederlandsch-Indie* (Civil Code for the Netherlands Indies).

2. This is, in fact, the logical consequence of the principle of legal unification itself since with the nationalization of the country, the classification of the citizen as an object of national law is only understood as Indonesian or non-Indonesian, leaving all other classifications existing before independence, such as Chinese, European, Indian, Arab, etc. outside the new criteria.

3. Especially on the matter of interfaith marriage, the Marriage Law seems to follow the principles of religious law that ban marital relationships between people of different faiths.

4. Article 57 of the Marriage Law states: "What is meant as mixed marriage in this Law is the marriage between two people complying in Indonesia with different laws due to different citizenships and one of the parties is an Indonesian citizen."

5. Article 6 of the *Regeling* stated very clearly that mixed marriages could be contracted by following the law of the husband in the marriage (*'De voltrekking van gemengde huwelijken geschiedt volgens het voor den man geldende recht, behoudens de toestemming der aanstaande echtgenooten, welke steeds wordt vereischt.'*). Article 7 of the same Regeling stated that the differences in religion, geographic location, or ethnic origin were not obstacles to a marriage contract (*'Verschil van godsdienst, landaard of afkomst kan nimmer als beletsel tegen het huwelijk gelden'*). See Engelbrecht & Engelbrecht (1960), *supra* note 5 on pp. 745–46.

6. S. Pompe, "Mixed Marriages in Indonesia: Some Comments on the Law and the Literature". *Bijdragen tot de Taal -Land- en Volkenkunde* 144 (1988): 262–64.

7. See Nani Soewondo et al., *Analisa dan Evaluasi Hukum Tidak Tertulis tentang Hukum Kebiasaan dalam Perkawinan Campuran* (Jakarta: Proyek Pusat Perencanaan Pembangunan Hukum Nasional, Badan Pembinaan Hukum Nasional, 1991–92), pp. 41–42.

8. Article 2(1) of the Universal Declaration of Human Rights states very clearly that: "Everyone is entitled to all the rights and freedoms set forth in this Declaration, without distinction of any kind, such as race, colour, sex, language, religion, political or other opinion, national or social origin, property, birth or other status." See online: <http://www.unhchr.ch/udhr/lang/eng.htm>.

9. Nani Soewondo (1991–92), *supra* note 7.

10. The data on those local government and departmental letters is as found in the attachment of the book in Nani Soewondo (1991–92), *supra* note 7.

11. The example of the case of legal circumvention and its impact in the future of marital relationship can be shown in the case of *Tati Djuwati v. Tr. Aritonang*. In this case, the wife (Tati Djuwati) as a

plaintiff brought the case to the Religious Court of Cirebon that since her husband (Aritonang) reverted to his previous religion after marriage, their marital relationship was not harmonious anymore. The court, as espoused in the letter No. 612/82 dated 22 October 1982, decided that the marriage had dissolved. As a plaintiff in error, the husband then brought the case to the Religious Court of Appeal to appeal the judgement against him in the lower court. The judgement of the Court of Appeal, however, supported the judgement of the lower court (Letter of Judgment No. 12/1983, dated 3 February 1983). Dissatisfied with that judgement, the husband brought the case to the Supreme Court in Jakarta. As explained in the Supreme Court Judgement No. 32 K/AG/1983, dated 22 September 1983, the appeal of the husband was rejected, so that the decisions of the lower courts were basically supported by the Supreme Court. The marital relationship was thus dissolved.

12. The marriage registration undertaken in the office of KUA for Muslims and KCS for non-Muslims is based on Article 2(2) of Law No. 1 of 1974 and Article 2(1-2) of the Government Regulation No. 9 of 1975 on the Implementation of the Marriage Law. See also marriage registration in general in Law No. 32 of 1954. The organization of the Office of Civil Registration is based on the Presidential Decision No. 12 of 1983. On this matter, see also the Decision of Secretary of the Interior No. 221a of 1975. The role of religious experts to help the registrar in the KCS for Christian, Hindu, and Buddhist marriage is based on the Decision of Secretary of the Interior No. 97 of 1978.

13. On the discussion of religious concept of interfaith marriage see Jørgen S. Nielsen, "Islam and Mixed Marriages", *20 Research Papers: Muslims in Europe* (1983): 8–13; Guy Harpigny, "Muslim-Christian Marriages and the Church", *20 Research Papers: Muslims in Europe* (1983): 18; in the case of Indonesia, see S. Pompe, *supra* note 6 (1988): 259–75.

14. The best example of the decision of the local government issued in relation to the many cases of interfaith marriage happening in society is the decision of the Governor of the Special Region of

Jakarta in 1986, No. 2185/-1.755.2/CS/1986. See the explanation of
the letter and its complicated impact in the previous pages.

15. It is interesting to note that a lot of cases of interfaith marriage
    brought to the primary courts ended with the judges giving
    permission to the parties to undertake their marriages. The judges
    were of the opinion that Law No. 1 of 1974 does not regulate the
    interfaith marriage; hence the use of the Dutch law as explained in
    S. No. 158 of 1989 on mixed marriage was accepted as valid. See for
    instance the cases of the decision of the Primary Court of Surakarta
    (Central Java) No. 140/1983/ Pdt/P/PN.Ska., dated 2 March 1983 in
    Hartoyo and Etty Endang Poedjo Moelyati v. State, the decision of the
    Primary Court of North Jakarta No. 71/Pdt/P/1985/PN.Jkt.Ut., dated
    2 February 1985 in *Victor Simon Paat & Puji Aryanti v. the State*, and
    the decision of the Primary Court of Ciamis (West Java) No. 56/
    Pdt.P/1985, PN. Cms., dated 22 April 1985.

16. This was based on the letter of the Office of Religious Affairs (KUA)
    No. K.2/NJ-1/834/III/1986, dated 5 March 1986, and the letter of
    the Civil Registration Office (KCS) No. 655/1.1755.4/CS/1986, dated
    5 March 1986.

17. On the regulation of the office, see note 9 above.

18. The decision of the Primary Court of Central Jakarta Number 382/
    PDT/P/1986/PN.JKT.PST.

19. See also the legal explanations of the judges in the Primary Court in
    Z. Asikin Kusumah Atmadja, *Beberapa Yurisprudensi Perdata yang
    Penting serta Hubungan Ketentuan Hukum Acara Perdata*, 2nd ed.
    (Jakarta: Mahkamah Agung RI, 1990), pp. 409–13.

20. The decision of the Supreme Court No.: 1400 K/Pdt/1986, dated
    20 January 1989.

21. Article 27(1) of the 1945 Constitution states: "All citizens have
    equal status before the law and in government and shall abide by
    the law and the government without any exception." This is the
    text of the Constitution quoted before the amendments. The text
    has, however, basically not changed with the amendments.

22. See the explanation in Asikin Kusumah Atmadja, *supra* note 20
    (1990): 55, 414–19.

23. It is interesting to note here that due to many cases of interfaith marriage in the society, the Supreme Court sent a letter to the Minister for Religious Affairs and the Secretary of the Interior on 20 April 1981, No. KMA/72/IV/1981 containing legal opinion concerning interfaith marriage as well as an appeal of the Primary Court to the Ministry of Religious Affairs and related government offices to ease the implementation of interfaith marriage. It is interesting to note also that in this letter the Primary Court used the term "mixed marriage" rather than "interfaith marriage". There were at least three ideas presented in the letter: first, the pluralism of Indonesian society will make interfaith marriage basically unavoidable in the community; second, the Marriage Law is in fact silent on the case so that, based on Article 66 of that Law, the Dutch regulation (S. No. 158 of 1898) is valid as a reference for judging the case of interfaith marriage; third, since marriage contract in the country is in essence a state matter (*staatshuwelijk*), it is thus the responsibility of the government to manage interfaith marriage so that it does not become a contract that is based upon a lie.

24. See a number of interfaith marriage cases brought to the courts presented in note 12 above.

References

Assad, Dawud. "Mixed Marriages". *Research Papers: Muslims in Europe* (1983): 3–7.

Atmadja, Z. Asikin Kusumah. *Beberapa Yurisprudensi Perdata yang Penting serta Hubungan Ketentuan Hukum Acara Perdata*, 2nd ed. Jakarta: Mahkamah Agung RI, 1990.

Engelbrecht, W.A. and E.M.L. Engelbrecht. *Kitab-Kitab Undang-Undang dan Peraturan-Peraturan serta Undang-Undang Dasar 1945 Republik Indonesia. De Wetboeken Wetten en Verordeningen Benevens de Grondwet van 1945 van de Republiek Indonesië*. Bruxelles and Leiden: Les Editions A. Manteau S.A. and A. W. Sijthoff's Uitgeversmaatschappij N.V., 1960.

Harpigny, Guy. "Muslim-Christian Marriages and the Church". *20 Research Papers: Muslims in Europe* (1983): 18–28.

Jafizham, T. "Hukum Perkawinan Islam dan Masalah Perkawinan Campuran". *Hukum dan Pembangunan* 12 (1982): 130–34.

Nielsen, Jørgen S. "Islam and Mixed Marriages". *20 Research Papers: Muslims in Europe* (1983): 8–17.

Pompe, S. "Mixed Marriages in Indonesia: Some Comments on the Law and the Literature". *Bijdragen tot de Taal -Land- en Volkenkunde* 144 (1988): 259–75.

Soewondo, Nani et al. *Analisa dan Evaluasi Hukum Tidak Tertulis tentang Hukum Kebiasaan dalam Perkawinan Campuran.* Jakarta: Proyek Pusat Perencanaan Pembangunan Hukum Nasional, Badan Pembinaan Hukum Nasional, 1991–92.

Laws

Asian Human Rights Commission (2005). Certified translation of the 1945 Constitution of the Republic of Indonesia. Available online at <http://indonesia.ahrchk.net/news/mainfile.php/Constitution/34?alt=english>.

Decision of Secretary of the Interior No. 221a of 1975.

Decision of Secretary of the Interior No. 97 of 1978.

Departemen Kehakiman. *Himpunan Putusan-Putusan Pengadilan Negeri 1990.* Jakarta: Dirjen Badan Peradilan Umum and Peradilan Tata Usaha Negara, 1990.

Government Regulation No. 9 of 1975.

Huwelijkordonnantie Christen-Indonesiërs Java. Minahassa en Amboina (HOCI) (Ordinance for Christian Indonesians). *Staatsblad* 1933 No. 74.

Law No. 12 of 1983.

Law No. 32 of 1954.

National Marriage Act (1974) Law No. 1, Article 57, Article 66.

Presidential Decision No. 12 of 1983.

Staatsblad 1898 No. 158.

Staatsblad 1936 No. 607.

United Nations (1996–2005) Universal Declaration of Human Rights. Available online at <http://www.unhchr.ch/udhr/lang/eng.htm>.

Chapter 3

PRIVATE LIVES, PUBLIC CONTENTION
Muslim-non-Muslim Family Disputes in Malaysia

Maznah Mohamad, Zarizana Aziz
and Chin Oy Sim

INTRODUCTION

Conventionally, ethnic riots or recurrent violence are often used as distinct markers of ethnic conflicts in society. However, the prevalence of ethnic tensions can also be evidenced by other processes, such as the inability of legal institutions to resolve everyday conflicts involving family relationships. In Malaysia, this has become an important manifestation of emerging ethnic divides. Recent disputes involving interreligious relationships or Muslim-non-Muslim marriages, as in the Lina Joy, Shamala, and Subashini cases, have brought forth issues of legal significance with enormous political implications. The contentious nature of these cases is being dictated by a larger contest to control and influence reforms within both Islamic and civil law.

The force behind the Islamization movement is not solely provided by the Islamic political opposition, but also by a rising, urban-based Islamic civil society. The latter is driven by a newly-emergent Malay-Muslim middle-class, comprising scholars, professionals, and political activists who are able to mobilize and lobby effectively for Islamic dominance in all aspects of governance, the law being one of the most important institutions of control. This process has posed various problems, not least because it is being waged within a multicultural context, with about 45 per cent of the Malaysian population being non-Muslims.

The impetus to Islamize various branches of society may be read positively by its proponents — as a project to re-capture the indigenous elements of history once lost to colonial domination (Horowitz 1994). However, this is not always achievable without grave social costs, one of which is its impact on race relations. As the Malaysian legal system moves closer towards accommodating syariah, the laws, policies, and regulations which emanate from this process have influenced the resolution of interreligious family concerns and disputes. Many of these regulations unequivocally limit the boundaries of interethnic relationships. Together with an unrelenting social movement to carve out an exclusive framework of governance for Muslims, the evolving judicial trend has been extremely divisive.

This chapter documents some of the Muslim-non-Muslim cases which have been subjected to the above contestation. It describes the conflict which has arisen between those who advocate Islamic legal predominance in the system on the one hand, and those who rally behind the Constitution against such a dominance on the other. In this environment it is difficult for the judicial system to resolve interreligious family disputes. A just resolution of the three cases described in this chapter is highly improbable. In the Shamala and Subashini cases, there are lingering questions as to whether a dual system of court justice will ever allow for the equal treatment of non-Muslims in a Muslim-majority nation. In the Lina Joy case, there is the question of what amounts to fundamental human rights for a Muslim citizen.

On a larger plane, these contentious legal cases of interreligious marriage have opened up debates as to who could be considered as the guardians of constitutional liberties in Malaysia — the civil courts, the state, or an incipient people's movement yet to be born? Our central postulation in this chapter is that the contestation over laws and jurisdictional boundaries inevitably leads to difficulties in resolving interreligious litigations due to an overwhelming pressure to conform to a perceived Islamic hegemony in the system. By quoting at length some of the judgements made in these cases we hope to show how legal opinions seem to be in tandem with this trend, to the detriment of private well-being.

BACKGROUND OF STATE ISLAMIZATION

The period of Islamic political ascendance in Malaysia coincided almost synchronically with the rise of UMNO, the Malay-Islamic ruling party in Malaysia during the post-1969 years.[1] After the 1969 riots, the New Economic Policy (NEP) was implemented as an affirmative action programme for Malays and other indigenous communities. The numerous socio-economic programmes to leapfrog Malay advancement in the fields of urban employment and higher education were all done within a very short period, which proved to be socially and culturally dislocating for the Malays. Between the early 1970s and the mid-1990s there was a proliferation of influential Islamic movements to address these manifestations of alienation, such as the ABIM (The Malaysian Islamic Youth Movement), the Darul Arqam, the Jemaat Tabligh as well as a more strengthened PAS (Islamic Party of Malaysia) (Nagata 1980). The latter reinvented itself as a hard line Islamic opposition party to ride on this Islamism wave (Farish Noor 2004). This phase of Islamization saw an intense competition among claimant Islamic groups of various streams to gain followers and establish their authority among the general Muslim population.

The competition for power and adherents was fought along ideological lines such as whether Islam meant the ultimate concept of Islamic statehood or just about the infusion of Islamic values in society. All of these movements were ultimately in competition with the UMNO-led state. Various strategies were thus employed by UMNO in order to blunt the radical influence of these movements — from cooptation of their leaders into the UMNO-dominated government, to "out-Islamizing" the Islamic party. On the latter, UMNO tried to infuse more Islam into the system to counter PAS's agenda for Islamization. The state ultimately won as it was able to fashion a statist Islam that would ensure the containment of radical Islam to appease the non-Muslims while establishing a widespread project of official Islamization to please the Muslims.[2] The state as represented by UMNO acted as guardian and arbitrator as to which of the "Islams" would be the rightful one for national adoption.

The successful capture of Islam by the state meant the mainstreaming of Islam, or its integration into governance. From about 2000 onwards, the institutionalization of Islam by the state had been quite well-extended and deep enough for it to affect the multireligious citizenry in palpable ways. Conflicts over freedom of religion and the suppression of minority religious expressions had already become a recurring feature of the country since the 1980s although this never boiled over into open violence

(Lee 1988). There was a sense of a rising, but stabilized Islamic piety among Muslims who had by then occupied higher or middle-class ranks in society. At the same time, the competition between the various streams of Islam, between the radical, militant, and statist ones or between UMNO and PAS had almost levelled out, with clear lines drawn between the "right" Islam and the "wrong" Islam. The UMNO-led government was firmly in power while the NEP had achieved its maximum or optimal reach with no public institutions left untouched by *bumiputra/* Malay dominance. There was also an overall perception that Muslim interests had been met while non-Muslim discontent was under control, even assuaged. If one were to use the 2004 election results (where the UMNO-led ruling coalition was voted in with an overwhelming majority) as a gauge of societal sentiments towards government policies, it seemed that the Malay-Muslim hegemony over the multireligious citizenry had been securely won.

Abdullah Badawi succeeded Mahathir Mohamad as prime minister in 2002 after the latter's twenty-two-year rule. A fresh, convincing mandate given to Abdullah in the 2004 national election prompted him to promise more reforms and political openness. Some saw the Abdullah period as opening an opportunity for reversing some of the ethnically-divisive trends. But what eventually came to pass was a series of episodes which confirmed just the opposite of what was hoped for. Not only was there a public realization that Islamization had become well-entrenched within the state, but also that it may well be contributing towards the shattering of a hitherto well-managed, if not friction-free, state of ethnic relations.

What really postponed the open outbreak of discontent among non-Muslims was the fact that the execution of more Islam in society had been largely effected through procedural, even democratic means. Much legal and political arguments were made around the constitutional clause found in Article 3(1) of the Federal Constitution which states that Islam is the "religion of the Federation", hence supporting the argument that Islamic law is the supreme law for persons professing Islam. The historical origin of this clause has been subjected to much probing and debate, but it is becoming the "constitutional crutch" upon which proponents of the Islamic state have depended to defend their case (Fernando 2006).

Not surprisingly, it is at this stage too that the process of Islamization began to take on a more discriminatory and divisive approach. Islam's identity politics had become more intolerant. Among the authorities, there appeared to be an unrelenting mission to fuse Islam with the Malay identity in a formalistic and legally coercive way. Through Islamization, it was as though the identity of the Malay could be sacralized without recourse to an exit voice. As we shall describe in the following sections of this chapter, syariah compliant norms have been implemented in such a wide-ranging and thorough way that even the civil courts are circumspect about making independent decisions when it comes to the question of freedom of religion and culture for Malays and Muslims.

The process of mainstreaming Islam by the state and of turning Islam into an instrument of social control had become quite deep. The use of procedural democracy such as law-making (in support of the policy for Islamization) to determine how the secular judiciary and court system would function became one of its features. State Islamization can be traced largely to the expansion of the Islamic bureaucracy and the Syariah Court system. However, in effect, it went further than that — particular Islamic values, norms, and conforming mechanisms had influenced how Muslim members of the secular judiciary were thinking. In the later part of this chapter we will see how certain arguments made in the civil courts were even supported by religious quotes from the Qur'an.

ISLAMIC LAW REFORMS AND THE EXPANSION OF THE ISLAMIC BUREAUCRACY

The 1952 Enactment of the Administration of Islamic Laws in Selangor can be traced as the first piece of legislation which established the manifest place of syariah in a post-colonial Malaysia. This was followed by the passing of other state enactments. As the Federation of Malaysia has thirteen states, and Islam is under the purview of state rulers, thirteen separate enactments were each passed by a state legislature.[3] This early post-colonial process of entrenching Muslim laws took place between 1952 and 1974. The formalization of the Muslim or Syariah Court was also effected through an intermittent process, from it being totally cut off from the court system (with the passing of the 1948 Courts Ordinance) to it being recognized as a lower court within the court system hierarchy (as in the 1965 Syariah Court Act) (Ahmad Ibrahim 1999).

However, with the passing of the Federal Territory Administration of Islamic Laws Enactment in 1984, the re-centralization and augmentation of the syariah system happened swiftly and in a very substantial way. The 1984 Enactment paved the way for the establishment of a more uniform set of Muslim laws, which before this were administered distinctly and separately by the various state legislatures. More importantly, this new legislation allowed for an empowered and enlarged Syariah Court system. This was done by separating the office of the Mufti and the Islamic Religious Council from the Syariah Court administration itself. The Syariah Court was then expanded with the establishment of three levels of courts — the Syariah Lower Court, the Syariah High Court and the Syariah Appeals Court. With this single new legislation the syariah state bureaucracy experienced a multifold expansion almost overnight. The thirteen other states quickly emulated the provisions of the Federal Territory enactment within their own state laws. By 1991, all thirteen states within the Federation had established the three-tier syariah court system. At the same time, the Islamization of the state bureaucracy was enhanced with the separation of the offices of the Islamic Religious Council from the court system. The office of the Mufti, as head of the Religious Council, also began to take on a more prominent profile in the larger scheme of an eventual staking out of the "Islamic state".

The social consequences arising out of the reform process above led to an increase in the number of Islamic legal scholars, legal practitioners, and administrative functionaries who worked within this enlarged legal-bureaucratic structure. A vocal Islamic civil society was also one of the outcomes, and indeed came to represent the conscience of this new and empowered Islamic state bureaucracy. In this milieu of a spreading Islamization, there grew a strong Islamic civil society and a swelling Muslim middle class, among whom were the Islamic politico-legal elites who became confident enough to test the strength of the syariah, particularly the extent of its jurisdiction. We shall term this pressure group the Syariah Islamists, as they are at the forefront of trying to establish a re-Islamized judicial system. It made sense that they would coalesce around legislative instruments to further their cause because they were in actual fact modernists and had none of the illusions of previous groups such as the banned Darul Arqam which operated on the basis that Islam could be more genuinely activated through non-state, neo-Sufist, or millenarian communal movements detached from statist engagements (Ahmad Fauzi Abdul Hamid 1999).

"BLANK CHEQUE" ISLAMIZATION THROUGH THE RULE OF LAW

It was said that during the period of the 1980s and early 1990s there was a process of a "blank cheque" Islamization. It was a situation of how anything or everything done to strengthen Islamization, especially the passing of new laws or the amending of the Federal Constitution, could be done with an almost cavalier glibness.[4] There were two new laws which profoundly influenced litigations involving applications for religious conversions and other interreligious dispute settlements. Both of these legislations were amendments to previous laws to accommodate the demands of the rising Syariah Islamist community. The first was to fulfil a demand for the recognition of the syariah system to be on equal standing with the civil court system, and for it to be given full powers over wide-ranging matters that concern Islam and its constituents. This was done through Article 121(1A) of the Federal Constitution, which was amended in 1988 to allow for the separation of jurisdiction. The second was to impose compulsory notification of all Malays and Muslims (practising or nominal) as professing the Islamic religion. For this purpose, an administrative law was amended in 1999 to make it mandatory for all Muslims to state categorically the religion of Islam on their identification papers. This requirement is stipulated in the National Registration Regulations 1990.

Article 121(1A) (amendments 1988) of the Federal Constitution now states that the high courts of Malaya, Sabah and Sarawak, "shall have no jurisdiction in respect of any matter within the jurisdiction of the syariah courts". While the amendment did not enlarge the jurisdiction of the syariah courts in any way, it prohibits the civil court from assuming concurrent jurisdiction over a matter which is within the jurisdiction of the syariah courts. Effectively, the rights of citizens (both Muslims and non-Muslims) to have access to one common, equitable, and universal court system has been removed with the affirmation of this jurisdictional distinction. Cases heard in the Syariah Court cannot be brought for appeal at the Federal Court as judges have ruled that these cases are not within their jurisdiction. There is still a legal contention on this as even cases involving fundamental rights, as defined by the Constitution (such as rights to freedom of religion), have been considered the purview of the Syariah Court whenever it concerns a Muslim. Other legal opinions assert that fundamental rights involving civil liberty must not come under the purview of the syariah as long as they affect all citizens, including Muslims. As for the National Registration Regulations 1990, some relevant portions were amended in this law to specify that any person registering for an identity card shall give a list of particulars to the registration officer, which among others, include, "iv) his race" and "(iva) his religion (only for Muslims); wef, 1.10.1999".

Both of the above laws reflect how the state has tried to accommodate the interests of the Syariah Islamists, particularly through attempts at "harmonizing" civil laws with syariah, or even to make civil laws "syariah compliant". Some of the distinctive outcomes of these developments are as follows:

- The closure of the constitutional avenue for Muslims who seek to exercise civil liberty in their choice of faith and freedom of religion, because matters with regard to Islam have been interpreted to be the exclusive purview of the syariah courts without any interference from the civil courts.
- The emergence of legal conundrums in family cases involving litigants of overlapping or differing religious faiths, specifically between Muslims and non-Muslims, because even as these members may be bound biologically and socially, they will

be subjected to differing legal jurisdictions. This will be contentious as many provisions of the syariah family laws are at variance with those of civil family laws.

- The imposition of absolute Islamic legal sovereignty over Muslims when family and personal matters are conflated with their civil rights status; both of these areas are treated as falling within the purview of the syariah.

What is most significant in all this is that Muslims themselves were to bear the brunt of this reformed and prevailing syariah. Muslims would actually lose the protection of the civil court as the extent of the civil court's jurisdiction has been confined whenever it came to matters related to Islam. In fact, the civil judiciary did little to defy the pervading Islamic orthodoxy. Islam had overwhelmed almost all levels of the judiciary. Fear of an imagined heresy against Islam among the Muslim judges in the civil courts created some of the most inconsistent, if not unjust, judgements for some of the litigants in the cases — both Muslims and non-Muslims.

CONTROL OVER THE MALAY-ISLAM IDENTITY; CONTROL OVER THE *UMMAH*

In this section we discuss how the question of identity had been captured by the prevailing Syariah Islamism. To begin with, the definition of a Malay is already constitutionally determined through his religious identity, which is Islam. Article 160(2) of the Federal Constitution fixes this definition of the Malay as a person who professes the faith of Islam, habitually speaks the Malay language and conforms to the Malay custom, and who is a descendant of persons, one of whom was domiciled in the Federation or Singapore before Independence. So integral is being a Muslim to the Malay that abandonment of Islam is equivalent to desertion by a Malay of his/her community, of his/her "Malayness". In fact, to some, being Muslim is so synonymous with being Malay that the demand of non-Malay Muslim converts for their own mosques where sermons and religious instructions could be delivered in the vernacular language is viewed with suspicion and ascribed questionable motives.

Lately this fixity of the Malay-Muslim identity has been reinforced by the National Registration Regulations 1990. The Lina Joy case (which will be discussed below) specifically illustrates how this national regulation, which is outside the syariah system, has acted in tandem with Islamic norms to control and prevent the exit by members of the Malay or Islamic community into another religious faith. By the creation of this explicit, exact, and irreversible civil definition of the Islamic identity, that "the Malay is forever a Muslim", it is inferred that Malayness, by virtue of its sacred association with Islam, cannot be repudiated by any court system.

The application by Muslims to disavow their Islamic religion has actually been brought before the courts quite frequently. One of the earliest cases of Muslims applying through the court[5] to convert out of Islam was in the case of *Soon Singh A/L Bikar Singh V Pertubuhan Kebajikan Islam Malaysia (PERKIM) Kedah & Anor.*[6] The appellant, Soon Singh, had appealed to the highest court of Malaysia, the Federal Court, to recognize that he was no longer a Muslim. At the age of seventeen, Soon Singh who was born to Sikh parents, had converted to Islam without the consent of his widowed mother. At that time, he was still a minor. By the time he reached the age of twenty-one, Soon Singh changed his mind and went through a baptism ceremony in the Sikh faith, thereby renouncing Islam. This was followed by a deed poll and an application to the High Court to declare that he was no longer a

Muslim. At this hearing, the Religious Department of Kedah objected on the grounds that the High Court did not have the jurisdiction to hear this case because it involved a Muslim conversion. It argued that such cases should fall under the purview of the Syariah Court. The High Court upheld the objection of the Religious Department, and the Federal Court rejected Soon Singh's appeal against this. In arguing for the plaintiff, counsel for Soon Singh referred to Article 12(4) of the Constitution which states that the religion of a person under eighteen years of age shall be decided by his parent or guardian. They also referred to Article 11(1) of the Federal Constitution which states that every person has the right to profess and practise his religion. However, these lines of defence did not succeed in convincing the judges that Soon Singh had valid constitutional grounds to revert to his original faith. What was evoked by the judgement was the issue of jurisdiction, that is, the civil high court could not decide on what was deemed a jurisdiction of the Syariah Court. The civil court decided that it could not deal with an issue involving a Muslim's rights to commit apostasy. Subsequent judgements on the question of the renouncement of Islam would cite the Soon Singh precedent to distance the civil court from having any say in this matter.

Lina Joy's application to renounce Islam sometime around the early 2000s was one of the heights of non-Muslim anxiety over the rising climate of Islamic control within the judiciary. Another was the case of Kamariah Ali. From 1992 till 2005 Kamariah Ali and four others had applied to the High Court to declare that they were no longer Muslims. However, they were told to apply to the Syariah Court instead. They were soon to discover that there existed a "no exit" rule for Muslims.[7] At the Syariah Court their application to renounce Islam was not unexpectedly rejected.[8] The custodians of Islam could not be expected to approve any application by a Muslim to leave Islam.

Apostasy is more than a crime, it is a divine sin by ecclesiastical rules. Hence, in 1992 Kamariah Ali and four others served a jail term imposed by a lower Syariah Court in Kota Baru for engaging in deviationist practices (deviating from Islam). Soon after her release, she was arrested with several others for being a follower of the "sky kingdom" cult (deemed as deviant Islam by those in authority). This group was led by a self-styled preacher, Ayah Pin. Kamariah affirmed a statutory declaration renouncing Islam in 1998. Later as a way of escaping charges under the Islamic Criminal Offences law, Kamariah again declared herself to be a non-Muslim, but was instead charged under Section 7 of the Syariah Criminal Offence Enactment (Takzir) Terengganu (2001) for professing to be an apostate (Murali 2008). After a three-year trial, she was found guilty in 2008 and sentenced to a two-year imprisonment, her second bout of incarceration. Whether it be Soon Singh, Lina Joy, or Kamariah Ali, all would have to seek licence which is "conditioned on permission from the group representatives", to leave — a licence that the representatives would refuse to give (Thio 2006, p. 6).

PROHIBITING MUSLIM-NON-MUSLIM MARRIAGES

Cross-religious marriages, specifically Muslim-non-Muslim marriages, are prohibited through a series of laws, both Islamic and civil. Syariah marriage laws which govern Muslims disallow Muslim-non-Muslim marriages. Consistent with this, the civil law in the form of The Law Reform (Marriage and Divorce) Act, 1976, is not applicable for cross-religious marriages. This civil law makes the conversion to Islam by one party a ground for establishing the breakdown of a marriage. Section 10 of the Islamic Family Law (Federal Territories) Act 1984 states that no Muslim man may marry a non-Muslim woman who is not a *kitabiyah*,[9] while no Muslim woman may marry any non-Muslim man. While there is an exception given to Muslim men, this exception is almost impossible to fulfil because the definition of who constitutes a *kitabiyah* is very stringent.[10] In tandem with this, laws on apostasy (under the syariah) make it an offence for Muslims to convert out of the Islamic faith, hence disallowing a Muslim to convert out of Islam in order to legalize a marriage with a non-Muslim partner.

One of the most sensationalized cases of attempts at intermarriage was one between a Malay-Muslim woman, Nor'aishah bte Bokhari, and Joseph Arnold Lee, a Chinese-Christian. It created a massive media and public furore in the country. In order to marry Joseph, Nor'aishah decided to convert to Christianity. She prepared a statutory declaration renouncing Islam before a commissioner for oaths on 22 October 1997. When her family learnt about this, they disapproved of her action and decided to keep her under house confinement. Nor'aishah, through her lawyer, then filed a *habeas corpus* action in the law courts, seeking the courts' assistance in obtaining her release. The hearing was postponed three times — first scheduled for 12 December 1997, it was moved to 7 January 1998 and finally to 19 January 1998. In the meantime, a huge media frenzy was building around this case and it had taken on a political dimension with both government and opposition parties keen to intervene in the course of events. Nor'aishah's conversion had rocked the communal and religious sensibilities of Muslims, putting enormous pressure on Nor'aishah to withdraw her intention to convert out of Islam.[11]

On 30 December 1997, Nor'aishah escaped from her parents' house.[12] A police report was lodged by her family alleging that Joseph Arnold Lee had kidnapped her. The police conducted extensive investigations and ultimately produced Leonard Teoh, Nor'aishah's advocate and solicitor, before the Magistrate's Court of Pontian, Johore. Leonard Teoh was remanded for seven days for refusing to release information on Nor'aishah's whereabouts.

He claimed that communication between solicitor and client was subject to legal privilege, and challenged the remand order at the High Court. The High Court dismissed his challenge and ruled that the remand was lawful. Legal privilege, the court held, did not extend to the furtherance of a criminal act. In delivering this judgement, Justice Abdul Malik Ishak peppered his words with quotes from popular pop songs and the greatest romance literature.

> Leonard Teoh acted for one Nor'aishah bte Bokhari ('Nor'aishah'), a Malay lady of 25 years of age. She was born a Muslim and at the material time professing the Islamic religion and was working with Citibank in Kuala Lumpur. Trouble reared its ugly head when she fell in love with one Joseph Arnold Lee, a Christian Chinese. The cupid arrow must have struck Nor'aishah right smack into her heart so much so that she lost all sense of balance. He must have used love potion number 9, for she seemed to be on cloud nine. As Francis Bacon once remarked: 'It is impossible to love and be wise'. Shakespeare too in 'A Midsummer Night's Dream' once said: 'The course of true love never did run smooth'. Reverting back to the mainstream of the case, Nor'aishah decided to renounce the Islamic faith and was bent on embracing Christianity. Leonard Teoh was retained by Nor'aishah to advise her on her conversion to Christianity and on her instructions prepared for her a statutory declaration renouncing Islam which she duly affirmed before a commissioner for oaths on 22 October 1997.[13]

At about this time the judicial process was overtaken by the executive, given the potentially divisive outcome of the whole proceedings. Muslim-non-Muslim public anger over this case was defused through a top-down directive, notably through media control. The Nor'aishah issue was basically removed from public purview. Almost overnight the media blacked out their news on Nor'aishah. At the same time, the minister in the Prime Minister's

Department in charge of Islamic Affairs was quoted as saying that everyone should abide by Article 11 of the Federal Constitution which guarantees freedom of religion.[14] After the initial flurry had simmered down, nothing more was heard of Nor'aishah and her whereabouts. Presumably her renouncement of the Islamic faith through the Statutory Declaration could not be legally rejected.[15] Although there was general disapproval from the Malay-Muslim community of the Nor'aishah-Joseph relationship, it was generally accepted at that time that there was no legal sanction against a Muslim who forsakes Islam. As long as no more political capital could be gained by any party out of this issue, it fizzled into obscurity. This was helped by the fact that the state had come down hard with its own authoritarian measures to resolve further tensions from spilling over.[16]

The litigation around intermarriage could take on several forms. In the case of *Tongiah Jumali & Anor v Kerajaan Negeri Johor & Ors*[17] the plaintiff's application (Tongiah Jumali's) was to declare herself a Christian in order to validate her marriage to a non-Muslim. This application was struck out as the High Court did not consider it within its jurisdiction to adjudicate on the conversion of a Muslim to another faith. Justice Jeffrey Tan opined that,

> ...the jurisdiction to adjudicate on any purported renunciation of the Islamic faith lies with the Syariah Court even if express provisions are not provided in the State Enactment. Thus it was held by Mohamed Yusof SCJ, in Dalip Kaur, that the only forum qualified to answer the issue whether the deceased had renounced Islam during his lifetime is the syariah court (see also *Mohamed Habibullah bin Mahmood v Faridah bte Dato' Talib* 2 MLJ 793 (1992), where it was also held by Gunn Chit Tuan SCJ [as he then was] that the Syariah Court is the only forum qualified to answer whether a Muslim has renounced Islam).[18]

Similarly, in the case of *Priyathaseny & Ors v Pegawai Penguatkuasa Agama Jabatan Jal Ehwal Agama Islam Perak & Ors*[19] the plaintiff Priyathaseny applied to be declared a Hindu as she had renounced Islam some five years back. Her continued treatment by the Islamic authorities as a Muslim had subjected her to arrest, and to charges of cohabiting with her husband, and having two infant children by him (wrongful in Islam). She sought the court to declare that her continued treatment as a Muslim is unconstitutional under the Federal Constitution. This application was again dismissed by the civil court on grounds that it had no jurisdiction to hear cases involving conversions out of Islam. The judgement by Justice Abdul Hamid Embong states that,

> ...the central and substantive issue is whether the first plaintiff remains a Muslim despite her so-called renunciation of the Islamic faith and professing now, the Hindu faith and practice... I am now guided by and bound by the pronouncement of our apex court in Soon Singh that the jurisdiction of this court is now ousted from determining the merits of this application.[20]

Muslims who seek to opt out of the syariah jurisdiction are caught in a catch-22 situation. This is because an application for renunciation of Islam can only be made at the Syariah Court, even though by doing so, the applicant would be admitting to apostasy, that is, to the commission of a criminal offence, and would be liable to punishment. For example, section 13 of the *Enakmen Jenayah (Syariah) Perak 1992*[21] states that, "Any Muslim who wilfully either by his action or words or in any manner claims to denounce the religion of Islam or declares himself to be a non-Muslim is guilty of an offence of deriding the religion of Islam and shall on conviction be liable to a fine not exceeding three thousand ringgit or to imprisonment for a term not exceeding two years or both". In all states, except the state of Negeri Sembilan, which subjects a Muslim apostate to mandatory rehabilitation, no express provision is made for a Muslim to register or formalize his conversion out of Islam.[22] A recent study reveals that out of eighty-four applications in Negeri Sembilan over a period of ten years from 1994 to 2003, only sixteen applications were allowed whilst twenty-nine were dismissed and thirty-nine are "on hold". In 2005, out of thirteen applications, five were allowed, one was dismissed, five withdrew their applications and returned to Islam, while two others are "on hold".[23]

In the next section we shall examine the three cases of Lina Joy, Shamala, and Subashini. These cases show how legal reforms started about two decades ago to assert Islam's dominance in governance have affected fundamental issues of citizenship rights and belonging. Invariably, personal lives are affected and personal tragedies fall upon families which are locked in acrimonious interreligious divorce battles or are deprived of rights to conjugal intimacy because of invalidated Muslim-non-Muslim marriages. While the contest to affirm one worldview over the other is waged within the public domain, laws and regulations which are the outcomes of this power struggle pervade the private realm in deeply unsettling ways.

THE CASES

Case 1: Lina Joy

Background of Case
Lina Joy, whose name was originally Azlina binti Jailani, was born in 1964 to Malay parents, and hence born a Muslim. When she was twenty-six years old she began practising the Christian

faith and was baptised in 1998.[24] Since being a Muslim in Malaysia carries with it obligations that are legally enforceable as well as a different set of personal laws, Lina no longer wished to be considered a Muslim.[25] However, although the National Registration Department (NRD) approved her application to change her name, it refused to accept her repeated requests to modify her national identity card to reflect her change of religion. The NRD felt it had no jurisdiction to remove the entry of her religion, Islam, on the identity card without confirmation from the Syariah Court or an appropriate Islamic authority that she had renounced Islam.[26]

The Court Decisions

Lina commenced legal proceedings at the High Court in May 2000 to seek declarations that would establish her status as a Christian.[27] After the High Court dismissed the suit in April 2001, Lina appealed to the next higher court, the Court of Appeal, in May 2001. Four years later, on 19 September 2005, her appeal was dismissed by the Court of Appeal, by a two-to-one majority decision, with two judges concurring and one dissenting.[28]

Two of the judges decided that the NRD's policy of requiring an Islamic religious authority to confirm Lina's assertion was reasonable. The dissenting opinion was that of Justice Gopal Sri Ram. He held that since the reason for the NRD's questioning of Lina's change of religion was to ascertain the truthfulness of that assertion, it should be her baptism certificate, and not a Syariah Court order that should be considered the relevant documentary evidence.

> The form she attempted to submit on January 3, 2000 makes it clear in column 31 that she no longer wished to be a Muslim. In these circumstances, an order from the Syariah Court does nothing to support the accuracy of the particular that the

appellant is a Christian. However the baptismal certificate dated May 11, 1998 produced by the appellant in evidence amply supports the accuracy of the particular that the appellant is a Christian...In the appellant's case, she stated that her reason for the change of name was that she was now a Christian. Accordingly, there is nothing in Regulation 4 (cc) (xiii) that supports the action of the Director General in this case...It follows from what I have said thus far that an order or certificate from the Syariah Court is not a relevant document for the processing of the appellant's application. It is not a document prescribed by the 1990 Regulations.[29]

In April 2006 Lina took her appeal further, this time to the highest court of the country, the Federal Court. On 30 May 2007, with more than 100 Muslims holding vigil outside the court, the Federal Court delivered its decision in upholding the Court of Appeal decision by a majority of two to one. Thus, the final stage of her appeal to remove the word "Islam" from her identity card was dismissed by this court. In the public eye, it was confirmed that this case "establishes the syariah court as the sole judicial institution in the country in regard to all things Islam".[30] The renunciation of Islam by Muslims cannot now be decided by any other court except the religious court. Even though Malaysia is a signatory to the United Nations Universal Declaration on Human Rights (one provision of which is freedom of religion), this does not deter the national courts from pronouncing such a decision, as it has been argued that such international conventions merely serve as "persuasive authority" and are only used where there is a lacuna in national laws.[31]

The then Chief Justice, Ahmad Fairuz, delivered the majority decision and held that matters pertaining to conversions to Islam were within the jurisdiction of the syariah courts and by implication, conversions from Islam were similarly within the same jurisdiction. Thus the NRD's policy in requiring an Islamic religious authority to confirm Lina's renunciation of Islam was correct, according to the highest court of the land. Chief Justice Ahmad Fairuz (whose judgement was in Malay) decided that,

> The federal court is of the opinion that it is appropriate and legal that the Syariah Court which has been given the powers to decide on conversions into Islam, would also by implication have the powers to decide on matters concerning the conversion of Muslims out of Islam or apostasy. I do not see any flaws in the judicial decision of the federal court. As such I do not have any other choice but to answer to question three by stating that the Soon Singh case had been decided correctly.[32] (Translation)

It was only Chief Justice (Sabah and Sarawak) Richard Malanjum who dissented from the other two judges. In his dissenting judgement he quoted with approval the dicta from another 1988 Supreme Court[33] case in which, "we have to set aside our personal feelings because the law of this country is still what it is today, secular law".[34] Although the question appears to be substantially an administrative question, "beneath it lurks fundamental constitutional issues involving fundamental liberties". Furthermore, he saw the Lina Joy application as touching on constitutional matters,

> Since constitutional issues are involved especially on the question of fundamental rights as enshrined in the Constitution it is of critical importance that the civil superior courts should not decline jurisdiction by merely citing article 121(1A). The article only protects the Syariah Court in matters within their jurisdiction which does not include the interpretation of the provisions of the Constitution. Hence when jurisdictional issues arise civil courts are not required to abdicate their constitutional function. Legislations criminalizing apostasy or limiting the

scope of the provisions of the fundamental liberties as enshrined in the Constitution are constitutional issues in nature which only the civil courts have jurisdiction to determine.[35]

All these arguments were to have wide-ranging implications on the status of human rights in Malaysia and formed the basis of heated public debates, setting the stage for the ever widening divide between those supporting regulated or restricted freedom of religion and those supporting unfettered freedom of religion as a constitutional right.[36] This also intensified the already existing arguments on Malaysia's status as a secular or an Islamic state.

Case 2: Shamala

Background of Case

Shamala a/p Sathiyaseelan and Jeyaganesh a/l C. Mogarajah, both Hindus at the time, were married according to Hindu rites in November 1998 and their marriage was registered under the civil marriage law. About four years later, Jeyaganesh converted to Islam and, within a week, converted their two young sons (then aged about two and three years) to Islam without Shamala's knowledge or consent.

Shamala filed a suit in the civil High Court in late December 2002 to seek custody of the children. On 7 January 2003, however, unknown to Shamala, her husband filed an *ex parte* application in the Syariah Court also for custody (*hadanah*) of the children. On 27 March 2003 the Syariah Court issued a warrant of arrest on Shamala for failure to attend the court hearing. A month after that, on 17 April 2003, the High Court granted Shamala interim custody of the children, with weekend visitation rights for her husband. Notwithstanding this decision, on 8 May 2003, the Syariah Court granted custody of the children to their father. This was a case of two separate courts deciding on the same application (that is, for child custody) by two people, one Muslim and the other non-Muslim.

The Court Decisions

On whether the Syariah Court order applied to her, Justice Faiza Tamby Chik ruled that the order giving custody of the children to Shamala's husband (who converted to Islam) was not binding on Shamala herself as she is a non-Muslim.[37] According to Justice Faiza Tamby Chik, the *hadanah* custody order "did not change the status" of the interim order given earlier by the civil court itself. He went on to state that the interim order was "made by a court of competent jurisdiction and is binding on the plaintiff wife and the defendant husband equally".[38] Justice Faiza opined, more than once, that the "husband's obligation under the Hindu marriage cannot be extinguished or avoided by his conversion to Islam".[39] He also stated unequivocally that, as a non-Muslim, Shamala was not subject to the Syariah Court's jurisdiction and that the Syariah Court had no jurisdiction to deal with any matter where one party was non-Muslim.[40] Justice Faiza Thamby Chik even remarked on the joint responsibility of both parents over their children,

> I pause here to remind parties about the equality of parental rights under s 5 of the Guardianship of Infants Act 1961 ('Act 1961') which provides that the mother of an infant shall have the like powers of applying to the court in respect of any matter affecting the infant as are possessed [by] the father and in relation to the custody and upbringing of an infant, a mother shall have the same rights and authority as the law allows to a father and the rights and authority of mother and father shall be equal. In this case, the children Saktiswaran and Theiviswaran are still infants under the said Act 1961.[41]

Shamala's other application was to get a court declaration that her husband's unilateral conversion of their two children, done without her knowledge or consent, was invalid as it violated her right to determine their religious upbringing.[42] She contended that Article 12(4) of the Federal Constitution[43] must be construed to mean that a child's religion is to be determined jointly by both the mother and father. She relied on Section 5 of the Guardianship of Infants Act 1961 ('Guardianship Act'), which confers each parent equal guardianship rights over their children. In April 2004, Justice Faiza dismissed Shamala's application to declare the conversions of her two minor children by her husband null and void. He held that one parent's consent sufficed since both provisions use the term "parent" in the singular. This decision of Justice Faiza Thamby Chik seemed to differ from the earlier opinion,

> The consent of a single parent is enough to validate the conversion of a minor. Any other interpretation would give an unjust result.[44]

In addition to that, although his earlier judgement had noted that Section 5 of the Guardianship Act grants equal parental rights to a mother,[45] here he found the provision unhelpful to Shamala as he determined that the Act was inapplicable to her husband, who had become a Muslim.[46]

> Notwithstanding what I said earlier about s 95 (b) of Act 351, I am of the opinion that the said section is not applicable to the husband in the circumstances of the present case because he is a Muslim...The wife never questioned the validity of the husband's conversion. In my view, on construction of art 12(4) of the Federal Constitution, read in conjunction with s 95(b) of Act 505, the husband as a natural parent — a Muslim father has the capacity to convert the two minors into Islam.[47]

On the question of which court has jurisdiction to determine the validity of the conversion, Justice Faiza began his analysis with the supposition that "the two minors are now Muslim".[48] He consequently held that "the syariah court is the qualified forum" to determine their status, all the while acknowledging that Shamala, as a non-Muslim, could not go to the Syariah Court for legal redress.

> Upon careful consideration of all evidence and of the surrounding circumstances, I have come to the conclusion that by virtue of art 121(1A) of the Federal Constitution, the Syariah Court is the qualified forum to determine the status of the two minors. Only the Syariah Court has the legal expertise in hukum syarak to determine whether the conversion of the two minors is valid or not. Only the Syariah Court has the competency and expertise to determine the said issue.[49]

The decision is reflective of the increasing ambiguity in questions of access to justice and of jurisdiction in matters pertaining to Islam, as well as an increasing tendency of the civil superior courts to defer to the syariah courts, notwithstanding the fact that the consequence would be a denial of legal redress for non-Muslim individuals. This is perhaps best illustrated by the advice offered by Justice Faiza to Shamala, while dismissiing her application:

> [The plaintiff] Being a Non-Muslim the Syariah Court has no jurisdiction to hear her. What then is for her to do? The answer to that is, it is not for this court to legislate and confer jurisdiction to the Civil Court but for Parliament to provide the remedy... as the law stands today I think the only way open for the Wife is to seek the help of [the State Religious Council]...[50]

In July 2004 Justice Faiza granted Shamala day-to-day custody of the children, with legal custody to be shared with her husband.

He ordered her to raise the children as Muslims and not expose them to her Hindu faith. Shamala and her husband have filed separate appeals against the High Court's decisions. This seemed to be a compromise solution, but hardly a satisfactory or a comforting one.

Case 3: Subashini

Background of Case
Subashini a/p Rajasingam's dilemma is not unlike Shamala's. Subashini and Saravanan a/l Thangathoray registered their marriage in July 2001 under civil law. A Hindu wedding ceremony was performed about seven months later. Their elder son, D, was born in May 2003 and their younger son, S, in June 2005. Subashini in her affidavit said that they began to have marital problems sometime in October 2005 and Saravanan had not returned home from February 2006 until D's birthday on 11 May 2006. On that day, she continued, he and his family members verbally abused her, alleging that S was not his son and threatening to kill her if she did not leave the home. He also alleged that he had converted to Islam and that he would cut her off from D. Shortly after that, she was forced to leave the house and allowed to take S with her but not D.

Saravanan[51] officially converted to Islam a week later, on 18 May 2006, at which time he also converted D without Subashini's agreement. He adopted the name Muhammad Shafi bin Abdullah for himself and also changed D's name to reflect their new religion. The next day, he applied to the Syariah Court for their marriage to be dissolved, based on the state Islamic law enactment, although the marriage had been registered under civil law. He also applied for interim custody of D from the Syariah Court, which was granted to him on 23 May 2006.

Subashini denied that she was aware of her husband's actions prior to receiving a notice from the Syariah Court, dated 14 July 2006, announcing the custody hearing date. On 4 August 2006, she petitioned the civil High Court for divorce, custody of both children, and maintenance for her and her children. On 7 August 2006 she applied for an *ex parte* injunction to prohibit her husband from converting the children to Islam and from commencing or continuing any Syariah Court proceedings relating to the marriage or the children.

The Court Decisions

The Court of Appeal heard Subashini's appeal in early January 2007. The arguments presented by each side reflected the widening divide in viewpoints on Islam's role in law and governance. Muhammad Shafi's contention, which had gained increasing currency in some Muslim quarters, was that since Article 3(1) of the Federal Constitution provides that Islam is the "religion of the Federation", Islamic law is the supreme law for persons professing Islam. As such, any law that is contrary to Islamic law is, therefore, *ultra vires* and void. Subashini challenged this reasoning on the premise that this constitutional provision could not detract from the clause that the Constitution is the supreme law.[52] On 13 March 2007, the court dismissed Subashini's appeal in a majority decision with Justice Gopal Sri Ram dissenting.[53]

Justice Suriyadi Halim Omar applied the principles of Islamic law to the marriage, although the marriage between Subashini and her husband was contracted under civil law. He stated that the principles which dictated the marriage ended upon Saravanan's conversion. He refrained from deciding whether the Syariah Court had jurisdiction to dissolve the marriage, since Subashini was not a Muslim, but stated that Muhammad Shafi (formerly Saravanan) was constitutionally entitled to choose the Syariah Court, instead of the civil court, in matters relating to the marriage. According to him, since both Subashini and Muhammad Shafi wanted their marriage dissolved, it "made no sense for her to object merely on the ground that the syariah court was constitutionally set up only for Muslims".[54]

Justice Suriyadi even quoted Qur'anic verses to dismiss Subashini's application to restrain the Syariah Court from resuming proceedings and to argue on the competence of syariah judges to deal with parliamentary laws:

> This judge, who must have practised syariah law and its jurisprudence, appreciative of all Islamic orthodoxy (correct interpretation of myths) and orthopraxy (correct interpretation of rituals), traditional teachings, theology, and naturally the Five Pillars, before being elevated to his posts, not only must boast experience, but also the scholarship to deal with issues that are infused with Islamic tenets. Surely that Syariah judge must be more than equipped to be given the confidence to deal with subject matters promulgated by Parliament. His position would squarely fall under these Quranic revelations:
>
> *And We have set you on a road of Our Commandment (a Syariah, or a Sacred Law of Our Commandment, Syaria'tin min al-amr); so follow it, and follow not the whims of those who know not (45:18)* (see also Islam: A Sacred Law by Feisal v Abdul Rauf).[55]

Justice Suriyadi referred again to the Qur'an in calling for a solution to the present state of jurisdictional divide,

> Parliament has to cap any obvious lacuna promptly and as equitably as possible to harmonise the two systems. Justice is never irreconcilable. The universal concept of justice and equity, and Islamic law, is not dissimilar as the al-Quran in surah An-Nisa' had revealed that justice is for mankind.[56]

Justice Hasan Lah also held that Subashini's appeal should be dismissed. He opined that Subashini should request the Syariah Appeal Court, rather than the civil court, to review whether her husband's application is within the Syariah High Court's jurisdictional limits. He stated unequivocally that the syariah courts had equal standing with the civil courts.

In his dissenting opinion, Justice Sri Ram cited both statutory and case law to support his finding that it was the civil court, not the Syariah Court, which had jurisdiction over the issues in Subashini's application for an injunction. He emphasized that the Syariah Court only had jurisdiction where all parties were Muslims (and where state legislature had expressly legislated on a matter). He found the husband's argument, that Islamic law principles prevailed over statutory law because Islam was the religion of the federation, to be baseless, and stated that Malaysia's constitutional jurisprudence was secular.

> It follows from the dichotomous approach adverted to by Lord President Salleh Abas that our Constitutional jurisprudence is secular.[57]

The divergent approaches taken by the judges raise more questions than answers, and illustrate how divided opinions are on the question of jurisdiction and the relative status of the two judicial systems as well as the status of Islam under the Constitution. As these opinions were given out, it is obvious that the Malaysian judiciary was split as to which court should ultimately decide on cases which involved the differing religious rights of the litigants. The court's decision received considerable media attention, and if the press coverage is any indication, reactions to the judgement tended to be critical. A few Islamic religious figures, a Cabinet Minister, and some individuals have voiced their support for the view that non-Muslims could be required to seek redress in the Syariah Court (Husna Yusop 2007). Several rights groups, however, along with non-Muslim religious groups, the Bar Council, and a relatively high number of members of the public wrote to the press to express alarm and outrage over the decision.[58]

ISLAMISTS VERSUS CONSTITUTIONALISTS

The above cases are but several of the numerous cases which had already surfaced around the issue of jurisdiction and constitutional liberty involving race and religion. By the 2000s this had prompted a mixed group of social activists, comprising lawyers, human rights advocates, religious leaders, and women's rights groups to call for the formation of a statutory body to be called the Inter-Faith Council (IFC). The first conference around the interfaith question was held in April 2005, with the participation of about 200 people representing all the major faith-based groups and various sectors of civil society. The IFC intended to deal with a number of legal cases which involved interreligious (Muslim/non-Muslim) tussles over issues such as conversions, marriage, child custody, and burials.

Originally several Muslim groups had given their support to the idea of the IFC, but subsequently withdrew from the pro-tem committee citing reasons such as not wanting to work with those whom they labelled as "deviant" Muslims or those who had specifically opposed the 2000 Bill on the Restoration of Faith (which empowers the state to act against Muslim apostates). A line was drawn between the defenders of "authentic Islam" and its "enemies" (non-Muslims and secular Muslims). The latter were those identified as pro-IFC advocates. One side of the divide was represented by the coalition of Muslim groups, which included the Islamic Party of Malaysia (PAS), the anti-IFC group, Badan

Anti-IFC (BADAI), and a Malay self-help movement, called the Teras Keupayaan Melayu. The coalition was named the Allied Coordinating Committee of Islamic NGOs (ACCIN). They drew a battle line against those who supported the IFC.

The coordinated effort of this body demanded that the government reject the idea of the IFC. The argument was that the IFC would threaten the supremacy of Islam as a "state religion" by suggesting that the IFC would subject the syariah system under its purview.[59] Responding to this call, the government officially instructed that the IFC be disbanded. The subsequent protest by the Muslim groups was meant to stir Muslim uneasiness by implying that if the government were to endorse the IFC, then Islam will be put on par with other religions.[60] Without the IFC, a few prominent cases would continue to be left in a state of legal limbo. The controversial cases of Shamala, Moorthy, Kamariah Ali, Nyonya Tahir, Lina Joy, Ayah Pin, and Rayappan evoked intense reactions from Muslim groups and angered non-Muslims, but were nevertheless exploited to mobilize a Muslim consensus against Islam's enemies.[61]

Despite the strident opposition of the Islamists, certain other sections of civil society continued to have faith in dialogue, and persisted to engage in this issue by setting up a new coalition called The Article 11, a direct reference to Article 11 of the Federal Constitution which reads, "Every person has the right to profess and practise his religion and, subject to Clause (4), to propagate it." This is likely to be the first constitutionalist movement in the country's history. The strategy this time was not to formalize the formation of any legal statutory bodies, but to raise awareness on the constitutional rights of citizens. It held or sponsored three forums to discuss the constitutional provisions on freedom of religion and the roles of the syariah and civil courts on matters of interreligious disputes. Despite collecting

20,000 signatures for a petition to the government, the coalition's stated objectives were still opposed by Muslim groups, which, by the middle of the year, had also gathered strength in terms of coalition membership and support from the Muslim masses. On two occasions when Article 11 forums were held, the Muslim opposition held demonstrations to protest against the group's alleged "hidden agenda" to revive the IFC. In Penang and Johor Baru, protesters heckled the panelists, and forced the events to end unceremoniously. Sensing the rising climate of interracial tension, the prime minister ordered all future Article 11 forums to be cancelled and that all public discussions on interfaith issues be banned. This came on the heels of a gathering of reportedly 10,000 Muslims at the National Mosque on 24 July 2006.

The mobilization of this Islamic "siege sentiment" was never really quelled even after the government ban on open discussions of interfaith issues. At a two-day conference held in November 2006 at the International Islamic University on the issue of apostasy, speakers included prominent members of the religious establishment, including a judge and an academic. They continued to argue the case for stiffer preventive and punitive measures against Muslims who intend to leave the faith. One of the panelists even called for apostates to be imprisoned without trial under the Internal Security Act (Fauwaz Abdul Aziz 2006).

It would be an extremely inaccurate reading of the situation if one were to say that this contestation outside the courtroom, between the Islamists and the constitutionalists, existed independently of whatever tussles were occurring within the judicial realm. There had been considerable pressure exerted by vociferous civil society organizations, both from the Islamic as well as the constitutionalist sides, to influence the direction of law reforms and court judgements in the country. The invocation of the separate jurisdiction between the syariah and civil court without reverting to constitutional supremacy involving civil law matters can be read as the triumph of Islamists who have elevated the role of Article 3 ("that Islam is the religion of the Federation") to defend and promote Islam (Thio Li-ann 2006). But constitutionalists will press on with the tenet that the Federal Constitution is the highest law of the land, especially invoking Article 4(1) which stipulates that all other laws and powers conferred by law must be constitutionally consistent (Surin 2007).

CONCLUSION

From the above cases, we may speculate that it is seldom that individuals in pursuit of happiness and personal choice are aware that boundaries laid by institutions such as the law can exert an exceedingly heavy toll on their quest. In a multiracial and multireligious society, challenging cultural and religious norms linked to legal sanctions can entail an even graver cost. In the 1950s, for example, all that thirteen-year-old Nadra "Maria" Hertogh wanted for herself was to be happy, where she was, with her Malay foster mother who brought her up from infancy. However, competing justices and nations did not see it that way.[62] As for Lina Joy, all the fever-pitched legal and political wrangling and the *cause celebre* status which her case had assumed seemed unable to capture the sad irony that she is , "… simply a person who wishes to marry and lead a quiet life, which the current legal regime poses obstacles to". (Thio op. cit.)

Resolving the issues by appealing to the courts has not brought private matters to rest. Conflict of jurisdiction between the civil and syariah courts has become more serious over the last decades. Lately however, there are small signs for optimism. The Federal Court is starting to affirm that the approach of the civil courts should start from the constitutionality of the law or decision brought before it. It is said that the issue of constitutionality is ultimately a matter for the civil High Court and not the religious court to decide.[63] Abdul Hamid Mohamad FCJ (currently the Chief Justice of Malaya), delivering a judgement of the court in July 2007, has these words for the judiciary to ponder upon,

> ...a situation can arise where the Legislature of a State makes law that infringes on matters within the Federal List. I am quite sure that there are such laws made by the Legislatures of the States after the introduction of cl (1A) of art 121 even though I shall refrain from mentioning them in this judgment. In such a situation the civil court will be asked to apply the provision of cl (1A) of art 121 to exclude the jurisdiction of the civil court. The civil court should not be influenced by such an argument. Clause (1A) of art 121 was not introduced for the purpose of ousting the jurisdiction of the civil courts. The question to be asked is: Are such laws constitutional in the first place? And the constitutionality of such laws are a matter for the federal court to decide — Article 128.[64]

This is an important acknowledgement of a festering public dissatisfaction with the state of the judiciary, but particularly of the laws and of the law-makers themselves who have been responsible for creating the enormous legal setbacks experienced by ordinary citizens.

To conclude, by analysing several legal cases of interreligious marital disputes and applications in Malaysia this chapter has examined some of the factors behind the public contention and the agony imposed upon private lives. This chapter has shown that these are connected to the nature and direction of law reforms and political battles within the system. The Malaysian legal system has gone through a distinctive process of change. Specifically, contemporary history of legal reforms in Malaysia has been strongly characterized by a move towards the infusion of more Islamic principles into the system, or the accommodation of syariah principles within the judiciary. Such a trend, while inevitable as the post-colonial nation tries to refashion itself according to the intentions of new power wielders and power holders, has also been the source of fissures within society. Islamic reformers, who lobby for more syariah on the basis of relative cultural rights, and human rights advocates, who argue for the supremacy of the secular constitution as the requisite foundation of civil liberty, have become major social actors in seeing to either the escalation or the resolution of these frictions. It is around these differences that interreligious family concerns have become the legal battlegrounds upon which the contest over law reforms and their entrenchment have been played out, much to the detriment of ethnic peace and human liberty; not to mention private happiness.

Notes

1. The country achieved its independence from British rule in 1957 and was subsequently ruled by a coalition of three ethnic parties, namely UMNO (United Malays National Organization), MCA (Malaysian Chinese Association), and the MIC (Malaysian Indian Congress). The year 1969 was a watershed year for Malaysia because of the post-elections racial riots. The conventional argument for the outbreak of the riot was that Malays had felt threatened by rising non-Malay assertion in the wake of UMNO's defeat in several key constituencies. A state of emergency was declared and the country was led by the interim National Operations Council (NOC) before fresh elections were called in 1974. It was during this transitional period that UMNO crafted a new political pact which ensured its pre-eminence in an enlarged coalition of about ten political parties, renamed the Barisan Nasional (BN — National Front).

2. Women were one of the more strategic constituents to be won over by both PAS and UMNO in this competition for the legitimization of authority over Islam. On this see Maznah Mohamad (2001).

3. Malaysia has three territories which come under federal purview. The Wilayah Persekutuan (Federal Territories) consists of Kuala Lumpur, Labuan, and Putra Jaya. The Islamic enactments for these territories are passed by Parliament. Islamic Muslim laws for these territories are contained in the 1984 Federal Territory Enactment on the Administration of Islamic Law.

4. For example, Haris Mohd Ibrahim, a Kuala Lumpur-based lawyer who served as counsel for several thorny interfaith cases in courts, and is one of the prime spokespersons on human rights has this to say, "For a long time, those pursuing an 'Islamisation' process in this country had a 'blank cheque' to do so. Laws passed, supposedly in furtherance of this process, were hardly scrutinised in the legislative assemblies. Non-Muslim legislators steered away from these proposed laws, thinking these were intra-Muslim issues. Muslim legislators, fearful of being castigated as anti-Islam if they challenged the appropriateness of such proposed laws in the context of our multi-racial, multi-religious, constitution-supreme way of life, offered little debate." See his website (not dated), "The Truth of the Matter", <http://www.accin-badailies.org/>.

5. A note on use of legal sources — the law reports listed in the reference section are used throughout for accessing judgements made in the relevant cases. These are written judgements. The reports are abbreviated accordingly. AMR (All Malaysia Review), CLJ (Current Law Journals), and MLJ (Malayan Law Journal) are all journals that report cases in Malaysia. Some cases are reported by all of them (the more important ones such as the federal court cases), and some cases may be reported by one of them, but not another. We can have a case, such as the Lina Joy's federal court case, being reported by all and may have either a CLJ or a MLJ or AMR citation, or two of them, or all three. It depends on which reporter(s) will be reporting the case. The citation will be listed as such [2004] 2 MLJ 628 or [2005]

5 MLJ 40 at 46. The figure stated within the parentheses refers to the year of publication or year that judgement was delivered, while the last figure refers to the section within the report from where the quotations are extracted.

6. MLJ 489 (1999).

7. [2005] MLJU 595 (2005).

8. Ibid.

9. *Kitabiyah* refers to the followers of the religion brought by David, Moses, or Jesus who are referred to as "people of the book".

10. The definition of *kitabiyah* here follows the Shafi'i School of Law. The woman must be descended from one of these: the Bani Ya'qub lineage, or of Nasrani ancestors who lived at the time before Mohammad became the prophet, or is a Jew by descent from the line of Jews who lived at the time before Isa became a prophet. See Ahmad Ibrahim (1999, p. 156).

11. Facts taken from *Re: The Detention of Leonard Teoh Hooi Leong*, 1 CLJ 857 (1998).

12. 1 MLJ 757 at 763 (1998).

13. 1 MLJ 757 at 761 (1998).

14. See a series of sensationalized daily reports on the issue in the Malay language newspaper, *Utusan Malaysia*, from 24–26 January 1998.

15. Facts taken from *Re: The Detention of Leonard Teoh Hooi Leong*, 1 CLJ 860 (1998).

16. Still, any whisper of potential renunciation of Islam by Malays is likely to cause heightened emotional and legal responses. For example, a rumour that Malays were being baptized at the Church of Our Lady of Lourdes in Silibin that spread through mobile phone short messaging in late 2006 nearly caused an ethnic/religious incident after a large crowd of angry Muslims gathered at the church to stop the baptism <http://www.malaysiakini.com/news/59100>. The fact that the rumour proved false as the actual function in the church was the first Holy Communion for 110 ethnic Indian children, only went to show how quick a reaction such fear could engender.

17. 5 MLJ 40 (2004).

18. 5 MLJ 40 at 46 (2005).
19. 2 MLJ 302 (2003).
20. MLJ 302 at 308 (2003).
21. *Syariah Criminal Enactment of Perak*, 1992.
22. Section 90(3) *Administration of Islamic Law (Negeri Sembilan) Enactment 1991*.
23. Dr Azam Mohamed Adil, as quoted in the news, "States' Approach to Apostate Issue Varies", *The Star*, 26 January 2007.
24. 6 MLJ 193 (2005).
25. Sections from court of appeal affidavit in support of the case.
26. This was stated during the court proceedings.
27. The judicial system consists of the subordinate courts (Magistrate's Court and Sessions Court) and the superior courts (High Court, Court of Appeal and the Federal Court). The Federal Court, formerly known as the Supreme Court is the highest judicial authority and final court of appeal in Malaysia.
28. 6 MLJ 193 (2005).
29. MLJU 345 (2005).
30. News titled, "Syariah Court Sole Authority on Islam", see *New Straits Times*, 7 June 2007.
31. MLJ 197 (2005).
32. 4 MLJ 585 at 616 (2007).
33. As the federal court was then called.
34. 4 MLJ 585 at 619 (2007).
35. 4 MLJ 585 at 598 (2007).
36. With concomitant arguments on human rights as entrenched in the Universal Declaration of Human Rights, of which Malaysia is a signatory.
37. 2 MLJ 241 (2004).
38. 1 AMR 317 at 329–30 (2004).
39. 1 AMR 317 at 323, 326 and 331 (2004).
40. 1 AMR 317 at 324, 325 and 330 (2004).
41. 2 MLJ 241 at 249 (2004).
42. This section is from 2 CLJ 416 (2004).

43. Article 12(4) of the Federal Constitution states, in relevant part: "... the religion of a person under the age of eighteen years shall be decided by his parent or guardian".

44. 2 MLJ 648 at 657 (2004).

45. 1 AMR 317 at 323 (2004).

46. 2 CLJ 416 at 423 (2004).

47. MLJ 648 at 657 (2004).

48. 2 CLJ 416 at 426 (2004).

49. 2 MLJ 648 at 660 (2004).

50. 2 CLJ 416 at 427 (2004).

51. Various documents in the record of appeal.

52. Article 3(4) states: "Nothing in this Article derogates from any other provision of this Constitution".

53. In the Lina Joy case, the only other dissenting judgement at the Court of Appeals level was that of Justice Gopal Sri Ram. The other two judges were Muslims. At the Federal Court level hearing it was Chief Justice (Sabah and Sarawak) Richard Malanjum who dissented from the majority opinion of the other two Muslim judges. Both Justices Gopal Sri Ram and Richard Malanjum are non-Muslims. This makes the issue rather obvious — that there is a division between the Muslim and the non-Muslim bench.

54. 2 MLJ 705 (2007).

55. 2 MLJ 705 at 738 (2007).

56. 2 MLJ 705 at 739 (2007).

57. 2 MLJ 705 at 729 (2007).

58. See for example, "Christian Group Troubled by Verdict on Non-Muslim", *The Star*, 24 March 2007. Subashini appealed to the Federal Court. Although the Federal Court dismissed Subashini's application on a technicality, the Court did find that the jurisdiction of the Syariah Court is limited to Muslims and the Syariah Court order dissolving the civil marriage had no legal effect in the civil High Court other than evidence of the fact that under Islamic law, the marriage was dissolved. Therefore Subashini was right to have sought her relief in the High Court. Reported in [2008] 2 CLJ 1.

59. In its press statement, it was said that "The IFC was intended to be an anti-Islam body initiated by the non-Muslims of the Malaysian Consultative Council of Buddhism, Christianity, Hinduism and Sikhism (MCCBCHS) to challenge, in the guise of Freedom of Religion, certain fundamental Islamic teachings such as prohibition of apostasy." See *ACCIN Press Statement on National Conference on Initiative towards the Formation of the INTER-FAITH COMMISSION (IFC)* held at Bangi, February 2005.

60. The spokesperson of ACCIN, Mustapha Ma, declared that "... Malaysia would have achieved Islamic state status if not for the interference of the colonial masters and the arrival of non-Muslims. Are we now witnessing the regression of our country into a secular state with Islam as a mere ornament?" (*Malaysiakini.com*, 1 March 2005).

61. See Johan Abdullah (2006) for an explanation of these cases.

62. The final judgement in the case of Nadra or Maria Hertogh, involving the tussle between her Malay foster mother and her Dutch natural parents, angered the Muslim community and culminated in the 1950 violent riots in Singapore. Later on, Maria herself grew up miserable in Holland, became estranged from her mother and was convicted for conspiring to murder her husband. A Dutch newspaper rather appropriately summed up the episode as one in which "justice triumphed but love defeated" (Haja Maideen 2000, p. 299).

63. 5 MLJ 101 (2007) (delivered by the Federal Court post-Lina Joy).

64. 5 MLJ 101 at 118 (2007).

References

Ahmad Fauzi Abdul Hamid. "New Trends of Islamic Resurgence in Contemporary Malaysia: Sufi Revivalism, Messianism and Economic Activism". *Studia Islamika* 6, no. 3 (1999): 1–74.

Ahmad Ibrahim. *Undang-Undang Keluarga Islam di Malaysia*. Kuala Lumpur: Malayan Law Journal Sdn. Bhd., 1999.

Farish A. Noor. *Islam Embedded: The Historical Development of the*

Pan-Malaysian Islamic Party PAS (1951–2003) (volume 2). Kuala Lumpur: Malaysian Sociological Research Institute, 2004.

Fauwaz Abdul Aziz. "Apostasy: Tighten Law says Negri Sembilan Mufti". *Malaysiakini.com*, 29 November 2006.

Fernando, Joseph M. "The Position of Islam in the Constitution of Malaysia". *Journal of Southeast Asian Studies* 37, no. 2 (June 2006): 249–57.

Haja Maideen. *The Nadra Tragedy: The Maria Hertogh Controversy*. Malaysia: Pelanduk Publications, 2000.

Horowitz, Donald L. "The Qur'an and the Common Law: Islamic Law Reform and the Theory of Legal Change". *The American Journal of Comparative Law* 42, no. 2 (1994): 233–93.

Husna Yusop. "Islamic Experts Tell Non-Muslims Not to Be Prejudiced Against Syariah Courts". *The Sun*, 23 March 2007.

Johan Abdullah. "The Slide in Ethnic Relations". *Aliran Monthly*, 7 October 2006.

Lee, Raymond L.M. "Patterns of Religious Tensions in Malaysia". *Asian Survey* 28, no. 4 (April 1988): 400–18.

Maznah Mohamad. "Women in the UMNO and PAS Labyrinth". In *Risking Malaysia: Culture, Politics and Identity*, edited by Maznah Mohamad and Wong Soak Koon. Bangi: Penerbit Universiti Kebangsaan Malaysia, 2001.

Mohd Asri Zainul Abidin. "It's the Faith that Matters". *New Sunday Times*, 4 February 2007.

Murali, R.S.N. "Sky Kingdom Member Jailed for 2 Years for Apostasy". *The Star*, 3 March 2008.

Nagata, Judith. "Religious Ideology and Social Change: The Islamic Revival in Malaysia". *Pacific Affairs* 53, no. 3 (Autumn 1980): 405–39.

Surin, Jacqueline Ann. "The Federal Constitution is the Highest Law of the Land". *The Sun*, 20 March 2007.

Thio Li-ann. "Apostasy and Religious Freedom: Constitutional Issues Arising from the Lina Joy Litigation". *The Malayan Law Journal Articles*, volume 2 (2006).

Law Reports
All Malaysia Reports — AMR
Current Law Journal — CLR
Malayan Law Journal — MLJ
Malayan Law Journal Unreported — MLJU

Laws
Administration of Islamic Law (Negeri Sembilan) Enactment 1991.
Syariah Criminal Enactment of Perak 1992.

Newspapers
Malaysiakini Online newspaper, various dates.
New Straits Times. "Syariah Court Sole Authority on Islam", 7 June 2007.
The Star. "States' Approach to Apostate Issue Varies", 26 January 2007.
The Star. "Christian Group Troubled by Verdict on Non-Muslim", 24 March 2007.
Utusan Malaysia, 24, 25 and 26 January 1998.

Chapter 4

LEGAL ASPECTS OF MUSLIM-NON-MUSLIM MARRIAGE IN INDONESIA

Mark Cammack

No legal issue has generated more controversy over a longer period in Indonesia than interreligious marriage. The Dutch first addressed the issue with a decree promulgated shortly after the first settlement in Batavia that prohibited all marriages between Christians and non-Christians. As the number of Europeans in the Indies increased, the effort to prevent cross-racial marriages was replaced with rules designed to regulate its consequences. Thus, under Dutch law that became Indonesian law upon independence, difference of religion was expressly stated not to be an impediment to marriage. This rule remained in effect for nearly three decades until the passage of the national marriage law in 1974.

The 1974 Marriage Law does not address interreligious marriage directly, and for many years the permissibility of marriage across religious lines was uncertain. This uncertainty has now been largely resolved. It is now generally accepted that marriage between persons of different religions is not allowed under Indonesian law. But while there is broad agreement in both the legal community and the public at large that the law prohibits marriage between persons of different religions, the legal authorities are far less certain on the issue. The difficulty in contracting interreligious marriage in Indonesia is based more on the actions of conservative Muslim groups in condemning marriages between Muslims and non-Muslims than it is on the application of law.

COLONIAL HERITAGE

The regulation of Muslim-non-Muslim marriage in contemporary Indonesia is shaped by the legacy of Dutch law. A brief summary of colonial marriage law is, therefore, necessary in order to understand the current situation.

The key fact about the law of the Netherlands Indies as it relates to contemporary regulation of marriage is that the law was personal rather than territorial (Gautama 1991). The law that governed a particular transaction depended on the "law group" to which the person belonged.[1] The three recognized law groups were, first, "Europeans", which included Dutch and other Europeans, but also Japanese and nationals of other countries whose family law was similar to that of the Netherlands; second, "foreign Orientals", which was comprised principally of Chinese, Arabs, and South Asians; and third, indigenous Indonesians.[2]

The situation with respect to the law of marriage was even more complicated, since distinctions were made within the main law groups. The marriage law for Europeans was based on the Dutch Civil Code (*Burgerlijk Wetboek*),[3] which stipulates that marriage is a purely civil relationship (Article 26). Marriage must be performed in the presence of the state registrar, and is concluded based on the declaration of the parties that they accept each other as husband and wife, and agree to fulfil the obligations imposed by law (Article 80). The marriage law for foreign Orientals distinguished between Chinese and all others. A regulation issued in 1917 extended most of the marriage provisions of the Civil Code to the Chinese (Stb. 1917 No. 129). The marriage of others in this group was governed by either the customary law or the religious law of the parties. Finally, Dutch policy for the indigenous Indonesian population was that marriage was to be governed by custom or *adat*. This resulted in a distinction between Muslims and non-Muslims. Non-Muslims were subject to the marriage law of the ethnic group to which they belonged. Because Islamic marriage doctrine was considered to have been assimilated into Indonesian custom, the marriage and divorce of Muslims were based on the Shafi'i School of Islamic Law. A third body of marriage doctrine applied to certain segments of the indigenous Christian population. A statute promulgated in 1933 (*Huwelijks Ordonantie Christen Indonesiers* (HOCI) Stb. 1933 No. 74) created a special set of marriage and divorce rules for Indonesian Christians on Java (which included the adjacent island of Madura), Minahassa, and Ambon. Christians outside these areas who were neither Chinese nor subject to European law remained subject to their customary marriage rules. Thus, the marriage law system at the end of the colonial period was as follows:

- The European group: The Dutch Civil Code
- Foreign Orientals:
  - Chinese: Civil Code
  - Others: Customary or Religious law
- Indigenous Indonesians:
  - Christians in Java, Minahassa, and Ambon: HOCI
  - Muslims: Islamic law
  - Others: *Adat*

The existence of different marriage laws for different elements of the population created an evident need for some mechanism to regulate marriages between persons belonging to different groups.[4] Although the matter had been dealt with previously, the most comprehensive treatment of mixed marriage was contained in the Regulation on Mixed Marriage promulgated in 1898 (*Regeling op de Gemengde Huwelijken* or RGH, Stb. 1898 No. 158). The RGH declared that difference of religion, nationality, or origin is not a hindrance to marriage (Article (7(2)); that marriage between persons from different law groups is to be performed according to the law applicable to the husband (Article 6(1)); and that a woman who marries a man belonging to a different law group thereby acquires the legal status of her husband (Article 2).

The complex system of multiple marriage laws was made even more complicated through the creation of two separate marriage registries. In 1849 the Dutch created the Office of the Civil Registry (*Burgerlijke Stand/Catatan Sipil*) to implement the registration requirement of the newly promulgated Civil Code (Stb. No. 25, 1849). Initially it was only European marriages performed according to the Civil Code that could be registered. The services of the Civil Registry were later extended to Chinese and then to Christians married under the HOCI by statutes promulgated in 1919 (Stbl. 1919 No. 81) and 1933 (Stbl. 1933 No. 75).[5]

The marriage registration system established by the Dutch was applicable to only a small segment of the population of the Indies. The group of non-Christian indigenous Indonesians, which comprised the overwhelming majority of the population, was not included in any of these statutes.[6] Shortly after independence, the newly established republican government addressed this gap in the law with a statute requiring registration of Muslim marriages (Law No. 22/1946). For reasons related to expanding political patronage, the task of registering Muslim marriages was not assigned to the existing Civil Registry, an arm of the Ministry of Home Affairs, but to a (then) newly created Office of Religious Affairs (*Kantor Urusan Agama*/KUA), which is administered by the Ministry of Religion.

Another important step concerning the administration of marriage was taken in 1966 in the immediate aftermath of the 1965 failed coup attempt. An instruction issued by the "Presidium Cabinet" in 1966 extended the services of the Civil Registry to all Indonesians (Presidium Cabinet Instruction No. 31/U/IN/12/ 1966). By this action provision was made for the registration of marriages of non-Muslims not covered in the Dutch-era registration statutes. Finally, in 2006 the legislature enacted the Law on Civil Registration that overhauled the existing system of population registration and replaced the diverse collection of colonial (and independence) era laws and regulations with a single statute (Law No. 23/2006). While the 2006 law abolished most of the colonial legacy of religious and ethnic differentiation in the registration system, one feature of the previous system that is preserved in the Act is the existence of separate marriage registries for Muslims and non-Muslims. The Ministry of Religion and its local offices of religious affairs administer the marriage and divorce of Indonesian Muslims, while responsibility for registration of the marriage of non-Muslims is assigned to the Home Affairs Ministry and its local civil registry officials.

INTERRELIGIOUS MARRIAGE IN INDONESIA

The Dutch structure of multiple law groups and multiple marriage laws became Indonesian law when Indonesia achieved independence after World War II.[7] This included the 1898 Mixed Marriage Regulation that expressly authorized marriages across religious lines.

In the mid-1950s the RGH and the principle of interreligious marriage received the unqualified endorsement of the Indonesian Supreme Court. The case involved a Muslim woman, Soemarni Soeriaatmadja, who wished to marry Ursinus Elias Medellu, a Christian man.[8] The KUA refused to register the marriage on the grounds that marriages between Muslim women and non-Muslim men are not allowed under Islamic law.[9] Soemarni then petitioned the local District court, which found no legal grounds to prevent the marriage, and the couple was married in a ceremony presided over by a Protestant pastor.

The woman's father, who was also an official at the Ministry of Religion, opposed the marriage and filed a suit in the Jakarta District court to have it annulled.[10] The Jakarta District court denied his petition, and Soemarni's father sought a review of the District court's decision in the Supreme Court.

The Supreme Court upheld the lower court's decree permitting the marriage and rejected the contention that religious doctrines can interfere with an individual's freedom to marry a person from a different religion. The Court first affirmed the validity of the Mixed Marriage Regulation. Permission to enter into an interreligious marriage cannot be denied on the grounds of difference of religion, according to the Court, since to do so would enable the religious law to effectively prohibit what the statute expressly permits.

Having disposed of the petitioner's claim the Court went on to address broader issues relating to interreligious marriage and the relations between state law and religion generally. Noting the religiously and ethnically diverse character of Indonesian society, the Court concluded that the rule permitting interreligious marriage is a practical necessity to avoid the legal and social consequences of illegitimacy. The Court next addressed the jurisprudential premises of its decision. The Court acknowledged that in authorizing marriages between Muslim women and Christian men, the statute permits a type of marriage that the religious law forbids. However, this inconsistency presents no real conflict, according to the Court, since religious law and the law of the state operate in different spheres. The purpose of all laws applicable in this world is the regulation of social life, whereas religion is principally concerned with salvation in the hereafter.

The Supreme Court's endorsement of the principle of interreligious marriage was answered by an equally emphatic rejection of Muslim-non-Muslim marriage by the local Muslim community. In September of 1952 an estimated 5,000 protestors gathered at a mosque in the Tanah Abang district of Jakarta to voice their opposition to the marriage of Soemarni and Ursinus. The organizers of the event produced a resolution that was sent to President Soekarno and other government officials. The resolution stated, among other things, that the marriage between Soemarni and Ursinus was invalid from the perspective of Islamic law, called for the withdrawal of the Mixed Marriage Regulation pending the enactment of a new law, and urged the government to declare the marriage between Soemarni and Ursinus invalid (Gautama 1991, pp. 136–37).

THE MARRIAGE LAW OF 1974

The goal of replacing Dutch marriage legislation with national law was an announced priority from early on in Indonesia, and efforts to enact marriage legislation began shortly after independence. Although a number of marriage law proposals were debated in the 1950s and 1960s, none of the proposals was enacted. The principal point of contention was whether to enact a single set of marriage and divorce rules applicable to all

Indonesians, the position generally favoured by secular nationalists, or to provide different marriage laws for different religious/cultural communities, the approach favoured by Muslim advocates of state enforcement of Islamic law.

The impasse was finally broken in the mid-1970s. It was the opinion of the Soeharto government at the time that circumstances were then ripe for passage of a secular national marriage law. The government had scored a decisive electoral victory in 1971, the first election held following Soeharto's assumption of power after the 1965 coup (Mackie & MacIntyre 1994, pp. 12–13). After the election the government further consolidated its hold on power by disbanding all existing political parties and forcing them into two new parties — the Unity Development Party (*Partai Persatuan Pembanguan*, PPP), made up of all existing Muslim parties, and the Indonesian Democracy Party (*Partai Demokrasi Indonesia*, PDI) that included the secular nationalists and non-Muslim religious parties (Id.).

The government presented its marriage law proposal in July 1973.[11] By this time many Muslims had come to believe that the Soeharto government was intent on marginalizing Islam as a political force, and the marriage law proposal was interpreted as yet another assault on Muslim interests. To begin with, Muslim organizations, including the Ministry of Religion, were completely excluded from the preparation of the legislation (*Tempo*, 8 September 1973, pp. 6–7).[12] Muslim opponents of the proposal were most concerned, however, with the substance of the draft, which was believed to deviate in several respects from Islamic law. The provision that attracted the greatest criticism was Article 2 which set forth the requirements for a valid marriage. This Article, which was reflective of the fundamentally secular character of the bill generally, made registration with the state the basic condition for creation of a valid marriage. Another provision that provoked significant opposition was Article 11 regarding marriage between persons of different religions. That Article, which largely tracked the language of the Dutch RGH, stated:

> Differences of nationality, ethnic group, country of origin, place of origin, religion, belief, and descent are not an impediment to marriage.

The proposal to authorize marriage between persons of different religions without restriction drew a predictably harsh response from certain Muslims.[13] The opposition to Article 11 was based in part on the perceived incompatibility of the provision with Islamic doctrine. Although Muslim jurists have expressed a range of opinions on the permissibility of Muslim-non-Muslim marriage, the most widely held opinion approves one category of marriages between Muslims and non-Muslims — marriages between Muslim men and non-Muslim women who adhere to a religion with a divine revelation (*ahli kitab*), that is, either Christians or Jews.[14] Marriages between Muslim men and women who are not *ahli kitab* and all marriages between Muslim women and non-Muslim men are forbidden.

A second more divisive objection to Article 11 was based on a claim that the rule was intended to serve the ulterior motive of converting Indonesian Muslims to Christianity (Rasjidi 1974).[15] Among those believed to be behind the Christianization programme was the Centre for Strategic and International Studies (CSIS), a think-tank with a number of prominent Catholics and close ties to the Soeharto government. It was suspected that the eventual goal of CSIS was the establishment of a Catholic dominated government in Indonesia similar to the one that existed in Buddhist South Vietnam (*Tempo*, 8 September 1973, pp. 6–7).

The government's proposal had the support of a majority of the members of the legislature. The governing GOLKAR party, the PDI, and the Armed Forces, which occupied a block of unelected seats as part of its "dual function", expressed varying degrees of support for the measure. The only party that opposed the bill was the Muslim-based PPP. More important than the opposition within the legislature, however, was the reaction to the government's proposal by the broader Muslim community, which condemned the draft in harsh and uncompromising terms. The Soeharto government's dismissive treatment of Muslim interests was compared unfavourably to the actions of the Dutch who, according to the critics, had at least consulted Muslims before going forward with a proposed marriage reform in the 1930s. Muslim preachers condemned the bill during Friday prayers, and demonstrations against the bill in Jakarta and elsewhere threatened to become violent (*Tempo*, 25 August 1973, p. 6).

Concerns that the situation might spiral out of control and threaten the country's security were made worse by the fact that the controversy over the marriage law occurred during a period when students were staging mounting protests against growing economic inequality and government reliance on foreign capital. The volatility of the situation became clear in January 1974, just weeks after the Marriage Act was approved, when riots broke out in Jakarta in protest against the visit of the Japanese prime minister.

The intensity of Muslim opposition to the marriage law proposal apparently persuaded Soeharto that he had overreached himself. The task of resolving the controversy was assigned to the military. In late November representatives from the Armed Forces faction in the legislature met with representatives of the Muslim PPP to work out a compromise. The agreement, which reportedly had the approval of Soeharto (Mudzhar 1993, p. 53),[16] promised Muslim interests that Islamic law and Islamic legal institutions would not be diminished or altered. It was also agreed that

Article 2 regarding the requirements for marriage would be revised to give overriding effect to the religious law of the parties. The representatives of the PPP agreed in return to a requirement that marriages be registered in the interest of administrative regularity and to the implementation of measures to prevent arbitrary divorce and polygamy.

In early December a ten-member parliamentary working group that included all four parliamentary factions was formed to revise the law according to the terms of the agreement (*Tempo*, 15 December 1973, p. 6). The discussions within the working group quickly deadlocked, however. After seven meetings and despite the intervention of the Ministers of both Religion and Justice, the working group could neither agree on the formulation of the bill's first article nor agree on a way forward. The governing GOLKAR group and the Armed Forces faction were both willing to compromise, but the Indonesian Democracy Party (PDI) and the Muslim PPP were intransigent. The nationalist-oriented PDI declared that it was not bound by an agreement to which it was not a party. For its part, the PPP projected an attitude that no compromise was necessary, and that its interests would ultimately be vindicated. In a prescient analysis published in the final days before the bill was completed the news magazine *Tempo* wryly suggested that, despite the impasse in the negotiations, PPP's apparent optimism might yet prove justified. "In spite of everything", the article stated, "a fair wind may still blow in the direction of [PPP] if the way is opened once again for lobbying from 'high places'" (*Tempo*, 22 December 1973, p. 11). The anticipated intervention was apparently forthcoming, and the law was finalized in time to meet the government's announced deadline — Indonesian Mothers' Day.

The statute that was enacted differs fundamentally from what was originally proposed. The difference is apparent in the key provision of the law that defines the requirements for a valid marriage. Article 2 of the Marriage Act makes the formation of marriage dependent on compliance with religious requirements. A marriage is "valid" under this Article if it is performed according to the religious law of the parties. This differs from the original proposal, which envisioned marriage as a purely civil relationship. Insofar as compliance with religious requirements is the only means of creating a valid marriage it also differs from the law as it existed prior to the passage of the Act. Prior to 1974, Indonesian law permitted both religious marriage and civil marriage performed by the Office of Civil Registry. The elucidation to Article 2 states that "there is no marriage outside the religious law of the parties", suggesting that civil marriage is no longer recognized in Indonesia.

A number of articles were dropped from the government's proposal pursuant to the agreement that all matters contrary to Islamic law would be removed. Among the articles from the draft that did not appear in the statute is Article 11 concerning interreligious marriage. No official explanation was given for the removal of Article 11, and the Statute contains no provision specifically addressing interreligious marriage. The Statute does, however, include a section labelled "Mixed Marriage", which was also included in the draft. The rules contained in this section have generally been interpreted as applicable to marriages between persons subject to different marriage law because of differences in nationality, and not to marriages of persons of different religions.

The absence of an explicit treatment of the subject of interreligious marriage in the Marriage Act has created considerable confusion and uncertainty.[17] The failure to provide a clear answer to such an important question was not a result of oversight, but reflects the inability of either the supporters of a right to interreligious marriage or those who opposed it, to have its position written into law. It can be assumed that the government was unwilling to implement the restrictions on interreligious marriage favoured by Muslim groups, but at the same time, did not want the issue to prevent the law from being approved. The permissibility of interreligious marriage was intentionally left ambiguous in anticipation that a definitive interpretation of the statute on the issue would ultimately be achieved in negotiations within the bureaucracy.

The provisions of the Marriage Act that bear on interreligious marriage are subject to differing interpretations. The legal arguments concerning the permissibility of interreligious marriage focus primarily on whether the subject of marriage between persons of different religions is covered or regulated by the Act. That issue assumes importance because of Article 66, the Act's transitional provision, which specifies the effect of the Marriage Act on prior law. Article 66 states that existing marriage legislation, including the Dutch Regulation on Mixed Marriage, remains in effect to the extent matters treated in those laws are not covered in the Marriage Act. Thus, if interreligious marriage is not regulated by the Marriage Act, it remains permissible under the Mixed Marriage Regulation, and the requirements for concluding a marriage between persons of different religions are those stated in the Regulation. Those favouring a right to marry persons of a different religion argue that the matter of marriage across religious lines is not covered in the Act because Article 11 that addressed the subject was removed prior to enactment.

The argument that the Marriage Act limits or prohibits marriages between persons of different religions is premised on a contention that the colonial Mixed Marriage Regulation was superceded by the Marriage Act. In particular it is argued that the permissibility of marriage between persons of different religions is governed by the provisions of the Act regarding the general requirements for creating a valid marriage. In other words, the permissibility of a marriage between persons of different religions depends on whether the marriage is permitted under Article 2 by the religious law of the parties.

The first official pronouncements concerning the permissibility of interreligious marriage under the Marriage Act came from the Supreme Court and the Department of Internal Affairs, both of which issued instructions on the application of the Marriage Act in 1975. Neither pronouncement addressed the issue of interreligious marriage directly, but both statements intimated that the Regulation on Mixed Marriage remained in effect after the passage of the Act. The Supreme Court directive simply reiterated the substance of Article 66 of the Marriage Act stating that the Act repeals prior laws only insofar as those laws are regulated by the Marriage Act.[18] The Court then cited, among other things, the Regulation on Mixed Marriage. The Department of Internal Affairs' pronouncement was similarly oblique. The purpose of the statement, which was issued on 1 October 1975, the date the Marriage Act took effect, was to instruct local registry officials on the implementation of the Act. The brief statement simply instructed local registrars to continue to register marriages and divorces under existing registration laws until such time as a comprehensive civil registry law could be enacted. The statement then cited four colonial era statutes — the three registration statutes and the Mixed Marriage Regulation. The Decision did not purport to interpret the Marriage Act, but the citation of the Regulation as a legal basis for registration implied that it remained in force and that marriages authorized by the Regulation continued to be permissible.[19]

The Department of Religion signalled a different interpretation of the Marriage Act in a letter written in March 1976.[20] The letter was written by Wasit Aulawi, the Religion Ministry official with responsibility over the Islamic Courts, and was addressed to the mayor of the East Javan city of Malang. Copies of the letter were also sent to the Departments of Justice and Home Affairs. The Mayor had directed an enquiry regarding the legal status of a marriage between a Muslim man and a non-Muslim woman to the Provincial Governor and the Department of Justice. The Religion Department letter was apparently prompted by the Department's disagreement with the position taken by the Department of Justice.

The letter first addressed the relevance of the Marriage Act's provisions on "mixed marriage", concluding that those articles were concerned with marriages of persons of different nationalities, not different religions. The letter stated next that a marriage is considered valid and may be registered only if it is valid according to the religion of the parties. "Therefore, a marriage between persons of different religions can be considered valid only if it is valid according to the religious law of the parties." Under Islamic law, according to the Religion Department official, a Muslim man may marry a non-Muslim woman who is a Person of the Book (*ahli kitab*), which includes a Christian. Since the case that was the subject of the inquiry involved the marriage of a Muslim man and a Christian woman, the marriage was valid under Islamic law, and therefore also valid under the Marriage Act.

The legal status of the Mixed Marriage Regulation and the permissibility of interreligious marriage came before the Indonesian Supreme Court in the latter part of the 1980s. The case involved a Muslim woman named Andi Vony Gani who wished to marry Andrianus Petrus Hendrik Nelwan, a Protestant man.[21] The couple sought to marry at both the Office of Religious Affairs and the Civil Registry, but both offices refused to register their marriage. Andi Vony then sued in the District Court in Jakarta challenging those decisions. Quoting both the Qur'an and the New Testament, the District Court ruled that the marriage was prohibited by the religious law of both parties and rejected the request for permission to marry. Andi Vony then sought a review of the District Court's decision in the Supreme Court.

The Supreme Court declined to follow either of the conventional approaches to the issue. The Court rejected the authority of the Mixed Marriage Regulation, but not on the usual ground that interreligious marriage is regulated by the Marriage Act. The Court expressly found that the Act does not address marriages between persons of different religions, but refused to apply the Dutch era law because the secular premises of the RGH are incompatible with the religious conception of marriage reflected in the Marriage Act. The Court then turned to Article 2 as the legal authority most directly pertinent to the issue. That Article has generally been interpreted as requiring, in the case of interreligious marriage, that the law according to which the marriage is performed permit marriage between persons of different faiths. Thus, a Christian woman may be married to a Muslim man in an Islamic ceremony provided such marriages are permitted in Islamic law. The Supreme Court interpreted the rule that marriage be performed according to the religious law of the parties as requiring fulfilment of the marriage law of both parties to the marriage. In the case of a marriage between persons of different religions, this means that two sets of rules are applicable at the same time, which is an impossibility. On that basis the Court concluded that Article 2 applies only to marriages between persons of the same religion.

Although the Supreme Court interpreted the Marriage Act to require persons wishing to marry to be subject to the same law, the Act does not thereby preclude marriage between persons of different religions. There is nothing in the Marriage Act indicating that difference of religion is a bar to marriage, the Court wrote, and the constitutional guarantee of equality before the law arguably encompasses a right to marry citizens of different religion. Considering that interreligious marriage is not prohibited by Indonesian law, and may in fact be guaranteed as a constitutional right, the Court found that the absence of provision for interreligious marriage constitutes a gap or "vacuum" in the law. Given the principle that difference of religion is not a bar to marriage, and the reality that many persons of different religions wish to marry each other, the Court concluded that the gap in the law should not prevent such marriages from taking place. The question, then, is how this is to be accomplished. Because the powers of the Office of Religious Affairs are limited to presiding over marriages between Muslims, the office, therefore, cannot officiate over a marriage involving a Christian. On that basis the Court concluded that the Civil Registry is the appropriate agency to perform marriages of mixed religion couples. Beyond the question of jurisdiction, however, Article 2 of the Marriage Act requires that the parties to a marriage be subject to the same law. The Court found a solution to that problem by assuming that the petitioner in the case, Andi Vony, had effectively renounced Islam. By filing her petition to be married with the Civil Registry, Andi Vony implicitly indicated that she wished to submit to a non-Muslim marriage. Finding that the petitioner no longer considered herself a Muslim, the Court ordered the Jakarta Civil Registry to perform the marriage.

The Andi Vony decision is the most authoritative statement on the permissibility of interreligious marriage under the Marriage Act, and the case has generated a large commentary in keeping with its perceived importance.[22] In an analysis of the decision published in 1991 Sebastiaan Pompe (1991) concluded that the

Court intended to use the decision to send a message to Civil Registry officials that marriage requests from mixed marriage couples should be honoured. If that was the Court's intention, which seems likely, the decision stands as a spectacular failure since it had almost no impact beyond the parties before the court. The Supreme Court released its ruling on 20 January 1989, and shortly thereafter, the couple was married in a civil ceremony at the Jakarta Civil Registry. Ironically, however, the case that was intended to establish the legality of interreligious marriage was the last such marriage ever performed by the Jakarta Civil Registry. On 1 January 1989, three weeks before the Supreme Court issued its decision on the Andi Vony case, the Jakarta Civil Registry adopted the policy that civil marriages would no longer be recognized.[23] The new policy required that all marriages be performed by religious officials, and restricted the function of the Civil Registry to recording marriages that had been previously formalized by religious authorities.

The decision by the Jakarta Civil Registry to discontinue the practice of performing civil marriages did not on its face address the issue of marriage between persons of different religions. But conflict over interreligious marriage was clearly the reason for the change. The policy reversal in January 1989 was preceded by a period of intense criticism of the Civil Registry's role in performing interreligious marriages. The eventual ban on interreligious marriage is generally attributed to a series of occurrences in Jakarta in mid-1986 (Mujiburrahman 2006, pp. 185–87). In June 1986 Jamal Mirdad, a popular Muslim singer, was married to Lydia Kandou, a well known Protestant actress, in a civil ceremony at the Jakarta Civil Registry. The marriage created a minor uproar among the public and sparked a round of recriminations within the bureaucracy. The Jakarta Regional Council of Muslim Religious Scholars expressed strong disapproval of the marriage in letters to the Governor of Jakarta and other provincial officials. The Civil Registry responded to the criticism by issuing a decision stating that marriages such as that of Jamal and Lydia involving Muslim men and non-Muslim women should be performed by the Muslim Office of Religious Affairs, but marriages of non-Muslim men and Muslim women fall within the purview of the Civil Registry.[24] This was not the response the critics of interreligious marriage were looking for. Three weeks after the release of the Civil Registry's decision, the Ministry of Religion issued its own statement expressing a different interpretation of the matter. In a letter addressed to the Governor of Jakarta, the Religion Ministry official stated that marriages between Muslim women and non-Muslim men are not permitted under the Marriage Act, and that in any event the Office of Civil Registry has no authority to register marriages involving Muslims.[25] The Governor of Jakarta quickly came to the defence of the Civil Registry with a letter endorsing its position.[26]

In December 1988, the Jakarta Civil Registry adopted the policy that it would no longer perform civil marriages. This was more than two years after the controversy over the marriage of Jamal and Lydia. I was told by individuals who were working at the Civil Registry during this period that the immediate cause of the change in policy was the appointment of a new director of the Civil Registry in 1988. It is clear as well, however, that events in Jakarta were part of a broader discussion on national policy regarding interreligious marriage.[27] Within a few months after the change of policy in Jakarta the Ministry of Home Affairs issued instructions that resulted in the abolishment of civil marriage throughout the country. In a circular letter to provincial governors dated 17 April 1989, the Minister for Home Affairs stated that only religious marriages would receive legal recognition and that registration by the Civil Registry must be preceded by a religious ceremony performed by appropriate religious authorities.[28]

INTERRELIGIOUS MARRIAGE PRACTICE

The decision to discontinue performing civil marriage and limit state recognition to marriages performed by religious authorities did not resolve the question of the permissibility of interreligious marriage in Indonesia. This decision simply recast the issue as a matter of religious rather than state regulation.

It is not my intention to undertake a comprehensive analysis of the teachings of all Indonesian religions on interreligious marriage. It is sufficient for present purposes to make two general points. First, religious doctrine is generally ill-suited to the task of resolving questions of state marriage law, and achieving definitive answers to questions concerning interreligious marriage is often difficult or impossible. Second, despite, and also because of, the indeterminacy of religious law, it can be stated with confidence that interreligious marriage is not entirely banned by the religions represented in Indonesia.

The Marriage Act is based on an assumption that the teachings of each of the country's religions includes a body of marriage rules that are sufficiently definite and stable to be applied by a modern state bureaucracy. That assumption is problematic when applied to Islam. The "marriage law" of most of Indonesia's other religions is considerably less well developed than that of Islam, and the problems associated with relying on the teachings of these religions to regulate marriage are accordingly greater.

Mention has been made of the fact that the majority opinion within Islamic law has historically recognized a limited right of Muslim men to marry non-Muslim women. But it cannot be said that this states the rule of Islamic law on interreligious marriage.

There is no central legal authority in Islam, and Islam contains no set of universally recognized legal doctrines. The existence of legitimate difference of opinion in matters of legal interpretation is demonstrated by the fact that official opinion in Indonesia with respect to Muslim-non-Muslim marriage has itself changed over the decades. By 1989 all of Indonesia's major *fatwa* bodies (those entitled to rule on a point of law or dogma) had rejected the traditional rule and issued *fatwa* declaring all marriages between Muslims and non-Muslims impermissible. The Nahdlatul Ulama, which issued a ruling in 1960 declaring that marriage between Muslims and non-Muslims is forbidden, was the first to take this step.[29] The Indonesian Majelis Ulama issued a similar decision in 1980,[30] and the *fatwa* committee of the Muhammadiyah declared interreligious marriage impermissible in 1989.[31] But these rulings, and the very existence of multiple *fatwa* bodies, demonstrate that Islamic law provides no definitive answer to the question.

Although diversity of opinion on the subject of interreligious marriage within Islamic law is undeniable, it might be argued that the Indonesian government has effectively resolved the issue of difference of opinion with respect to matters found in the Compilation of Islamic Law. The Compilation is an Indonesian language code of marriage, inheritance, and *waqf* (donation for pious purposes) rules that was promulgated for use by the Islamic courts in 1991. An early draft of the Compilation would have permitted marriages between Muslim men and non-Muslim women who were either Christians or Jews. However, the provision on interreligious marriage was revised before the Compilation was released, and in the final version Muslim-non-Muslim marriages of all types are completely banned.

The Compilation is now generally regarded as authoritative by the Islamic courts. It could be argued, therefore, that whatever the diversity within Islamic doctrine, the Compilation constitutes the authoritative version of Islamic law for institutions of the Indonesian state. This is a plausible position, but it does not have universal approval, and the issue continues to be debated. The principal objection to recognition of the Compilation as an authoritative statement of Indonesian Islamic doctrine is based on its lesser status in the hierarchy of laws under Indonesian law. The Compilation was not submitted to the legislature, but was promulgated by means of a presidential order.

The marriage law of most of Indonesia's other religions is considerably less well developed than the marriage law in Islam; some of the religions found in Indonesia barely speak of the issue. Next to Islam, the marriage law of the Catholic Church is probably the most detailed and definite of the religions found in Indonesia. The Catholic position on interreligious marriage is probably more restrictive than the country's other religions. But even within Catholicism, interreligious marriage is not entirely prohibited. While the other four religions recognized in Indonesia limit or discourage interreligious marriage to some degree, it is manifestly not the case that all six of Indonesia's recognized religions categorically prohibit marriage across religious lines.

It may generally be said of all legal systems that the question of what the relevant legal authorities really "mean" is less important than the question of what courts, administrators, and other legal actors actually do. The extent to which religious officials in Indonesia, in fact, refuse to marry their followers to persons of a different religion is difficult to ascertain. It is certain, however, that some religious officials from both Islam and Indonesia's other religions perform such marriages. The practice of marrying Muslims to non-Muslims according to Islamic law has attracted particular attention in connection to groups that offer what is best described as an interreligious marriage service.

The most prominent group engaged in performing interreligious marriage was affiliated with the progressively-oriented Paramadina University in Jakarta. Paramadina stopped performing marriages in 2005, but another group known as the Inter-Religious Forum has since emerged to offer the same services. These groups facilitate marriages between persons of different religions by providing the services of a private *"penghulu"* to preside over the exchange of the offer and acceptance of marriage as required by Islamic law. Although Islamic law does not require the participation of religious officials in the marriage ceremony, under Indonesian law, the marriage contract must be performed in the presence of a quasi-clerical official from the Office of Religious Affairs. The participation of this official, commonly referred to as the *penghulu*, is so well-ingrained in Indonesian marriage practice that popular opinion has come to regard the presence of the *penghulu* as a necessary part of the marriage ceremony. In the case of Paramadina marriages, the function of *penghulu* was performed by a member of the University's faculty and a scholar of Islamic law who publicly affirmed the permissibility of interreligious marriage under Islamic law. Although the attendance of the Paramadina official contributes nothing to the validity of the marriage under either Indonesian or Islamic law, the association of the marriage with an Islamic legal scholar and a scholarly justification is significant in the eyes of the parties and the public at large. On a more practical level, Paramadina and its successor organization work with the local Civil Registry so that the marriages performed under their supervision can be registered.

In addition to the question of whether an interreligious marriage can be formalized, there is a separate question of whether the marriage can be registered. Since the Marriage Act does not require registration for a marriage to be valid,[32] the category of nominally valid marriages does not necessarily coincide with the category of registered marriages. In fact, as many as half of all marriages in Indonesia are not registered.[33] As a practical matter, registration is often more important than validity. A child born to a valid but unregistered marriage, for example, has a legal relationship with his mother, but not his father. Indeed, "validity" according to the law of the state adds little if anything to a marriage beyond the religious legitimacy that arises independently of the state's endorsement.

Because many of the benefits of marriage are dependent on registration, a prohibition of registration of interreligious marriages would be as onerous, if not more so, than a prohibition against formalizing such marriages. Whether or under what circumstances a marriage between a Muslim and a non-Muslim could be registered at the Civil Registry was for many years uncertain. The 1989 pronouncement by the Minister for Home Affairs states that a marriage can be registered only after it has been formalized by the appropriate religious officials. This instruction was generally interpreted by Registry officials to mean that the Civil Registry has no role in performing marriages, but simply verifies the occurrence of actions that are under the authority of religious officials.

Although the Civil Registry has renounced its role in performing marriage or specifying the requirements to marry, Registry officials I spoke to in 2006 stated that only marriages between persons who share the same religion can be recorded, and that in cases in which the identity cards of the parties indicate different religions, proof of conversion is required before the marriage can be recorded. While this is probably an accurate characterization of practice generally, the policy was apparently never as strict as it was represented to be. The registration of interreligious marriages performed by Paramadina was mentioned above. Church officials also told me in 2006 that the Civil Registry sometimes records marriages of mixed religion couples without proof of conversion if the non-member party to the marriage promises to permit the member spouse and the couple's children to continue to practise the religion.[34]

The law on civil registration that was approved in December 2006 includes a provision on registration of interreligious marriage that may make marriages between Muslims and non-Muslims more easily contracted. The oblique manner in which the issue is treated reveals the sensitivity of the subject and shows how difficult it is to address the question directly. Marriage between persons from different religions is not mentioned in the statute itself, but only in the official elucidation that accompanies it. Article 35 states that one type of marriage that is subject to the registration requirement is "marriages that have been decreed by a court". The explanation for this phrase in the elucidation states that it refers to "marriages that are performed between communities (*antar-umat*) with different religions". Though phrased in unnecessarily obscure terms, this clearly refers to marriages between persons with different religions, and will likely be understood as an invitation to mixed religion couples to request permission to marry from a court. There is as yet no specific authorization for such a procedure, but the general courts are hearing requests from mixed religion couples for permission to marry based on a provision in the 1974 Marriage Act that authorizes the courts to hear an appeal against a decision by a marriage register not to register a marriage.[35]

The civil registration law does not change the law pertaining to marriage between persons of different religions. Moreover, in requiring a court decree in order to register an interreligious marriage, the Act adds to the burden of registering such a marriage rather than making registration easier. But this stealth strategy for legal change is well practised within the Indonesian legal system, and depending on how the courts respond, the veiled invitation contained in the civil registration law may prove beneficial to mixed religion couples wishing to marry.

The procedures applicable to the KUA differ from those of the Civil Registry. KUA officials both preside over the marriage and complete the registration. While the publicly stated position of the Ministry of Religion is that interreligious marriage is not allowed, the practice is apparently not so inflexible. The official handbook for Muslim marriage registrars published by the Ministry of Religion authorizes one type of interreligious marriage. The handbook's instructions for marriage registrars contain a list of ten types of marriages that are prohibited under Islamic law (*syari'at Islam*). Marriage between persons of different religions is listed here as among the marriages that are not allowed. Later in the same section, however, this absolute prohibition is qualified. The handbook states:

> A Muslim man is prohibited from marrying a non-Muslim woman, and a Muslim woman is similarly prohibited from marrying a non-Muslim man. However, a Muslim man is permitted to marry a woman who belongs to a religion that possesses a divine revelation (*ahli kitab*), that is, a woman who is either a Jewess or a Christian. This rule is an example of diversity of doctrine, which need not be discussed here (Department of Religion 2003, p. 31).

INTERRELIGIOUS MARRIAGE AS A FUNDAMENTAL RIGHT

Constitutional norms have historically played only a minor role in the development of Indonesian law, and the permissibility of interreligious marriage has so far been debated primarily within the framework of the Marriage Act. With the end of the Soeharto era and the move to establish legal limits on state power, the situation has begun to change. Among the constitutional reforms passed by the post-Soeharto People's Consultative Assembly (Majelis Permusyaratan Rakyat/MPR) was the addition to the Constitution of a broad set of fundamental rights based on the Universal Declaration of Human Rights. The catalogue of Constitutional rights includes several rights that might be used to challenge limitations on the right to marry. For example, Article 28(B) guarantees the right to form a family, Article 28(E) guarantees freedom of religion and association, and Article 28(I) guarantees the right to be free from discriminatory treatment. To be sure, none of these provisions clearly encompasses a right to marry a person of a different religion, but constitutional norms commonly express broad general values that take more definite shape in the process of application.

Even more significant than the passage of a constitutional bill of rights was the creation of a Constitutional Court with the power to invalidate legislation that is in conflict with the constitution. The establishment of a Constitutional Court was approved by the MPR in the 2001 round of constitutional amendments, and in 2003 the justices were appointed to the Court and it began to hear cases. In its first few years in operation the Court has demonstrated a willingness to use its powers to enforce conformity with the Constitution. The Court has issued a number of important and controversial decisions striking down a variety of laws dealing with, *inter alia*, privatization of the electrical power industry, anti-terrorism, and the rights of former Communists to stand for elective office.

From what has been said, a petition to the Constitutional Court would appear to offer a promising strategy for challenging the ban on interreligious marriage. The prospects for success in such a suit, however, are poor. While the Court's previous decisions suggest that it might be sympathetic to the merits of the claim, the problem for those wishing to challenge the constitutionality of the ban on interreligious marriage is getting the issue before the Constitutional Court. The Constitution limits the Court's legislative review powers to a review of the conformity of legislation (*undang-undang*) with the Constitution (Article 24C(1)). Under the enabling act implementing the Constitutional grant of authority (Law No. 24/2003), the Court's review authority is defined as including the power to decide whether the "substantive content (*materi muatan*) of an article, paragraph, and/or section of a statute conflicts with the Constitution" (Article 51(3)(b)).

CONCLUSION

It is generally regarded as common knowledge in Indonesia that marriage between persons of different religions is not allowed. While there is a virtual consensus that interreligious marriage is not allowed, the legal authorities on which that belief is based are far less certain. The ban on marriage between persons of different religions is assumed to be derived from the language of Article 2 of the Marriage Act. But a prohibition against interreligious marriage is not apparent on the face of Article 2, and it has never been authoritatively interpreted to encompass such a prohibition.

For practical purposes, it scarcely matters whether the belief that interreligious marriage is prohibited is correct (whatever that might mean) so long as those charged with implementing the law refuse to recognize such marriages. The refusal of Registry officials to sanction marriages across religious lines has more to do with avoiding criticism from Muslim opponents of the practice than with the terms of the law. The process by which the views of this one segment of the population came to exert such a powerful influence is complicated. Certainly, the adoption of a restrictive rule for fellow Muslims is one of the ways by which Muslims opposed to interreligious marriage have been able to prevent or discourage the practice. But the declarations in the Compilation of Islamic Law and recent *fatwa* that interreligious marriage is not permitted under Islamic law appear to have had an effect that reaches beyond Muslims. The Marriage Act recognizes marriages carried out according to any of the country's six religions, and the fact that interfaith marriage is not permitted by Muslim religious law does not prevent the performance of interreligious marriage by Protestant or Confucian authorities. Similarly, the pronouncements of Muslim opponents of interreligious marriage on the permissibility of interreligious marriage under Islamic law have no direct bearing on the Civil Registry. The Civil Registry deals exclusively with marriages performed according to the law of a religion other than Islam. All marriages based on Islamic law must be registered at the KUA.

The announcement by Muslim leaders of a total ban on interreligious marriage under Islamic law does not directly affect the permissibility of interreligious marriage performed by other religions, but the restrictive policy adopted by Islam has been an important factor in promoting the perception that interreligious marriage is prohibited generally. This is in part a result of confusion or lack of understanding of the significance of the Islamic doctrine in Indonesian law. Because most Indonesians are Muslims, it is, no doubt, generally assumed that a ban on interreligious marriage under Islamic law means that interreligious marriage is banned for Muslims. The adoption of a restrictive rule for Islam also promotes the perception that interreligious marriage is banned generally in more direct ways. Some Protestant church leaders told me that they refrain from marrying their members to persons of different religions, but their reason for refusing to perform interreligious marriage is not that church law forbids it. The reason given for not marrying people of different religions is to avoid criticism by Muslims.

Muslim opinion has always been a potent force in shaping Indonesian family law policy. The ability of Muslim opponents of interreligious marriage to pressure other religions to renounce interreligious marriage is probably strengthened by the hard line position they themselves have taken on the issue. Indeed, the strategic advantage of declaring a total ban on all interreligious marriage may help explain why, on this particular question, Indonesian Islam has adopted a position that is more conservative than the mainstream. If Indonesian Muslim leaders were to adhere to the majority rule and marry Muslim men to non-Muslim women, they could hardly fault Christian churches for marrying Muslim women to Christian men. But by declaring a complete ban on interreligious marriage, Muslims are in a much better position to denounce other religions who fail to do the same.

The historical process that led the Civil Registry to discontinue the practice of performing civil marriages suggests that the same dynamic that explains the refusal of some religious leaders to perform interreligious marriages is also at work in the Civil Registry. Registry officials ceased to perform civil marriage in response to criticism by Muslim leaders of the Registry's role in performing interreligious marriage. The action that was taken at the time did not address interreligious marriage directly; the Registry stopped performing civil marriages and announced that only marriages formalized according to religious doctrine would be recognized. This change was responsive to Muslim criticism to a point, since civil marriage had been used to unite couples who did not share the same religion. But the objections that prompted the change were not to civil marriage *per se*, but to any marriage of a Muslim woman to a non-Muslim man. Inasmuch as the announced policy that only religious marriage would be recognized did not fully address Muslim criticisms, it is reasonable to infer that the Civil Registry quietly took the further step of refusing to register any marriage in which the parties did not share the same religion.

The subject of Muslim-non-Muslim marriage continues to incite controversy, and the current approach to the issue has the full approval of almost no one. The legal system has accommodated the disagreement that exists within society by maintaining a degree of uncertainty and ambiguity in the law. This lack of clarity has allowed for a certain flexibility in the application of the law that opens avenues for mixed religion couples to marry while at the same time preserving the pretense that marriage between Muslims and non-Muslims is not allowed. This approach is manifest most recently in the 2006 Law on Civil Registration. On its face, the Law creates no new rights to interreligious marriage. The only mention of the issue is a vague reference to a non-existent court procedure for recognition of such marriages. While the statute does little to clarify whether interreligious marriage is permitted under Indonesian law, it may have the effect of providing mixed religion couples regular and predictable means both to marry and have their marriage registered. For now, that is perhaps the most that supporters of a right to interreligious marriage can reasonably hope for.

Notes

1. This system had its origins in Article 109 of the *Regerings Reglemement* of 1855. In 1926 that provision was incorporated as Article 163 of the *Indische Staatsregeling*. As Lindsey (2005, p. 43) has pointed out, this classificatory scheme was not the product of any single moment in history, but emerged through a long historical process.

2. The boundaries of these groups were not impermeable. Foreign Orientals and Indonesians could become subject to the law of a different group through a process of "assimilation" (Gautama 1991, p. 150).

3. The Civil Code for the Indies was approved in 1846 and took effect on 1 May 1848.

4. More to the point, perhaps, the Dutch wished to assert control over the inevitable unions between Dutch citizens and Indonesians or other non-Europeans in the Indies. See Stoler (1992).

5. Although the Civil Registry recorded vital statistics for all three groups, separate registries were maintained for each.

6. A 1920 enactment (Stbl. 1920 No. 751) provided for the registration of births and deaths of indigenous Indonesians in most parts of the colony, but the regulation did not address registration of marriages.

7. The 1945 Indonesian Constitution declares that existing laws shall continue in force until replaced by new legislation (Transitional Provisions, Paragraph II).

8. Reg No. 245 K/Sip/1953.

9. The Regulation on Mixed Marriage stated that marriages between persons from different law groups are to be governed by the law of the prospective husband. Before the couple may marry it must be shown that the marriage does not violate marriage law requirements applicable to the prospective wife. Compliance with this requirement must be proven with a written declaration from the official having jurisdiction over marriages of the woman's law group. For Muslims, the official with authority to issue the declaration is the head of the local office of Religious Affairs. If the registry office refuses to permit the marriage the woman has the option of petitioning the local court for a review of the registrar's decision.

10. The petition argued that the marriage was invalid because the petitioner, as the girl's father and guardian (*wali mudjbir*), had not given his consent to the marriage as required under Islamic law.

11. For a discussion of the marriage law controversy with particular emphasis on the issue of interreligious marriage, see Mujiburrahman (2006), pp. 163–80.

12. The question who wrote the bill was never answered, but Muslims suspected that it originated with General Ali Murtopo and Catholic members of GOLKAR who were close to Murtopo (Mujiburrahman 2006, p. 166). While the Murtopo group may have been consulted on the proposal, the bill was probably drafted under the direction of the office of the State Secretariat, based on input from a variety of sources. However, the theory of the Catholic origins of the proposal was consistent with Muslim suspicions that the law was intended as an attack on Muslims. For Muslim critics the theory also seemed to be borne out by the content of the proposal, which proposed a secular marriage law to be enforced by the secular district courts.

13. See e.g., *Beberapa Pasal Masalah, Tempo,* 8 September 1973, pp. 9–10.

14. The allowance for this type of marriage is based on Qur'an 5:4 which states, according to the translation of Mohammed Marmaduke Pickthall, "This day are (all) good things made lawful for you. The food of those who have received the Scripture is lawful for you, and your food is lawful for them. And so are the virtuous women of the believers and the virtuous women of those who received a divine revelation."

15. The most prominent advocate of this "covert Christianisation" thesis was Professor H.M. Rasjidi, a respected modernist and the country's first Minister of Religion. See Rasjidi (1974).

16. Atho Mudzhar reports that the decision to accede to Muslim demands followed a visit to Soeharto by two prominent leaders from the Nahdlatul Ulama, K.H. Bisri Sansuri and K.H. Masykur.

17. For a discussion of the various interpretations of the Act as it relates to interreligious marriages, see Pompe (1988).

18. *Nomor MA/Pemb./0807/1975, Petunjuk-Petunjuk Mahkamah Agung Mengenai Pelaksanaan Undang Undang Nomor 1 Tahun 1974 dan Peraturan Pemerintah Nomor 9 Tahun 1975, 20 August 1975.*

19. Another executive branch decree issued in 1983 implied that the Mixed Marriage Regulation was no longer valid. In February 1983 Soeharto issued a Presidential Decision regarding the organization

and functioning of the Civil Registry (*Keputusan Presiden No. 12/1983 tentang Panataan dan Peningkatan Pembinaan Penyelenggaraan Catatan Sipil*). The legal considerations for the Decision listed all the other colonial era registration statutes except the Regulation on Mixed Marriages. I am not aware that registry officials attached any significance to this omission, but subsequent events proved the Decision to be a portent of future policy.

20. *DIV/4N/2260/76, Pelaksanaan Undang-Undang No. 1/1974 Peraturan Pemerintah No. 9/1975, 4 March 1976.*

21. *Mahkamah Agung Reg. No. 1400/K/Pdt/1986, 20 January 1989.*

22. Prominent English language discussions of the case include Pompe (1991), Butt (1999), and Bowen (2003).

23. Sudhar Indopa interview with Mark Cammack, July 2006.

24. *Keputusan Kepala Kantor Catatan Sipil Propinsi DKI Jakarta No. 2185/1.755.2/CS/1986 tentang Petunjuk Penyelesaian Pelaksanaan Perkawinan "Antar Agama" pada Kantor Catatan Sipil.* The Decision came after a high-level consultation on the subject of interreligious marriage organized by the Office of Civil Registry. The meeting was attended by, among others, representatives of BAIS, the Armed Forces, the State Intelligence Service (Bakin), the Police, and the regional office of the Department of Religion.

25. *Departemen Agama Direktorat Jenderal Pembinaan Kelembagaan Agama Islam No. EV/HK.03.4/2803/86, 3 September 1986.*

26. *Gubernur Kepala Daerah Khusus Ibukota Jakarta, No. 2009/-1.755.2, 27 September 1986.*

27. Pompe (1988, p. 272) reports that it was decided in a meeting by the Ministers for Religion, Justice, and Home Affairs in January 1987 that civil marriages would no longer be permitted. I have not been able to confirm this decision.

28. *Menteri Dalam Negri No. 893.3/1558/PUOD, 17 April 1989.*

29. NU reiterated the ruling that all marriages between Muslims and non-Muslims are prohibited in *fatwa* 1962, 1968, and 1989 (Masyuri 1997, pp. 225–26, 339–41).

30. *No. 05/Kep/Munas II/MUI 1980, 1 June 1980.*

31. *Keputusan Sidang Seksi I Muktamar Majelis Tarjih Mujhammadiyah ke XXII, 15 February 1989.*
32. Language that would have made registration necessary for a valid marriage was removed in response to Muslim objections.
33. This is the marriage registration rate cited by Siti Musdah Mulia, former Special Assistant to the Minister for Religion. While I am not aware of the empirical support for this figure, there are good reasons to accept it as reliable. A comparison of the number of divorces processed by the Islamic courts with an estimate of the number of self-reported divorces demonstrates that only about one-half of all divorces by Indonesian Muslims are processed by the courts (Cammack et al. 2007, pp. 119–20). It is reasonable to assume that the rate of unregistered marriage is comparable to the rate of unregistered divorce.
34. There is to my knowledge no reliable information on the frequency of marriage between persons of different religions in Indonesia. One impediment to obtaining data on the extent of interreligious marriage is the fact that many such marriages are contracted after one of the parties has converted to the other party's religion, and therefore these marriages would not be recorded as marriages between persons of different religions. More fundamentally, the extreme sensitivity of the issue has discouraged efforts to research the subject.
35. I am grateful to Marcus Lange for calling this to my attention.

References

"Beberapa Pasal Masalah". *Tempo*, 8 September 1973, pp. 9–10.

Bowen, John R. *Islam, Law and Equality in Indonesia: An Anthropology of Public Reasoning*. Cambridge: Cambridge University Press, 2003.

Butt, Simon. "Polygamy and Mixed Marriage in Indonesia: The Application of the Marriage Law in the Courts". In *Indonesia: Law and Society*, edited by Timothy Lindsey. Sydney: Federation Press, 1999.

Cammack, Mark E., Helen Donovan and Tim B. Heaton. "Islamic Divorce

Law and Practice in Indonesia". In *Islamic Law in Contemporary Indonesia: Ideas and Institutions*, edited by R. Michael Feener and Mark Cammack. Cambridge, Massachusetts: Harvard University Press, 2007.

Departemen Agama. *Pedoman Pegawai Pencatat Nikah*. Jakarta: Direktorat Jenderal Pembinaan Kelembagaan Agama Islam, Departemen Agama R.I., 2003.

Gautama, Sudargo. *Essays in Indonesian Law*, 2nd ed. (1993). Bandung: Citra Aditya Bakti, 1991.

Lindsey, Tim. "Reconstituting the Ethnic Chinese in Post-Suharto Indonesia: Law, Racial Discrimination, and Reform". In *Chinese Indonesians: Remembering, Distorting, Forgetting*, edited by Timothy Lindsey and Helen Pausacker. Victoria, Australia: Monash University Press, 2005.

Mackie, Jamie and Andrew MacIntyre. "Politics". In *Indonesia's New Order: The Dynamics of Socio-Economic Transformation*, edited by Hal Hill. Honolulu: The University of Hawaii Press, 1994.

Masyhuri, K.H. Aziz, ed. *Masalah Keagamaan Hasil Muktamar dan Munas Ulama Nahdlatul Ulama*. Surabaya, Indonesia: Dinamika Press, 1997.

Mudzhar, Mohammad Atho. *Fatwas of the Council of Indonesian Ulama: A Study of Islamic Legal Thought in Indonesia 1975–1988*. Jakarta: Indonesia-Netherlands Cooperation in Islamic Studies, 1993.

Mujiburrahman. "Feeling Threatened: Muslim-Christian Relations in Indonesia's New Order". Ph.D. dissertation, Utrecht University, 2006.

Pompe, S. "Mixed Marriages in Indonesia: Some Comments on the Law and Literature". *Bijdragen tot de Taal-, Land- en Volkenkunde* 144, nos. 2/3 (1988): 259–75.

———. "A Short Note on Some Recent Developments with Regard to Mixed Marriages in Indonesia". *Bijdragen tot de Taal-, Land- en Volkenkunde* 147, nos. 2/3 (1991): 261–72.

Rasjidi, M. *Kasus R.U.U. Perkawinan Dalam Hubungan Islam dan Kristen*. Jakarta: Bulan Bintang, 1974.

"RUU (Rancangan Undang-Undang) Perkawinan, Aksi dan Reaksi". *Tempo*, 8 September 1973, pp. 6–7.

"RUU (Rancangan Undang-Undang): Yang Didrop dan Diubah". *Tempo*, 15 December 1973, p. 6.

"RUU (Rancangan Undang-Undang): Masih Pasal 1". *Tempo*, 22 December 1973, p. 11.

Stoler, Ann. "Sexual Affronts and Racial Frontiers: European Identities and the Colonial Politics of Exclusion in Colonial Southeast Asia". *Comparative Studies in Society and History* 34 (1992): 514–51.

"Suara Khatib dan Ancaman Gregorius". *Tempo*, 25 August 1973, p. 6.

Chapter 5

THE POLITICO-RELIGIOUS CONTESTATION
Hardening of the Islamic Law on Muslim-non-Muslim Marriage in Indonesia
Suhadi Cholil

The study of Muslim-non-Muslim marriage in Indonesian Islamic law is intriguing because it will not only show how Islamic law has been practised in the largest Muslim country in the world, but also how Indonesian Muslims interpret their religion for the sake of communal need. In this chapter, I will investigate some pertinent issues on Muslim-non-Muslim marriage in Indonesia from two angles: the discourse on interreligious marriage in the Islamic tradition, and the current discourse on Muslim-non-Muslim marriage, as well as analyse legal changes that have taken place in recent times and the political motives behind them.

Religio-political contestation lay behind the Islamic law prohibiting Muslim-non-Muslim mixed marriage in Indonesia. As a result of the contestation, interreligious marriage became impossible for Muslims, both men and women. The political contestation involves a number of Muslim organizations. *Fatwa* or religious decrees prohibiting interreligious marriage were successively issued by the Muslim organization, Nahdlatul Ulama (NU) (literally Ulama Awakening), in 1960, the Majelis Ulama Indonesia (MUI) or Indonesian Ulama Council in 1980, and Muhammadiyah (the Indonesian reformist Muslim organization), which is the second largest Indonesian Islamic organization, in 1989. While the socio-political reason behind the NU religious decree was fuzzy, both the MUI and the Muhammadiyah decrees on Muslim-non-Muslim marriage take very clear positions. According to them, interreligious marriage will lead Muslims astray to convert to other religions. To a large extent, the religious political contestation in Indonesia is manifested in the two largest religious communities, the Muslims and the Christians.

DISCOURSE OF THE ISLAMIC TRADITION

There are three Qur'anic verses dealing with Muslims marrying non-Muslims, namely, idolaters (*musyrik*), unbelievers (*kuffâr*), and people of the Book (*ahl al-kitâb*).

> And do not marry idolatresses (*al-musyrikât*) till they believe. And indeed a slave woman (*amah*) who believes is better than an idolatress (*musyrikât*), even though she pleases you... (Al-Qur'an 2:221).

> O you who believe, when believing women (abandon the enemy and) ask for asylum with you, you shall test them. Allah is fully aware of their belief. Once you establish that they are believers, you shall not return them to the disbelievers. They are not lawful to remain married to them, nor shall the disbelievers be allowed to marry them. Give back the dowries that the disbelievers have paid. You commit no error by marrying them, so long as you pay them their due dowries. Do not keep

disbelieving wives. You may ask them for the dowry you had paid, and they may ask for what they paid... (Al-Qur'an 60:10).

This day are (all) things good and pure made lawful unto you. The food of the People of the Book is lawful unto you and yours is lawful unto them. (Lawful unto you in marriage) are (not only) chaste women who are Believers, but chaste women among the People of the Book, revealed before your time, when ye give them their due dowers (mahr), and desire chastity, not lewdness, nor secret intrigues (Al-Qur'an 5:5).

Muslim scholars have generally understood the first two verses as prohibition of Muslim-non-Muslim marriage. Sura 2, verse 221, prohibits Muslim marriage to those who believe in gods other than Allah (musyrikun/musyrikat). Moreover Sura 60, verse 10, prohibits Muslims from sending female converts, who have come to them, back to their unbelieving husbands.

Sura 5:5 is the primary source that has given rise to polemics in the history of Islamic law, due to its exceptional viewpoint which allows Muslims to marry "virtuous" or free (muhsanât) women of the People of the Book, commonly understood as Christians and Jews.

As mentioned by Kecia Ali, these basic tenets of Islamic law presuppose two kinds of hierarchies: that Muslims take precedence over non-Muslims, and husbands over wives (Ali 2006, p. 14). But in Indonesia, the exception allowed by the surah 5:5 has been denied. We need to understand the religio-political motives behind this elimination of any possibility of Muslim-non-Muslim marriages.

Religio-political consideration in Islamic law is not something new, having existed since the era of Prophet Muhammad and his disciples. Some classical Muslim scholars were aware that Muslim men are permitted to marry women of ahl al-kitâb, but because of political (*as-siyâsah*) considerations, they turned it into a prohibition. In this instance, the consideration refers to an instruction of Umar bin Khattâb who asked other disciples of Muhammad to divorce their wives of *ahl-al-kitâb*.

> When Umar asked the disciples of the Prophet to divorce their *ahl al-kitâb* wives, all the disciples obeyed the instruction, except Huzaifah. Then Umar asked of Huzaifah again — 'Please divorce her'. Huzaifah said, 'Would you (Umar) be the witness that marrying a woman of *ahl al-kitâb* is prohibited (*harâm*).' Umar answered, 'She will cause slander (*fitnah*), please divorce her.' Then Huzaifah repeated what he had said before and Umar responded again — 'She is a slander'. Finally, Huzaifah said: 'Actually I knew that she will cause slander, but she is permitted (*halâl*) for me.' After Umar left him, Huzaifah divorced his wife of *ahl al-kitâb*. A disciple asked him: 'Why did you not divorce her when Umar asked of you?' Huzaifah replied, 'I do not want people to know that I hold an improper attitude' (Qudamah vol. 6, p. 590).

Besides Al-Qur'an 5:5, the verse which gives Muslims the right to wed free women of the scriptures was included in a very late, if not the latest, period of the revelation. According to some traditions, it was revealed during the Prophet's last pilgrimage (*hajjat al-wadâ'*) in the year 10 A.H./632 A.D. (Al-Wahidî 1968, pp. 126–27; As-Suyûtî).[1] Yohanan Friedmann writes that if this traditional dating is accepted, permission to wed Jewish and Christian women was granted after the "break with the Jews", that is, after the Prophet decreed their exclusion from Medina and after the conquest of Khaybar. If we interpret Al-Qur'an 5:5 according to the predominant view, in which the permission to wed *ahl al-kitâb* women is a symbol of Islamic superiority, the timing of the permission becomes understandable: once the great victory of Islam over its enemies had been assured, the time had come to symbolize this victory by permitting the Muslims to take women of the conquered in matrimony (Friedmann 2003, p. 191).

VOICES OF INDONESIAN MUSLIM SCHOLARS AND THE STATE ISLAMIC LAW

The issue of Muslim-non-Muslim marriage in Indonesia has become of striking interest among Islamic law scholars (*fuqahâ'/ 'ûlamâ'*). It has also been receiving a great deal of attention from law experts and practitioners. Indonesian Muslim scholars often do not only articulate their own opinions, but they represent the voice of their religious organizations. Here, we will explore the positions and theological arguments of the three largest Muslim organizations in Indonesia, namely the NU, MUI, and Muhammadiyah.

The NU had earlier given a short statement on the issue of Muslim-non-Muslim marriage. The largest Muslim organization in Indonesia, NU was formed by Hasyim Asy'ary, a charismatic Javanese *ulama* (Islamic scholar). Since its establishment in 1926, the organization has held periodic meetings (*muktamar, munas, konbes*), of which one of the agendas was to issue religious decrees. An NU religious decree on Muslim-non-Muslim marriage was issued in a Jakarta meeting in 1960, following which nineteen religious decrees (*fatwa*) were published. The Muslim-non-Muslim marriage decree started with a question: "What is the decree for a Muslim man marrying a *kafir* woman?" The decree was only stated very briefly: "It is prohibited (*haram*) and is illegal (*tidak sah*), if the *kafir* woman is not a *kafir kitabi*, which means, her ancestors were not members of the original religion before the era of Muhammad's prophethood." The scholars of the NU had referred to the text of Al-Syarqawi in a literal manner (Masyhuri 2004, pp. 184–85). To some extent, it is common practice for the organization to issue its religious decrees in the light of the classical literature of the *ulama* (*kitab kuning*) without further argumentation, rationalization, and explanation.[2] Besides the doctrinal interpretation, there exists a political motive, but from this curt NU decree, it is not possible to trace the politics behind the rationale for the decree. Mujiburrahman mentions in his published Ph.D. dissertation that the NU's decree was related to the political tension between Muslim and Christian political groups that had existed since 1952 on the issue of interreligious marriage in the drafting of the Marriage Bill. Besides being a Muslim mass organization, the NU was a political party during the period 1952–73. He argued that the decree could be linked to the position of the NU as a political party at that time (Mujiburrahman 2006, pp. 160, 184). However I tend to see no indication of political undertones in the text of NU's decree. The contents of the decree differ from those of the Muhammadiyah and MUI.

While the NU religious decree was brief and unilluminating, the religious decree issued by MUI twenty years after NU's decree was very clear. On 1 June 1980, MUI issued a decree on Muslim-non-Muslim marriage.[3] The decree was a follow-up of a discussion on interreligious marriage in the MUI second annual conference in 1980. The decree has two significant aspects: first, a Muslim woman is not allowed to be married to a non-Muslim man; and second, a Muslim man is not permitted to wed a non-Muslim woman, including *ahl al-kitâb*. The absolute prohibition of a Muslim marrying a woman of *ahl al-kitâb* was a new development in the Indonesian religious discourse at that time. The NU did not have the courage in 1960 to present sophisticated polemics prohibiting marriage to women of *ahl al-kitab* in its religious decree. However MUI in 1980 explicitly declared the prohibition. MUI argued that the prohibition of marriage between Muslim men and women of *ahl al-kitâb* is based on *masâlih al-mursalah*, which is the principle of issuing a *fatwa* on behalf of Muslim interests.

The position of Muhammadiyah is as clear as the position of MUI. Initially, Muhammadiyah agreed with the opinion that Muslim men are permitted to marry women of *ahl al-kitâb* based on Al-Qur'an 5:5, arguing that the Prophet Muhammad had married Maria Qibtiyah, a Christian woman from Egypt. Besides that, many disciples of the Prophet also married women of *ahl al-kitab*. Nevertheless, Muhammadiyah reconsidered its position and asserted that the permission (*al-ibahâh*) for Muslim men to marry women of *ahl al-kitab* should be based on the intentions of the Muslim men. The intention of the Muslim man to convert the woman of *ahl al-kitâb* after marriage should be a point for consideration (*al-illah*) for granting permission. If however, circumstances are such that the Muslim man would be converted to the religion of his wife, the permission to marry turns into a prohibition (*harâm*).

Based on Muhammadiyah's view on the practice of Muslim-non-Muslim marriage, there are two dangerous threats when a Muslim man marries a non-Muslim woman. The first is due to Muslim men generally converting to the religion of their non-Muslim wives. The second is that children commonly adhere to their mothers' religion. Therefore, Muhammadiyah used the *saddu adz-dzari'ah* (avoiding disadvantage) theory to ban marriages between Muslim men and women of *ahl al-kitab*. For Muhammadiyah, the term *harâm* (forbidden) is not *harâm li dzatih* (forbidden in its existence), but *harâm li sadd adz-dzarî'ah* (forbidden in order to avoid disadvantage). Likewise this method in Islamic law was regarded as the application of the Islamic law principle of *ushûl al-fiqh: dar'u al-mafâsid muqaddamun ala jalbi al-mashâlih*, meaning "to prevent from destruction is paramount, rather than to gain benefit". According to the Islamic law objectives (*maqasid as-syari'ah*), this principle is a way to protect religion (*hifdz al-dîn*). All attempts should be made to avoid apostasy.[4] To sum up, Muhammadiyah's stance on Muslim-non-Muslim marriage is similar to that of MUI.[5]

The claim that marriage between Muslim women and non-Muslim men will invariably result in their children becoming non-Muslims seems to be only a prejudiced assumption. According to my recent ethnographical research, there is no conclusiveness in the trend of children's religious affiliation. There are some factors which influence their religious affiliation, such as the religion of extended family members who live with them, the religious beliefs of parents, and the schools they attend. It appears, therefore, that the prohibition of Muslim-non-Muslim marriage in Indonesia was constructed on the basis of an untenable assumption and fear that the proportion of Muslims in the population will decrease.

At the level of state Islamic law, there is still textual ambiguity in the laws on mixed marriage, including Muslim-non-Muslim marriage. The religious court, as a court for Muslims, adopts regulations from some law sources such as the *HIR/R. Bg.*,[6] *Law of Marriage No. 1/1974*, and *Instruction of President No. 1/1991 on Compilation of Islamic Law*. There are contradictions among these regulations. There is also a variety of interpretations among law scholars. The opinion that is frequently and tightly held by the judges of the religious court is that interreligious marriage between a Muslim man and a non-Muslim woman, or a Muslim woman and a non-Muslim man, is prohibited. This is derived from the Compilation of Islamic Law section (CIL) 40(c), which states, "It is prohibited for a man and a woman to get married in particular circumstances: (c) a woman is non-Muslim", and CIL section 44, which states, "A Muslim woman is not allowed to get married to a non-Muslim man". According to Ahmad Sukarja, the prohibition becomes stronger because the Marriage Law No. 1/1974 section 2 (1) states that a marriage is legal if it is performed based on each person's religious law and belief (Sukarja 1996, pp. 19–20).

In line with the prohibition of Muslim-non-Muslim marriage in the CIL 1991, some Indonesian Muslim scholars have argued that interreligious marriage leads to many problems that arise due to fundamental religious differences between the couple. According to them, we may find a mixed marriage couple getting along well and keeping their marriage intact, but these are rare cases that should not be cited as parameters for judging longevity of mixed marriages.

The CIL also refers to the past religious decrees of Indonesian Muslim scholars, in particular, the one issued by MUI ten years before the CIL. To circumvent the prohibition of Muslim-non-Muslim marriage, Muslim-non-Muslim couples usually register their marriage in the Civil Registry. However, this way out has been criticized by MUI Jakarta. According to MUI, under Government Regulation No. 9/1975 section 2 (2), the Civil Registry has no authority to register marriages between Muslims and non-Muslims.

In fact, there are no specific regulations in Indonesia that clearly prohibit Muslim-non-Muslim marriage. This lack of clarity gives rise to questions from the public and sometimes causes conflicts in the society. Moreover Indonesian Muslims generally tend to follow the CIL, which prohibits Muslim-non-Muslim marriage. To some extent, the CIL can be seen as a tool used to exact discipline in the Muslim social order. Seen from this perspective, the CIL, although not a proper law because of its low status in the legal hierarchy, has become an effective instrument for Indonesian *ulama* and scholars who do not wish to allow Muslim-non-Muslim marriage.

THE RELIGIO-POLITICAL DIMENSION BEHIND THE
ISLAMIC LAW OF MUSLIM-NON-MUSLIM MARRIAGE

At this point, I will examine the interest behind the Indonesian Islamic law on Muslim-non-Muslim marriage. As noted above, the statements of many, if not all, Islamic organizations and Islamic elites in Indonesia on Islamic Law, including those of MUI, NU, and Muhammadiyah, as well as the interest behind the CIL, agree with the prohibition of Muslim-non-Muslim marriage, including marriage between a Muslim man and a woman of the *ahl al-kitab*. The prohibition is in contradiction with the text of Al-Qur'an 5:5. Why do Indonesian Muslims, represented by their religious elites, prohibit Muslim men from marrying Christian or Jewish women? What is the issue behind this prohibition? I find that this question could be used as a point of departure for tracing the interest behind Muslim-non-Muslim marriage prohibition in the Indonesian context.

The political interest behind the prohibition of Muslim-non-Muslim marriage is explained clearly in Atho Mudzhar's work (Mudzhar 1993, p. 103). According to him, this prohibition was a result of competition for followers among religions. Religious figures considered it detrimental to the development of the Muslim community when its members abandon the religion, and therefore, the option of Muslim-non-Muslim marriage has to be completely closed, even for Muslim men to marry women of the *ahl al-kitâb* (Mudzhar 1993, p. 103). In many regions, this competition is actually one between Islam and Christianity. To some extent, the competition for followers worried the Indonesian Muslim elites who opined that many Muslims convert to other religions by marriage. I believe this is the central idea behind the prohibition of interreligious marriage in modern Indonesia. In this study, I will explore the construction of politico-religious contestation between Muslims and Christians.

The political tension between Muslims and Christians in modern Indonesia can be traced to the mid-1960s. After the military coup in 1965, the New Order Government required all Indonesians to choose one of five officially designated religions (Islam, Protestantism, Catholicism, Buddhism, and Hinduism) to show their anti-communist loyalty. Religion was incorporated into the school curriculum as one of the New Order strategies to disseminate anti-communist ideology. This anti-communist action opened the door for religious proselytization.[7] Christian missionaries successfully converted people who had been jailed for associations with the Indonesian Communist Party, and also people from the *abangan* groups in East Java and Central Java who were supporters of the Indonesia Communist Party (PKI) or the Indonesian National Party (Partai Nasional Indonesia/PNI).

The motives for religious conversion among PKI members and the *abangan*[8] people were very complex. One of them was the fear of Islam, because the mass killing of 500,000 PKI members or participants by the military forces at that time was supported by Islamic parties such as NU and its youth wing, Ansor. In Yogyakarta and Central Java, mass killing was also carried out by the Muhammadiyah through its paramilitary wing, Kokam (Komando Keamanan Muhammadiyah/Muhammadiyah's Security Command). Andree Feillard noted that the conversions from the 1960s to the 1970s were fewer than the 1.5 million reported by the missionaries, or less than two per cent of the total population at that time. In certain cities in Central Java, however, the number of Christians increased from one to two per cent before 1965 to more than ten per cent after 1965 (Feillard 2000, pp. 26–27).

In fact, the perceived large increase in numbers of Christians after 1965 worried the Indonesian Muslim elites and aroused the tension between them and the Christian elites. The government considered interreligious harmony an important ingredient for national stability. To reduce tension caused by religious proselytization, the government called for a meeting of religious leaders in Jakarta in November 1967, and asked each religion not to convert other religious adherents. Eventually the discussion centred on the *abangan* groups. For some Muslim elites, the *abangan* people are formally Muslims, who only needed to be "cleansed" of *syirik* (envy) and *bid'ah* (heresy). But the Christian religious leaders refused to accept this, arguing instead that the *abangan* people had not accepted Islam wholeheartedly. According to them, they were still looking for an appropriate religion, and thus, could convert to Christianity or any other religion.

The Christian missionary and evangelization efforts intensified at the end of the 1960s. The mission received support and financial aid from international mission networks. In the eyes of the Muslim political elites, this was a big challenge. Consequently, in July 1969, one of the Muhammadiyah leaders asked the Parliament to prohibit foreign aid for Christian missionary programmes. At the level of the grass roots, the intensification of Christian missionary activity created social unrest. For example, some churches were destroyed in South Sulawesi on 1 October 1967, a Methodist Church was destroyed in Meulaboh, Aceh, in 1967, and a Protestant church was destroyed in rural Jakarta in early 1969 (Feillard 2000, pp. 26–27). At that time, Muslim political elites perceived that the government ignored Muslim interests. The only government intervention to counter the Christian missions was the joint agreement of the Ministry of Religious Affairs and the Ministry of Domestic Affairs in 1969 requiring state permission for the establishment of religious buildings. The Muslim elites claimed that Christianization was flourishing, as the Christian population was increasing. To some extent, the claim was an assumption arising from Christianophobia. Population statistics of 1971–80 indicate that the Christian population was increasing and the Muslim population decreasing, but the trends were hardly significant (see Table 5.1).

TABLE 5.1
Number of Muslims, Catholics, and Protestants in 1971 and 1980

Religion	Population based on religious affiliation in 1971 ('000)	Population based on religious affiliation in 1980 ('000)
Islam	103,597 (87.5%)	128,462 (87.1%)
Catholic	2,692 (2.3%)	4,355 (3.0%)
Protestant	5,151 (5.1%)	8,505 (5.8%)

Source: The table is derived from population census data presented in *Statistical Year Book Indonesia* 1976, 1982, 1984, and 1986 (Jakarta: Biro Pusat Statistik). The Indonesian population was 118.367 million in 1971 and 145.703 million in 1980.

It can be seen that between 1970 and 1980, the percentage of Muslims decreased by 0.4 per cent, while the Christian (Catholic and Protestant) populations increased by 1.4 per cent. Of course, these statistics only provide a raw and general description, but they are often interpreted by Muslims as constituting a threat. Furthermore, to them, Muslim-non-Muslim marriage was a mode of Christian evangelization. The MUI religious decree in 1980 prohibiting Muslim-non-Muslim marriage was published in the context of this tension.

Besides the prohibition of Muslim-non-Muslim marriage, Muslim elites initiated government regulations to minimize Christian "penetration", which they felt was increasing through government policies. On 1 August 1978, the Minister for Religious Affairs, Alamsyah Ratuperwiranegara, issued Ministerial Rule No. 70/1978 "Guidance for Religious Mission" and No. 77/1978

"Foreign Aid for Religious Organisation in Indonesia". The Ministry of Religious Affairs and the Ministry of Domestic Affairs jointly issued the regulation entitled "The Religious Mission and Foreign Aid for Religious Organisations in Indonesia" to strengthen previous regulations (Lukman Hakim 1991, p. 8). The most important point in this regulation was the prohibition of proselytization to a person who already has a religion. Christian leaders objected to these regulations.

After 1965, the political situation in Indonesia was marked by increasing Islamic political militancy. This led to a consolidation of Christian political groups. In 1971, Ali Moertopo's group established a think-tank called CSIS (Centre for Strategic and International Studies). It was jointly led by Ali Moertopo, Sudjono Hoemardani, and Daud Yoesoef, a trio usually referred to as the *Tanah Abang* group. The CSIS played a significant role in Soeharto's bureaucracy for more than fifteen years, especially in foreign affairs. Furthermore, the political collaboration between CSIS, the Catholic right wing, and the Soeharto bureaucracy had been able to construct the Indonesian Islamists as a significant enemy of the government, similar to the old assumption developed by Snouck Horgronje in the Dutch colonial era. To some extent, Islamophobia, which was propagated by the Catholic political wing, was very strong in the early decades of the New Order era that ended in 1998. A political cadre system called the Khasebul (*Khalwat Sebulan*, etymologically a month's retreat), in which young Catholic political activists were trained by the CSIS, was established in 1965 by Pater Beek, S.J. (Ispandrihani 2000, pp. 24–25).

Daniel Dhakidae (2003, pp. 620, 636) does not mention *Khasebul* in his prestigious book, *Cendekiawan dan Kekuasaan Dalam Negara Orde Baru (The Intellectuals and Power in the New Order State)*. However he explains the ideology of the CSIS.

According to him, it should be noted that the CSIS was an alliance among the groups of Catholic politicians and intellectuals, as well as the Catholics in the army. Dhakidae also argues that CSIS's "theology" was based on the view of Karl Jaspers that when the church first began, it was without state authority, but after the conversion of Emperor Constantine into Christianity, there was a merging of the church and political power. Dhakidae indirectly says that the strong relationship developed by the Catholic political factions in Indonesia represented the concept of the "organic state". In his view, the Indonesian New Order is based on the concept of the organic state inherited from the Latin-Iberian tradition.

CSIS's political role started to decrease at the third GOLKAR National Conference in 1983. GOLKAR (*Golongan Karya*) was the Soeharto regime's political party. At this conference, the Tanah Abang group won only two seats, represented by Moerdopo (Vice-Chairman of Art and Culture Department) and Yusuf Wanandi (Vice-Chairman of Foreign Affairs). Previously, in the 1978 GOLKAR National Conference, the group had obtained many important seats such as those of secretary general and vice-chairman. Mochtar Mas'oed, a political scientist from Gadjah Mada University of Indonesia, said that the declining political power of Ali Moertopo and CSIS encouraged Soeharto's regime to see Soedharmono, a loyal cadre of GOLKAR, as suitable for the post of State Secretary, which subsequently became a "super bureaucracy" of the GOLKAR organization. Soeharto also thought that Soedharmono was less politically ambitious than the officers in the CSIS. Eventually, Soeharto recommended Soedharmono to be the top GOLKAR leader in the period 1983–88. Thereafter, GOLKAR started to accommodate the Islamic organizations. After some years, the political trend changed course to accommodate the demands of the Islamic political groups.

As the political situation changed, Muslim politicians proposed the adoption of Islamic regulations as state policies. In the early 1980s, the MUI issued a religious decree on the prohibition of Muslim-non-Muslim marriage, which became part of the civil discourse. To some extent though, this decree failed to regulate mixed marriage. About five years after it was issued, that is in the sixteen months from April 1985 to July 1986, 239 Muslim-non-Muslim marriages were registered in the Civil Registry in the Jakarta District, out of which 112 involved Muslim men marrying non-Muslim women, and 127 cases involved Muslim women marrying non-Muslim men (Sukarja 1996, pp. 19–20). Subsequently, after national politics aligned more closely with Islamic political groups, Muslim political leaders encouraged state regulation to prohibit Muslim-non-Muslim marriage.

In 1989, the Indonesian Government published a law governing the Religious Court, a special court for Muslims, with strong support from Muslim political wings. Although some Christian political factions showed resistance, this did not deter the president from issuing two years later in 1991, the Presidential Instruction, that is, the CIL, that prohibits Muslim-non-Muslim marriage.

CONCLUSION: CONSERVATIVE VIS-À-VIS MODERATE MUSLIM DEBATES

After the fall of the New Order Regime in 1998, a new discourse on interreligious marriage developed among Muslims and people of other faiths. In 2003, Paramadina Foundation, a progressive Indonesian Muslim group that was led by the late Nurcholish Madjid, published a book, *Fiqih Lintas Agama: Membangun Masyarakat Inklusif-Pluralis* (Fiqih Cross-Religion: Building Inclusive-Pluralist Society) (Sirry 2004). The spirit of the discourse in the book is very liberal, almost permitting anything forbidden by mainstream Muslim scholars. It comes as no surprise that, in a specific chapter of the book, the group permits Muslim-non-Muslim marriage. In 2002, the JIL (Jaringan Islam Liberal/Liberal Islamic Network) conducted a discussion on Radio 68H which disseminated the idea of freedom of interreligious marriage. In addition, in 2004, some progressive Muslim groups, led by Siti Musdah Mulia, proposed, in response to the CIL, a Counter Legal Draft (CLD)[9] which, among other things, permitted Muslim-non-Muslim marriage for male as well as female Muslims. Article 54 of the CLD states:

> (1) Muslim-non-Muslim marriage is permitted; (2) Muslim-non-Muslim marriage is carried out based on a principle of appreciation and respect for the rights of religious freedom of each other.[10]

In response to the development of ideas of religious freedom promoted in the CLD, MUI and MMI (Indonesian Mujahidin Council) asked the Ministry of Religious Affairs to withdraw the CLD.[11] In the last days of his ministerial position in 2004, Said Agil Munawwar banned the process of legislating the CLD. This situation shows how difficult it is to incorporate ideas of religious freedom in current regulations in Indonesia, even though the CIL has only existed for fifteen years as part of the Islamization of the state bureaucracy mentioned earlier. Contestation between progressive and conservative Muslims has intensified in recent decades, and the Muslim-non-Muslim marriage discourse is one of the most sensitive issues in this contestation.

In conclusion, the debate on Muslim-non-Muslim marriage is shifting from an interreligious debate between Muslims and Christians in the early 1970s, to a debate within interreligious groups, as well as between conservative and moderate Islamic groups. This new development has been the result of the changing of ideas about Islam and human rights within the last two decades. Finally, it is important to note that Muslim-non-Muslim marriage in Indonesia is not only a contestation in Islamic discourses, but also a socio-political contestation among interest groups.

Notes

1. As-Suyûtî, *Lubâb an-Nuqûl fî Asbâb an-Nuzûl*, vol. 1, p. 27, ll. 27–29: *...âkhiru sûratin nazalat al-mâida fa-mâ wajadtum fihâ min halâl fa-stahillûhu...*

2. For further explanation on how Nahdlatul Ulama scholars view Kitab Kuning, see, Wolfgang Marschall, ed., "Pesantren and Kitab Kuning: Continuity and Change in a Tradition of Religious Learning", in *Texts from the Islands: Oral and Written Traditions of Indonesia and the Malay World, Ethnologica Bernica* 4 (1994): 121–45.

3. The decree (*fatwa*) was signed by Hamka (Chairman of MUI) and Kafrawi (Secretary). It is interesting to note that the decree was also signed by Alamsyah Ratu Perwiranegara on behalf of the Religious Affairs Ministry, but MUI is an Islamic civil organization (non-state). See Atho Mudzhar *Fatwa-Fatwa Majlis Ulama Indonesia: Sebuah Studi tentang Pemikiran Hukum Islam di Indonesia 1975–1988*, English-Indonesia edition (Jakarta: INIS, 1993), p. 99.

4. This issue is discussed during the *Muktamar Tarjih Muhammadiyah XXII* in 1989. See Faturrahman Djamil, *Metode Ijtihad Majlis Tarjih Muhammadiyah* (1995), pp. 143–45.

5. For further infomation see Suhadi, *Kawin Lintas Agama: Perspektif Kritik Nalar Islam* (Yogyakarta: LKiS, 2006), Chapter II; point D on *Kawin Lintas Agama di Indonesia* (Interreligious Marriage in Indonesia), pp. 45–54.

6. HIR (Heriene Inlandsche Reglement)/R.Bg. (Rechts Reglement Buitengewesten) of 1855.

7. As mentioned by Andrée Feillard (2000), captives of the PKI were pressured to choose one of "five official" religions and to practise religious rituals. Most of them preferred to choose Christianity for

the reason that Islamic rituals such as the mandatory five daily prayers were strict compared with the Christian ritual of weekly prayers.

8. The term *"abangan"* derives from the Javanese word *"abang"* (the colour red) and is used to refer to nominal or non-practising Muslims. For further details, please read M.C. Ricklefs, *Polarising Javanese Society: Islamic and Other Visions (c. 1830–1930)* (Singapore: NUS Press, 2007), especially chapter 4 on "The Birth of The Abangan", pp. 84–104.

9. Siti Musdah Mulia's chapter in this volume explains the arguments involved in the Counter Legal Draft.

10. Tim Pengarusutamaan Gender Departemen Agama R.I. Jakarta *Pembaharuan Hukum Islam: Counter Legal Draft Kompilasi Hukum Islam*, an unpublished draft (Jakarta, 2004), p. 36.

11. This letter of protest was signed by Din Syamsudin (now a top leader of Muhammadiyah) and Umar Shihab (a well known Indonesian *ulama*).

References

Ali, Kecia. *Sexual Ethics & Islam: Feminist Reflection on Qur'an, Hadith, and Jurisprudence*. England: Oneworld, 2006.

Al-Wahidî. *Asbâb an-Nuzûl*. Kairo: Dâr al-Ittihâd al-'Arabî at-Tab'ah, 1968.

As-Suyûtî. *Lubâb an-Nuqûl fî Asbâb an-Nuzûl*. 2nd ed. Riyadh: Maktabah Riyâd al-Hadîtsah.

Dhakidae, Daniel. *Cendekiawan dan Kekuasaan dalam Negara Orde Baru*. Jakarta: Gramedia, 2003.

Djamil, Faturrahman. *Metode Ijtihad Majlis Tarjih Muhammadiyah*. Jakarta: Logos, 1995.

Feillard, Andrée. "Kaum Kristen dan Muslim di Indonesia dalam Kilas Sejarah Penjelasan tentang Terjadinya Kekerasan Baru Antaragama". Unpublished paper presented at Sanata Dharma University, Yogyakarta, 5 Oktober 2000.

Friedmann, Yohanan. *Tolerance and Coercion in Islam: Interfaith Relations in the Muslim Tradition*. New York: Cambridge University Press, 2003.

Ispandrihani, B. Suryoasmoro. *Penampakan Bunda Maria: Counter Hegemoni Gereja dan Rezim Orde Baru*. Undergraduate thesis published for a limited edition. Department Anthropology, Gadjah Mada University of Indonesia. Yogyakarta: KesAnt, 2000.

Lukman Hakim, ed. *Fakta dan Data: Usaha-Usaha Kristenisasi di Indonesia*. Jakarta: Media Dakwah, 1991.

Marschall, Wolfgang, ed. "Pesantren and Kitab Kuning: Continuity and Change in a Tradition of Religious Learning". In *Texts from the Islands: Oral and Written Traditions of Indonesia and the Malay World, Ethnologica Bernica* 4. Berne: University of Berne, 1994.

Masyhuri, K.H.A. Aziz. *Masalah Keagamaan Hasil Muktamar dan Munas Ulama Nahdlatul Ulama Kesatu/1926 s/d Ketigapuluh/2000*. Depok Indonesia: PPRMI & Qultum Media, 2004.

Mudzhar, Atho. *Fatwa-Fatwa Majlis Ulama Indonesia: Sebuah Studi tentang Pemikiran Hukum Islam di Indonesia 1975–1988*. English-Indonesia ed. Jakarta: INIS, 1993.

Mujiburrahman. *Feeling Threatened: Muslim-Christian Relations in Indonesian's New Order*. ISIM dissertation. Leiden: Amsterdam University Press, 2006.

Qudamah, Ibnu. *Mugni* Riyadh: al-Maktabah al-Riyadl al-Haditsah.

Ricklefs, M.C. *Polarising Javanese Society: Islamic and Other Visions (c. 1830–1930)*. Singapore: NUS Press, 2007.

Sirry, Mun'im A., ed. *Fiqih Lintas Agama Membangun Masyarakat Inklusif-Pluralis*. Jakarta: Paramadina, 2004.

Statistical Year Book Indonesia 1976, 1982, 1984, and 1986. Jakarta: Biro Pusat Statistik.

Suhadi. *Kawin Lintas Agama: Perspektif Kritik Nalar Islam*. Yogyakarta: LKiS, 2006.

Sukarja, Ahmad. "Perkawinan Berbeda Agama Menurut Hukum Islam". In *Problematika Hukum Islam Kontemporer*, edited by Chuzaimah and Hafiz Anshary. Book 1, 2nd ed. Jakarta: LSIK, 1996.

Tim Pengarusutamaan Gender Departemen Agama R.I. Jakarta. Pembaharuan Hukum Islam: Counter Legal Draft Kompilasi Hukum Islam. An unpublished draft. Jakarta, 2004.

SECTION II

LIVED REALITIES

Chapter 6

"NOT MUSLIM, NOT MINANGKABAU" Interreligious Marriage and its Cultural Impact in Minangkabau Society

Mina Elfira

INTRODUCTION

Bila seorang Minangkabau sudah tidak Muslim lagi,
Maka Minangnya sudah hilang. Yang tinggal hanya kabaunya saja

If a Minangkabau is no longer a Muslim, his/her Minang[1] will
vanish. What is left is only a water-buffalo.

This chapter contributes to the discussion on how "interreligious
marriages" (this term will refer to marriage between persons from
different religions) challenge cultural boundaries, in this case,
Minangkabau matrilineal-Islamic culture in West Sumatra,
Indonesia. The Minangkabau are not only well known as the
world's largest matrilineal society, but also as one that coexists
amongst the mostly Islamic societies within Indonesia, the country
with the largest Muslim population in the world.

The Minangkabau saying, "*Adat basandi syarak, syarak basandi Kitabullah*" (Minangkabau customary laws are based on Islamic laws; the Islamic laws are based on the Holy Book — Al Qur'an), is a Minangkabau ideological aphorism that conveys how *adat* (a collective term for Minangkabau laws and customs) has been greatly influenced by Islam which came into Minangkabau society around the sixteenth century (Abdullah 1966; Dobbin 1974). The pluralism of the legal system in West Sumatran Minangkabau society displays this convergence of influences, consisting of *adat* law, Islamic law, and Indonesian national law. In Minangkabau daily life, quite often the implementation of these legal systems contradict one another, especially in relation to property and inheritance, and marriage matters.

In this chapter I will focus on how the Minangkabau who are in established interreligious marriages utilize the ambivalent roles of agents of change and defenders of the *adat*, to maximize the advantages that can be gained from their dualistic position in relation to both their rights and privileges as Minangkabau people. The chapter is based on fieldwork conducted between 2002 and 2005. Respondents quoted in this chapter have been given pseudonyms to protect their privacy. Consequently, the focus of the analysis is the Minangkabau people who, in their effort to legitimize their marriages, have had to undergo religious conversion. The main issue that this chapter will investigate is the success these subjects have achieved in remaking the *adat* so that their status could be culturally recognized thereby reconstructing what is considered Minangkabau identity and family.

In order to explore these issues and to examine the lived experiences of Minangkabau people who have established interreligious marriages, I will rely more on qualitative data, obtained using qualitative methods. As Nancy Lopez argues, qualitative methods capture the contextual, real-life, everyday experiences of the individual interviewed (Lopez 2003, p. 7). However, this method, while providing rich contextual data, also has limitations. Its common limitation is that only a small number of cases can be studied in this intensive fashion (Lopez 2003, p. 7).[2] In addition, Clive Seale argues that "there is a danger here of imagining that a particular interaction format (the unstructured interview) is an automatic guarantee of the analytic status of the data that emerge" (Seale 1999, p. 209). Because of these limitations, I will also utilize quantitative data flexibly based on surveys conducted by both central and local Indonesian government institutions to support my analysis.

"MATRILINY" AND ISLAM: THE ESSENCES OF MINANGKABAU IDENTITY

In his paper "Ethnicity and Social Change", Daniel Bell contends that in the modern world "ethnicity has become more salient [than class] because it can combine an interest [an advantageous one], with an affective tie" (Bell 1975, p. 169). The main focus of ethnicity is, undoubtedly, ethnic groups. J. Milton Yinger generally defines an ethnic group as a segment of a larger society whose members regard themselves and are regarded by others to have a common origin and to share important segments of a common culture. In addition, these members participate in shared activities in which the (real or mythical) common origin and culture are significant factors that cause them to be perceived, either by themselves or others, as different (Yinger 1994, pp. 3–4). These significant factors constitute their basic identities.

According to Gordon Allport, identities tend to condense around symbols or cues (Horowitz 1975, p. 120).[3] A symbol of identity, however, "may be ignored or interpreted quite differently in the next [future], depending on the shape and significance of the underlying criteria of identity" (Horowitz 1975, p. 121). Nathan Glazer and Daniel P. Moynihan have hypothesized that "ethnic groups bring different norms to bear on common circumstances with consequent different levels of success — hence group differences in status" (Glazer and Moynihan 1975, p. 17). Therefore the deliberate ignorance or re-interpretation of a symbol of identity that is of the highest importance in one society is one strategy that an ethnic group may employ in order to survive or gain a better status in their world. These theories will be used in analysing the identity of Minangkabau, the sixth largest group of approximately one thousand ethnic and sub-ethnic groups that currently exist in Indonesia.[4]

Arguably, matriliny is the defining aspect of Minangkabau identity. By virtue of the society's matrilineal principles (descent and inheritance through the maternal line), Minangkabau women possess a privileged status and play significant roles in their communities. These roles include being bearers of descent, owners of ancestral property, and "managers" of their families. Minangkabau women also play a large part in determining the success or failure of decisions made by men in their positions as *mamak*, a maternal uncle, and *penghulu*, a clan leader. These claims are supported by the research of other writers on Minangkabau society and culture, including Joanne C. Prindiville (1981), Lucy A. Whalley (1993), Joke van Reenen (1996), and Peggy Reeves Sanday (2002). Because of these significant roles, Minangkabau women are symbolized as the *"limpapeh Minang, ranah Pagaruyuang"* (the central pillar of Minangkabau, the heartland of Pagaruyung).[5] When I conducted research in Minangkabau communities situated in West Sumatra, during my discussions with my informants, I formed the impression that large numbers of Minangkabau people, both male and female, proudly and strongly identified themselves as Minangkabau people and as being different from other ethnic groups, especially within the Indonesian nation. During my fieldwork, I discovered that some Minangkabau still persistently defined their adat *matriarchaat* (matriarchy),[6] indicating women's legitimacy in matters of power, although this concept has been rejected by most anthropologists within Minangkabau studies on the grounds that authority is still in the hands of men in their positions as brothers, mother's brothers, and the head of clan.

Besides matriliny, Islam appears integral to Minangkabau identity. Among Indonesians, besides Acehnese society, Minangkabau society is well known as one of the most religiously observant societies of Indonesia. Islam was not the first religion to arrive in Minangkabau: Hinduism and Buddhism had been important earlier influences. But, after penetrating into Minangkabau society, Islam has become one of the powerful centrifugal forces. After the coming of Islam, the word of "Islam" has become an inseparable part of the Minangkabau ideological aphorism, although its position in relation to *adat* has changed several times.[7] The recodification of *adat* can be seen from the establishment of *Adat Islamiah*. It means *adat* that is in accordance with Islamic principles. *Adat Islamiah* is ordained as *adaik nan sabana adaik* (*adat* which is truly *adat*) (Abdullah 1967; Azra 2003). There is no doubt that the dissemination of Islam into Minangkabau has significantly impacted on the structures of its social organization, especially in relation to its gender relations and inheritance systems. Matrilineal Minangkabau kinship system considers a husband/father an *outsider* (*orang lua*) of his wife's family. His children will automatically become part of their mother's family, and will bear the mother's clan name instead of their father's. Furthermore, it is *mamak*'s responsibility to take care of his sisters' children. The relationship between a *mamak*, maternal uncle, and his *kamanakan*, niece or nephew, is close, and is arguably even stronger than that between a father and his own son with *mamak* representing the "sociological father" of his sisters' children. *Mamak* also bequeaths his wealth to his *kamanakan*. His *sako*, inheritance of position, will be passed on to his nephews, while his *pusako*, inheritance of wealth, will be inherited by his nieces. Moreover, according to *adat*, traditionally the smallest family unit is known as *samande* (one mother) that is headed or owned by a woman, consisting of a mother and her children (Elfira 2005). However, based on research in West Sumatra by the Indonesian Supreme Court in 1976, *samande* has now been modified as a nuclear family, consisting of mother, children, and father who is regarded as the family's head ruler (Mahkamah Agung, *Proyek Penelitian Hukum Adat* 1980). This modification may partly be influenced by Islamic rule that positions the man as the head of the family (Al-Qur'an 4:34).[8]

Another impact of the imposition of Islamic values into *adat* can be seen from the change of the inheritance system in Minangkabau society. In order to integrate *adat* with Islamic laws, a Minangkabau assembly was held in Bukit Tinggi on 2–4 May 1953 consisting of the representatives of Minangkabau clan heads, village leaders, religious scholars and intellectuals, and an Indonesian Government representative who functioned as a witness. Members of the assembly, most of whom were men, launched a regulation that while *pusaka tinggi* (ancestral property) is still inherited based on matrilineal principle, *pusaka rendah* (self-acquired property) should be inherited based on syariah (Islamic law) (Hamka 1963, p. 7). According to syariah, sons should inherit twice as much as daughters. This consensus was made in order to avoid dispute between the rights of one's own children and one's sisters' children. This effort is an example of how Minangkabau people reconcile matrilineal laws and Islamic laws, which seemingly contradict each other, especially in relation to inheritance of property.[9]

The integration of Islam into Minangkabau *Adat* can also be seen from the way Minangkabau people define themselves. In the closing ceremony of *"Seminar Sejarah dan Kebudayaan Minangkabau* (Seminar of Minangkabau History and Culture)", held in Batusangkar between 1 and 7 August 1970 and attended by prominent Minangkabau scholars and *adat* leaders at that time,[10] the definition of *orang Minang* (Minangkabau people) was restated as:

> *Moyangnya turun dari gunung Merapi, sekarang berada dalam Negara Kesatuan Republic Indonesia. Berkiblat ke Baitullah* (Simulie 2002, p. xxi).

> [Their] ancestors came down from *Merapi* mountain, now [they] are in the Unitary State of Indonesian Republic. [When praying, they] orient themselves toward the Holy Mosque in Mecca.

In contemporary Minangkabau society, it seems that *Adat Islamiah* still exists and is used as the foundation of the Minangkabau way of life. For example, in the centre of Padang (the capital city of West Sumatra) there is a billboard stating that *"PERDA (Peraturan Daerah) anti maksiat merupakan perwujudan adat basandi syarak, syarak basandi kitabullah* (Local government regulations on immoral acts is a realization of Minangkabau customary laws which are based on Islamic law; the Islamic law is based on the Islamic Holy Book, Al-Qur'an)". The billboard, promoting the provincial government of West Sumatra's regulation on immoral acts, demonstrates how the government has intentionally deployed *adat Islamiah* laws in order to legitimize its official acts in public life in the homeland of Minangkabau, as well as speak of the continuation of the *adat*.

However, the interpretation and practice of the *adat* have been significantly influenced by changing political and social conditions and the penetration of views external to the culture itself. Conversely, Minangkabau subjects' new interpretation of *adat* may impact upon their local identity. Blackwood, for example, argues that the term *"adat"* constitutes the foundational discourse for Minangkabau identity and ethnicity (Blackwood 2001, p. 126).

The increasing influence of Christianization in Minangkabau society is another factor to consider. When I conducted my fieldwork in urban Padang, the Minangkabau community, there was concern about the spread of *"proses Kristenisasi* (the Christianisation process)" in *ranah Minang* (Minangkabau land)[11] as expressed by H. Rusydi Hamka, a respected Minangkabau Islamic scholar and a son of Hamka who is a prominent Minangkabau Islamic scholar:

> *Seperti informasi yang kita terima bahwa ada mahasiswa yang dihipnotis dalam rangka kristenisasi. Tidak boleh ada kristenisasi masuk sini. Karena tanah disini tanah adat, bikin aturan tidak boleh bikin gereja disini! (Posmetro Padang* 28 December 2003).

> Based on information we got that a student was hypnotized in the process of Christianization. Christianization is not allowed here [Minangkabau land]. Because this land is *adat* land, a regulation that building a church is not allowed should be made!

The comment of Rusydi Hamka, who criticizes contemporary Minangkabau people for having crises of identity and self-esteem (*Posmetro Padang* 28 December 2003), represents a fear among many Minangkabaus that they might become a target of Christianization. In my discussions on this issue with my informants, the case of Salmon Melianus Ongirwalu which received wide media coverage, was an example that was repeatedly mentioned not only by the Minangkabau who opposed the process of Christianization, but also by those who had converted to

Christianity, although the latter saw the case from a different perspective.

The case occurred in 1999 when Salmon Melianus Ongirwalu, a Christian man, was convicted in the Civil Court of having abducted and raped a sixteen-year-old Muslim girl in Padang.[12] Although the judge found Salmon guilty, some Minangkabau were still unhappy with the decision. This is because, as expressed by a member of the West Sumatran Islamic Community's Jihad Forum, an Islamic group that strongly and openly opposes the process of Christianization in Minangkabau society, the judge did not explicitly mention that "Salmon's action cannot be separated from the Christianising effort in Minang [kabau] territory".[13] This opinion may indicate that this case was of interest to some Minangkabau people because of the issue of Christianization. In retrospect, this case might not have become a national issue if the girl had been Christian by birth or non-Minangkabau. If the girl had been Christian by birth, the case might just have been considered a criminal case. In addition, *"Proses Kristenisasi"* (Christanization process) is still a sensitive issue in Indonesia, the country with the largest Muslim population in the world. Because of that, this case was used by some Indonesians as proof that the Christanization process has rapidly penetrated into Indonesian societies, even, without exception, into Minangkabau, well known among Indonesians as one of the strongest Islamic societies in Indonesia.

It is assumed that the Christianization process may occur through interreligious marriages between Minangkabau people (read: Muslim) and non-Muslim people. Interreligious marriages do not only involve those between Minangkabau and Christian people. For example, I got to know a Minangkabau man who converted to Buddhism. However, it seems that Minangkabau society focuses more on this issue of Christian-Muslim marriage since there is a strong tendency for interreligious marriages to occur between Minangkabau and Christians, and some Minangkabau have become Christians because of interreligious marriages.

INTERRELIGIOUS MARRIAGE IN MINANGKABAU SOCIETY: IN THEORY AND PRACTICE

The 1974 Marriage Law (Law no. 1 of 1974, article 57) defines *"kawin-campur"* (mixed marriages) as *"perkawinan antara dua orang di Indonesia tunduk kepada hukum yang berlainan, karena perbedaan kewarganegaraan dan salah satu pihak berkewarganegaraan Indonesia* (marriage between two people in Indonesia who obey different laws because of different citizenship and in which one of the party holds Indonesian citizenship)". The Law also states that those who wish to marry a person of different religion have to register their marriages at the *Kantor Catatan Sipil* (the Civil Registry Office) (Article 61, clause 1).[14] In addition, the Law guarantees the right to enter into such marriages. Since this Act was passed, public policy towards persons involved in interreligious marriages has changed. Despite this statute stating that mixed marriage is only between people of different nationalities, in the beginning it was broadly interpreted as not only marriages between people of different nationalities, but also between followers of different religions. Later the 1974 Marriage Law took on a narrower interpretation so that the term *"kawin-campur"* only refers to different citizenships.

The opportunity for Indonesian Muslim people to perform *kawin campur* has diminished further due to government policy. For example in 1983 President Soeharto directed *Kantor Catatan Sipil* to register marriages only if they did not involve Muslims (Bowen 2003, p. 241). Despite this change in policy, there is still opportunity for Indonesian people to perform valid "mixed marriages". The option is to perform the mixed marriage overseas and then register the marriage at the Indonesian Civil Registry. There are Indonesians who wish to contract *kawin campur* through this option, but as this option is relatively expensive, it is only available to those who can afford it. The other option is for the couple to undergo a formal marriage ceremony according to the rites of one of their religions. This means that one of them needs to *"pindah agama"* (leave his/her previous religion), either wholeheartedly or as a formality. According to Indonesian Law, this cannot be categorized as "mixed-marriage", but socially and culturally, in my opinion, it may be considered a "mixed-marriage", because the person who converts does so in a formal sense only, retaining his or her religion in practice and as part of his or her identity.

Despite the absence of records on mixed marriages in the data of the Civil Registry in Padang, I have met, in Padang, some Minangkabau people who were in mixed or interreligious marriages, as is evidenced by Nina's case. Nina is a forty-two year-old mother with two children. She married a Javanese Christian man in 1992. Initially they planned to get married in the Civil Registry Office as they had different religions. Since the procedure was quite difficult, they changed their minds. Nina agreed with her future husband's decision to get married according to Christian norms and rules. They then were married in a church in Jakarta. However, Nina told me that, to her, the process was only a formality in order to make their marriage valid according to Indonesian marriage law. She also told me that she was still a Muslim.

Based on Nina's explanation, it can be said that their marriage can be considered a mixed marriage. Nina is not the only Minangkabau person who has chosen this option. Based on my discussions and findings with informants, it can be argued that, in general, in Minangkabau, a marriage ceremony such as Nina's is the preferred choice of couples in interreligious marriages, especially for low and lower middle class Minangkabau people.

From my fieldwork and interviews in Minangkabau land, some general observations that could be drawn relate to the issue of interreligious marriages. It appears that Minangkabau society is more concerned about preventing marriages between Minangkabau women and non-Muslim men than *vice versa*. The first possible reason is that Islam, one of the foundations of Minangkabau *adat*, provides an opening for Muslim men, but not for Muslim women, to marry non-Muslim partners as long as the marriages are performed according to Islamic law (Al-Qur'an 5:5).[15] There are still debates among Islamic scholars whether this verse can be used to legitimize an interreligious marriage between a Muslim man and a non-Muslim woman. The late Nurcholis Majid, who married a few Muslim men and non-Muslim women, but never *vice versa*, was among the scholars who supported the idea (Bowen 2003, p. 245). Despite the debate, it seems that because of this verse, Minangkabau society is more tolerant of a Minangkabau man marrying a non-Muslim woman as long as the marriage is conducted according to Islamic law.

The other possible reason for the lack of acceptance of marriages between Minangkabau women and non-Muslim men is due to women's positions in their immediate families. As an Islamic society, the Minangkabau have absorbed many Islamic values such as a man's function as the head of his family and the guardian of his wife (Al-Qur'an 4:34). This concept is also supported by Indonesian laws (1974 Marriage Law, Article 31, clause 3,[16] and Article 34, clause 1).[17] My research indicates that most Minangkabau men and women have accepted this concept, formally or otherwise. It is, therefore, believed that since men as husbands have more authority within their own families, there is a possibility that they can easily "persuade" or "force" their wives to follow their ideologies or beliefs. An example was cited by my informant, Ratna, a forty-nine-year-old widow and traditional masseuse with seven children. One of Ratna's neighbours married a Christian Niasan man. Their marriage was carried out according to Islamic law so the Niasan man converted to Islam. However after a few of their children were born, the husband reverted to his previous religion of Christianity. He also asked his wife to become a Christian, failing which she would be divorced. According to Ratna, her neighbour was "forced" to follow her husband's decision because she was a poor and uneducated housewife who was financially dependent on her husband. The family then embraced Christianity.[18]

The third possible reason Minangkabau society prevents marriages between Minangkabau women and non-Muslim men, rather than *vice versa*, is due to the significant contributions that Minangkabau women make to this matrilineal-Islamic society, especially their functions as bearers of descent and defenders of Minangkabau *adat*. There is a strong assumption among the Minangkabau that Minangkabau women who participate in interreligious marriages may not completely fulfil these significant tasks.

Based on my observations, there is some credence to this assumption, with Piah's and Nina's cases exemplifying some of the difficulties that these women experience. Piah is a fifty-one-year-old mother with seven children. She married a Niasan Christian man in 1978. The marriage was conducted according to Islamic law. Piah's husband converted to Islam, although Piah told me that he was a *"Muslim KTP"*,[19] for example, her husband did not perform Friday prayers, which is compulsory for a Muslim man. In running her home or marriage, she preferred to apply

Minangkabau *adat* laws. For example, at home they communicated in Minangkabau language. She told me that her husband did not have any objection to these, as shown by the fact that it was he who moved in to Piah's family house.[20] Moreover, by virtue of the matrilineal system, Piah inherited a block of land and a house from her mother. Piah told me that these properties would be passed only to her daughters as based on matrilineal Minangkabau *adat*. Piah also brought up her children with Minangkabau values. When I asked some of the children whether they preferred to be known as Minangkabau or Nias, they told me that although they acknowledged their Nias blood, they felt and preferred to be called Minangkabau. Despite Minangkabau values being dominant in her home, Piah also implemented some values, considered un-Islamic, such as celebrating Christmas, which was usually held at the home of her husband's family. Because of this activity, Piah received a lot of criticisms, especially from her extended maternal family members. Piah told me she did it just to show respect to her husband's family who were Christians. Because of this "un-Islamic" practice, one of Piah's maternal cousins told me, *"kawinnyo tuh ndak kawin Islam doh tapi kawin campua"* (her marriage [life] cannot be categorized as an Islamic marriage but a "mixed marriage").

Nina, whose marriage ceremony was conducted according to Christian law, told me that Christian and Javanese values were dominant at her home. For example, her children were baptized and they spoke in Indonesian. The only Minangkabau way applied at home, according to Nina, who opened a Minangkabau foodstall in front of her home, was that food was cooked according to Minangkabau recipe and taste!

Moreover, the comment, expressed by Piah's cousin on Piah's marriage status (*kawin campua*), can be taken as an example that in everyday life, the term "mixed marriage" (*kawin campua*) is mostly used by Minangkabau people to refer to marriages between two persons from different religions. On the other hand, they usually use the term *kawin anta suku* to refer to marriages between two persons from different ethnic groups, but of the same religion, and *kawin anta nagaro*, to refer to marriages between two persons of different nationalities who hold the same religion.

Based on my observation, it can be said that, in general, Minangkabau people have a negative impression of *kawin campua* (read: interreligious marriages). For example, most of my informants freely spoke about their family members who were in *kawin anta suku or nagaro*, but they tended to cover up the cases of interreligious marriages in their families. The situation is quite different from the past when *kawin anta suku* or *kawin anta nagaro* was still a "taboo" or, at least, a non-preferred choice, as expressed by Tuti (60 years old) who married a Minangkabau man in 1970 on her maternal grandmother's advice:

> *Mengenai jodoh nenek membebaskan sepanjang orang Islam ... kalau bisa orang Minang. Karena menurut prinsip Beliau begini: "Sebaik-baiknya bangsa Indonesia tapi adatnya nggak sama dengan kita...nanti yang sulit kan kamu juga ... karena kalau kita sama adatnya berarti kita masuk ke lingkungan yang nggak sulit untuk berinteraksi.*

> Regarding a marriage partner, grandma let us choose as long as a Muslim ... if it is possible, a Minangkabau. It is because she had a principle that: "No matter how good an Indonesian [a non-Minangkabau] is, his customs are different from ours ... it might create a problem for yourselves ... if we [she and a marriage partner] have a similar adat, we come from a similar environment, it will not be difficult to interact".[21]

Based on Tuti's comment that even being a Muslim is not good enough to be chosen as a marriage partner, it seems that compared with the current situation, in the 1970s the *adat* played a more vital role in Minangkabau daily life. It may be argued that nowadays, there is a trend towards increased Islamization in Minangkabau society.

Out of the three reasons I have given above to explain why Minangkabau society is more concerned with preventing marriages between Minangkabau women and non-Muslim men rather than *vice versa*, the first two are generally used in all Muslim societies to prevent marriages between Muslim women and non-Muslim men, while the third is specifically used by Minangkabau society, which is matrilineal and considers women to be the central pillars of the society. Allowing Minangkabau women to participate in interreligious marriages may seriously impact the future of Minangkabau society, as expressed by one of my informants: *"Jiko padusi-padusi awak la diKristenkan capek atau lambek ranah ko lah jadi Kristen tantu la indak ado lai Minang ko."* (If our women are converted to Christianity, of course sooner or later this land will become a Christian land...As a result Minangkabau will vanish.)[22]

Based on the comment above, it may be argued that a more intolerant attitude towards interreligious marriages is one of the responses to the Christanization process in Minangkabau land. In order to prevent Christianization the Minangkabau have tightened the restriction on their women to enter into interreligious marriages. Because of this strong restriction, Minangkabau women who are already in interreligious marriages try to counter as best as they can, by playing the dual roles of agents of change and defenders of the *adat*. This strategy maximizes the advantages that can be gained from their ambivalent positions in relation to both their rights and privileges as Minangkabau. Reciprocally, Minangkabau people, who are against interreligious marriages, do the same things. In order to achieve their goals, quite often both parties "play" with the laws existing in their daily life.

"PLAYING" WITH THE LAWS: THE IMPLEMENTATION OF ISLAM, *ADAT,* AND INDONESIAN LAWS IN MINANGKABAU DAILY LIFE

In relation to interreligious marriage issues, a finding I gathered from my fieldwork in Minangkabau land is that Minangkabau people whose marriages were conducted according to Islamic law can still maintain their rights and responsibilities provided by the *adat.* Piah's case illustrates this. During our interviews Piah explained that despite receiving a lot of criticisms, especially from her extended maternal family, for participating in un-Islamic activities (e.g. celebrating Christmas), Piah can still exercise her rights and responsibilities as a Minangkabau, such as receiving ancestral properties from her maternal family which can be bequeathed to her daughters. Moreover, although Piah's extended family was suspicious of her husband's formal conversion to Islam, Piah's husband's position as *urang sumando* (in-marrying husband) is also acknowledged by her community. In addition, Piah's children are also formally and culturally accepted as members of the Minangkabau *adat* community.

Conversely, for those who were involved in interreligious marriages which were carried out according to another religion, Minangkabau society tended to dispense some sanctions. These sanctions can be either moral or material, or both. These people may lose their rights and responsibilities provided by the *adat.* They can even be excluded from the community of Minangkabau *adat,* as illustrated in Nina's and Lila's cases. Nina was a second daughter. After the death of her eldest sister, who was the eldest child, Nina replaced her sister as the representative of her family[23] and the successor of her mother's position. However, after her union with her husband in a Christian marriage, Nina's parents transferred all rights and responsibilities to Nina's younger sister. Nina and her children also lost their rights over maternal ancestral properties (*harato pusako*). Nina's mother told me that Nina would not even get the parents' self-acquired properties (*harato pancaharian*). Nina, who knew about her parents' decision, did not have any objections. Moreover, despite Nina still considering herself a Muslim, her *adat* community, as a result of her Christian marriage, did not acknowledge her as a Minangkabau anymore. Because of that, she could not claim her rights and responsibilities as Minangkabau. For example, although Nina's immediate family (Nina's parents and siblings) had accepted her, as well as her husband and children as a part of the family, they were not recognized as part of the *adat* family. This can be seen from the fact that Nina was never again invited to *adat* gatherings. It was her younger sister who represented her family.[24]

Lila is a thirty-five-year-old working mother with children. She married a Javanese man according to Islamic rites. Her marriage was celebrated with grand Minangkabau *adat* ceremonies, including a formal and cultural acceptance of Lila's husband, who converted to Islam, as a member of the Minangkabau *adat* community (as *urang sumando*). However, after they had several children, Lila's husband reverted to Christianity, and he also converted the children to Christianity. Lila was then excluded not only from her immediate family (parents and siblings), but also from her *adat* community. For example, as the only daughter, Lila used to accompany or represent her mother in *adat* gatherings, but her position was replaced by the wife of Lila's eldest brother. Lila's eldest brother became the family's representative. Lila also lost her rights over her ancestral maternal properties. However, unlike Nina, Lila, with the permission of her parents, still received a share of her parents' properties which were divided based on Indonesian law.

These instances also illustrate how the position of those whose marriages were not carried out according to Islamic law, could be destabilized in relation to inheritance. It depends on how successfully they can "soften" their family's "anger"[25] since they cannot automatically claim their rights over inheritance. The family might adopt any of the laws or a combination of these (*adat* law, Islamic law, and Indonesian national law) when making their decision, as can be seen from Nina's and Lila's cases. Nina could not receive any inheritance because her family decided to use only Minangkabau *adat* law. According to the *adat* law, a Minangkabau woman who has left Islam cannot be considered a member of the *adat* community. As such, she cannot claim her rights over inheritance — either *harato pusako* (ancestral property) or parents' *harato pancaharian* (parents' self-acquired property). Lila's family, however, used both Indonesian and *adat* laws when making their decision. Lila's parents implemented Minangkabau *adat* law regarding ancestral property (*harato pusako*). Thus, despite the fact that Lila was the only daughter who was supposed to inherit all *harato pusako*, she could not claim her rights over the ancestral property. However, Lila's parents practised Indonesian law regarding their *harato pancaharian*, so Lila could, at least, receive her share of her parents' self-acquired properties.

LEAVING ISLAM: LOSING MINANGKABAU IDENTITY

The other finding, gathered from my fieldwork in Minangkabau land in relation to interreligious marriage issues, is that those whose marriages are conducted according to religions other than Islam, may lose their identity as Minangkabau. For example, when I told an informant that I wanted to interview her neighbour, a Minangkabau woman whose marriage was performed according to Christian rites, she replied: "*Manga pulo inyo ka di wawancarai? inyo kan indak urang awak lai,*[26] *inyo lah jadi Nie!*" (Why should she need to be interviewed? She is no longer a member of our people [Minangkabau]; she has become a Nias.)

According to Rita Smith Kipp, among the Batak Karo, the Malay is partly identified with Islam. Because of that, Batak Karo call a person who has converted to Islam as becoming Malay (*menjadi Melayu*) and ceasing to be Batak Karo. While in Batak Karo society people use a term "*menjadi Melayu*" (becoming Malay) (Kipp 1996) to refer to people who have converted to Islam, in Minangkabau society in urban Padang, there is a term "*lah jadi urang Nie*" (becoming Niasan), to refer to people who have converted to Christianity. This may be because among the Minangkabau in urban Padang, the Niasan are identified as Christians. Because of this, they call a person who has converted to Christianity as "becoming Niasan" (Asnan 2003, p. 203; Colombijn 1994, p. 54)[27] and therefore ceasing to be Minangkabau. The fear of losing their identity as Minangkabau may be one of the main reasons some Minangkabau try to hide their religious conversion and abandonment of the Islam faith, as exemplified by Jamil's case.

Jamil is a sixty-year-old man who is an army pensioner. He converted to Christianity because of marriage. However, Jamil tried to conceal his conversion. None of his Minangkabau community members or extended maternal family members, except his elder brother and mother, is aware of his conversion. According to Jamil, this is because: "*Sepertinya tabu sekali bagi orang Minang untuk pindah agama [dari agama Islam] berat sekali resikonya....lebih-lebih kalau masih tinggal disana....sepertinya ndak ada tempat buat kita.*" (It seems to be extremely taboo for a Minangkabau to convert [from Islam] to another religion....the risk is great...especially if still living there [in the mainland of Minangkabau, West Sumatra] ...it is likely there is no place for us.)[28]

It is widely accepted among Minangkabau that Minangkabau persons whose marriages have been conducted according to the rites of a religion other than Islam cannot identify themselves as Muslim. As expressed by Jamil, Minangkabau society still strictly forbids its members from renouncing Islam. Leaving Islam is equivalent to leaving Minangkabau, either mentally or physically. That is why the Minangkabau who have left Islam usually leave *ranah Minang* by force or on their own accord. It is arguable that the consensus of "no Islam, no Minangkabau" has been accepted as an unwritten rule among the majority of Minangkabau who are the mainstream of the society. For example, when a Christian Minangkabau community in Jakarta planned to use the word "Minangkabau" for their Christian association, it instigated protest from the majority of the Muslim Minangkabau population. Their reason for protest was that "Minangkabau" represents many things: territory, culture, and ethnic group, and since the foundation of Minangkabau is Islam, as expressed by their ideological aphorism, Minangkabau people who left Islam have forfeited their right to use this word to refer to themselves. This issue became a national polemic.

Pressured by the Minangkabau people who were represented by some prominent Minangkabau scholars, and by *adat* and Islamic leaders in and outside ranah Minang, the Christian Minangkabau community eventually used the term "West Sumatran" for their association.[29] This example illustrates how tightly Minangkabau identity is still linked with Islamic identity in Indonesia. Another example can be taken from the billboard in the centre of Padang, which states that *"PERDA (Peraturan Daerah) anti maksiat merupakan perwujudan adat basandi syarak,*

syarak basandi kitabullah" (Local government regulations on immoral acts is a realization of Minangkabau customary laws which are based on Islamic law; the Islamic law is based on the Islamic Holy Book, Al Qur'an). The billboard, demonstrating the provincial government of West Sumatra's act in intentionally deploying *Adat Islamiah* laws in order to legitimize its official acts in public life in the homeland of Minangkabau, indicates the choice of *Adat Islamiah* by the majority of Minangkabau to reflect their identity in contemporary Indonesian society.

CONCLUSION

Based on the analysis above, this chapter's conclusion has three main points. Firstly, in Minangkabau society, the legal system is pluralistic as there is *adat* law, Islamic law, and Indonesian national law. As some of these cases of interreligious marriage have illustrated, in Minangkabau daily life, quite often the implementation of these legal systems can be contradictory. The new interpretation of the 1974 Marriage Law forbids interreligious marriage. Arguably one of the main reasons in prohibiting marriage between people of different religions is to prevent Muslim people from leaving Islam after such a marriage, but in reality, the end result is that more people change religion in order to marry. As shown by some cases in Minangkabau land, some Minangkabau people have become Christians in order to marry. Moreover, since Indonesian law implicitly "forbids" people from entering into interreligious marriages, some Minangkabau people whose partners are not Muslims have converted to other religions so that their marriages could be legitimized. Since their marriages are carried out according to the rites of their chosen religion, their marriages, in theory and according to Indonesian law, cannot be categorized as interreligious marriages. Nevertheless their daily life shows that often these people live in interreligious marriages.

Secondly, the analysis shows that Minangkabau who are in established interreligious marriages counter the societal consequences as best they can by playing both the role of agent of change as well as defender of the *adat*. This dualistic strategy maximizes the advantages that can be gained from their ambivalent positions with regard to both their rights and privileges as Minangkabau. However, Minangkabau people whose marriages are not conducted according to Islamic law are yet to succeed in remaking the Minangkabau *adat* so that their status can be culturally recognized. Neither have they completely succeeded in their efforts to reconstruct what is recognized as Minangkabau identity and family. Finally, both Minangkabau people who engage in interreligious marriages, and those who try to protect Minangkabau Islamic-matrilineal *adat*, quite often "play" with the pluralistic legal system in order to achieve their goals in their daily lives.

Notes

1. According to *tambo* (Minangkabau historical traditions), believed by most Minangkabau, the name Minangkabau derived from the word *manangkabau*, which means "the victory of the water buffalo". Minangkabau people call themselves *urang Minang* (Minang people). It can be said then *Minang* is the essence of Minangkabau identity. Indirectly it states that if a Minangkabau person converts into another religion, he/she will automatically lose his/her ethnic identity.
2. See also Caldwell et al. on the values and limitations of using qualitative methods, 1988.
3. Gordon W. Allport, *The Nature of Prejudice* (Cambridge: Addison-Wesley, 1954). Cited in Horowitz (1975), p. 120.

4. Based on the 2000 Population Census conducted by the Indonesian Central Statistics Bureau. It must be noted, however, that most ethnic and sub-ethnic groups sampled are very small in number. Actually only fifteen of the ethnic groups have a population of over one million. The major ethnic populations are Javanese (41.71 per cent); Sundanese (15.41 per cent); Malay (3.45 per cent); Madurese (3.37 per cent); Batak (3.02 per cent); Minangkabau (2.72 per cent); and Betawi (2.51 per cent) (Suryadinata et al. 2003).

5. Pagaruyung was the central government administration of the Minangkabau rulers. Aditiawarman, who was a descendant of the Majapahit royal kingdom, established the Pagaruyung in 1343 (Navis 1984, p. 15).

6. A term used by Dutch colonial officials in the nineteenth and early twentieth centuries to describe the Minangkabau *adat* (custom and tradition).

7. Minangkabau ideological aphorism originally stated *"adat basandi alur jo patut* (customary laws are based on proper context)". After the coming of Islam it was changed to *"adat basandi alur, syarak basandikan dalil* (customary laws are based on context; the religious laws are based on relevant passages of the Qur'an)". It shows that both values are equal and independent. Later it was modified as *"adat basandi syarak, syarak basandi adat* (customary laws are based on religious laws; the religious laws are based on customary laws)". This modification expresses their equality, but dependence on each other. This aphorism then once again has been changed to *"Adat basandi syarak, syarak basandi Kitabullah. Syarak, mangato, adat mamakai* (meaning Minangkabau customary laws are based on religious laws; the religious laws are based on the Holy Book — Al Qur'an; religious law orders, *adat* applies)". This explicitly shows that the status of *syarak* is officially higher than that of *adat*. This modified aphorism is still used in contemporary Minangkabau society. See Abdullah (1971), and Azra (2003) for more discussion.

8. It states: "Men are the protectors and maintainers of women, because Allah has made one of them to excel over the other, and because

they spend (to support them) from their means. Therefore the righteous women are devoutly obedient (to Allah and to their husbands), and guard in the husband's absence what Allah orders them to guard (e.g. their chastity, their husband's property)..." (*Translation of the Meanings of The Noble Qur'an in the English Language*, translated by Dr Muhammad Taqi-ud-Din Al-Hilali and Dr Muhammad Muhsin Khan [Madinah, KSA: King Fahd Complex for the Printing of The Holy Qur'an, 1419 H.]).

9. For more discussion on the relationship between Islam and Minangkabau *Adat*, see Hamka (1963, 1984). See also Hazairin (1950), Hazairin (1964), and Cammack (2002) for an extended analysis of the development of Islamic inheritance laws in Indonesia.

10. Some of them were Mohammad Hatta (former Indonesian first Vice-President), Buya Hamka (Minangkabau Islamic scholar), M.D. Mansoer (Minangkabau historian), H. Kamardi Rais Dt. P. Simulie (now head of LKAAM — *Lembaga Kerapatan Adat Alam Minangkabau* — of West Sumatran province), and Geoffrey A. Hodgson (scholar of Minangkabau studies).

11. I obtained this information not only from my discussions with some respondents, but also through the local media.

12. My informant who was a Christian Minangkabau person told me a different version of this story. According to him, Salmon did not kidnap the girl but only gave temporary shelter to a girl who had run away from home. The girl had willingly converted to Christianity before staying with Salmon. The interview was conducted in Jakarta on 20 August 2006.

13. As reported in *Forum Keadilan*, 27 September 1999. Cited in Bowen (2003), p. 238.

14. It states: "*Perkahwinan campur dicatat oleh pencatat yang berwenang* (Mixed marriage is registered by a competent registrar)".

15. It states: "(Lawful to you in marriage) are chaste women from the believers and chaste women from those who were given the Scripture (Jews and Christians) before your time when you have given their due *Mahr* (bridal money given by the husband to his wife at the

time of marriage), desiring chastity, i.e. taking them in legal wedlock, not committing illegal sexual intercourse, nor taking them as a girlfriend" (*Translation of the Meanings of The Noble Qur'an in the English Language,* translated by Dr Muhammad Taqi-ud-Din Al-Hilali and Dr Muhammad Muhsin Khan (Madinah, KSA: King Fahd Complex for the Printing of The Holy Qur'an, 1419 H.).

16. It states: "*Suami adalah kepala keluarga dan isteri ibu rumah tangga* (a husband is the head of the family and a wife is the housewife)".

17. It states: "*Suami wajib melindungi isterinya dan memberikan segala sesuatu keperluan hidup berumah tangga sesuai dengan kemapuannya* (It is compulsory for a husband to protect and give financial support to his wife)".

18. This interview was conducted in Padang in January 2004.

19. This is a term used to describe a person who does not fulfill his/her tasks as a Muslim (such as performing the five daily prayers). It is said that this person is a Muslim, based only on what is written in his/her identification card. Indonesian law requires every citizen to have a religion which is recorded in one's identification card (KTP).

20. Nias is a patriarchal society and its residence system is patrilocal.

21. Based on an interview conducted in Padang in October 2002.

22. Based on interviews conducted in Padang in December 2003.

23. As a result of its matrilineal principles, in Minangkabau, it is a daughter, not the son, who will be the bearer of family line. Because of that, a family is considered unlucky if it does not have any daughters. It means that the future of the family may vanish as the family line is passed on through daughters.

24. This information is based on an interview with Nina's parents and extended family in Padang in January 2003, and with Nina in Jakarta in February 2005.

25. My research shows that in general, Minangkabau people disagree with the concept of interreligious marriage, especially if the marriage is formally carried out according to non-Islamic rites.

26. Among Minangkabau, *urang awak* is a term used by Minangkabau to refer to themselves.

27. Niasan migrated to Minangkabau and were brought to Padang as slaves by the Acehnese and the VOC some time during the seventeenth century. Nias is a patrilineal society and most of its members embrace Christianity.

28. A confession of a Minangkabau person who converted to Christianity because of marriage. The interview was conducted in Jakarta on 20 August 2006.

29. This is based on an interview conducted in Jakarta on 20 August 2006.

References

Abdullah, Taufik. "Adat and Islam: An Examination of Conflict in Minangkabau". *Indonesia* 2 (1966): 1–24.

―――. *Minangkabau 1900–1927: Preliminary Studies in Social Development*. M.A. thesis, Cornel University, 1967.

―――. *Schools and Politics: The Kaum Muda Movement in West Sumatra*. Ithaca, N.Y.: Cornell University Modern Indonesia Project, Monograph Series, 1971.

Asnan, Gusti. *Kamus Sejarah Minangkabau*. Padang: Pusat Pengkajian Islam Minangkabau, 2003.

Azra, Azyumardi. *Surau: Pendidikan Islam Traditional dalam Transisi dan Modernisasi (Surau: Traditional Islamic Educational Institution in Transition and Modernization)*. Jakarta: Logos Wacana Ilmu Press, 2003.

Bell, Daniel. "Ethnicity and Social Change". In *Ethnicity: Theory and Experience*, edited by Nathan Glazer and Daniel P. Moynihan. Cambridge: Harvard University Press, 1975.

"Bincang-bincang Sejenak dengan Drs H. Rusydi Hamka: ABK SBK Hanya Retorika?". *Posmetro Padang*, 28 December 2003, p. 4.

Blackwood, Evelyn. "Representing Women: The Politics of Minangkabau Adat Writings". *The Journal of Asian Studies* 60, no. 1 (2001): 125–50.

Bowen, John R. *Islam, Law and Equality in Indonesia: An Anthropology of Public Reasoning*. Cambridge: Cambridge University Press, 2003.

Caldwell, John C., Allan G. Hill, and Valerie J. Hull, eds. *Micro-approaches to Demographic Research*. London: Kegan Paul, 1988.

Cammack, Mark. "Islamic Inheritance Law in Indonesia: The Influence of Hazairin's Theory of Bilateral Inheritance". *Asian Law* 4 (2002): 295–315.

Colombijn, Freek. *Patches of Padang: The History of an Indonesian Town in the Twentieth Century and the Use of Urban Space*. Leiden: Center of Non-Western Studies, Leiden University, 1994.

Din Al-Hilali, Muhammand Taqi-ud, and Muhammad Muhsin Khan, trans. *Translation of the Meanings of The Noble Qur'an in the English Language*. Madinah, KSA: King Fahd Complex for the Printing of The Holy Qur'an, 1419 H.

Dobbin, Christine. "Islamic Revivalism in Minangkabau at the Turn of the Nineteenth Century". *Modern Asian Studies* 8, no. 3 (1974): 319–56.

Elfira, Mina. "Gender and Kinship, Descent Systems and Islam: In East Asia, Southeast Asia, Australia and the Pacific". In *Encyclopedia of Women and Islamic Cultures 2*, edited by Suad Joseph. Brill: Leiden-Boston, 2005.

Glazer, Nathan and Daniel P. Moynihan. "Introduction". In *Ethnicity: Theory and Experience*, edited by Nathan Glazer and Daniel P. Moynihan. Cambridge: Harvard University Press, 1975.

Gordon, Milton M. "Toward a General Theory of Racial and Ethnic Group Relations". In *Ethnicity: Theory and Experience*, edited by Nathan Glazer and Daniel P. Moynihan. Cambridge: Harvard University Press, 1975.

Hamka. *Adat Minangkabau Menghadapi Revolusi*. Djakarta: Tekad, 1963.

———. *Islam dan Adat Minangkabau*. Jakarta: Penerbit Panjimas, 1984.

Hazairin. *Hukum Baru di Indonesia*. Djakarta: Bulan Bintang, 1950.

———. *Hukum Kewarisan Bilateral Menurut Al-Qur'an*. Djakarta: Tintamas, 1964.

Horowitz, Donald L. "Ethnic Identity". In *Ethnicity: Theory and Experience*, edited by Nathan Glazer and Daniel P. Moynihan. Cambridge: Harvard University Press, 1975.

Kipp, Rita Smith. *Dissociated Identities: Ethnicity, Religion, and Class in an Indonesian Society*. Ann Arbor: University of Michigan Press, 1996.

Lembaga Kerapatan Adat Alam Minangkabau Sumatera barat (LKAAM). *Bunga Rampai Pengetahuan Adat Minangkabau*. Padang: Yayasan Sako Batuah, 2000.

Lopez, Nancy. *Hopeful Girls, Troubled Boys: Race and Gender Disparity in Urban Education*. New York and London: Routledge, 2003.

Mahkamah Agung, Proyek Penelitian Hukum Adat. *Penelitian Hukum Adat tentang Warisan di Wilayah Hukum Pengadilan Tinggi Padang*. Jakarta: Mahkamah Agungm, 1980.

Navis, A.A. *Alam Terkembang Jadi Guru: Adat dan Kebudayaan Minangkabau*. Jakarta: Grafiti Press, 1984.

Prindivile, Joanne C. "Image and Role of Minangkabau Women". In *Southeast Asia: Women, Changing Social Structure, and Cultural Continuity*, edited by G. Hainsworth. Ottawa: University of Ottawa Press, 1981.

Reenen, Joke van. *Central Pillars of the House*. Leiden: Research School CNWS, 1996.

Sanday, Peggy Reeves. *Women at The Center: Life in a Modern Matriarchy*. Ithaca, N.Y., London: Cornell University Press, 2002.

Seale, Clive, ed. "Qualitative Interviewing". In *Researching Society and Culture*. London-Thousand Oaks-New Delhi: SAGE Publications, 1999.

Simulie, H. Kamardi Rais Dt. P. "Kata Pengantar: Bukan Seperti Seminar Biasa". In *Menelusuri sejarah Minangkabau*, edited by H. Kamardi Rais Dt. P. Simulie and Mestika Zed. Padang: Yayasan citra Budaya Indonesia and LKAAM Sumatra Barat, 2002.

Suryadinata, Leo, Evi Nurvidya Arifin, and Aris Ananta. *Indonesia's Population: Ethnicity and Religion in a Changing Political Landscape*. Singapore: Institute of Southeast Asian Studies, 2003.

Whalley, Lucy Anne. "Virtuous Women, Productive Citizens: Negotiating Tradition, Islam, and Modernity in Minangkabau". Ph.D. thesis. Indonesia: University of Illinois at Urbana-Champaign, 1993.

Yinger, J. Milton. *Ethnicity: Source of Strength? Source of Conflict?* New York: State University of New York Press, 1994.

Chapter 7

KHAO KHAEK
Interfaith Marriage between Muslims and Buddhists in Southern Thailand

Amporn Marddent

INTRODUCTION

Interfaith marriage among Muslims in Thailand has been discussed by many local religious leaders and senior village members as a worrying issue in the community. With the "Islamic Revival" that has taken place in Thai society over the last three decades, the debate over interfaith marriage has taken on a new dimension. Adherence to Islamic customs and beliefs among Muslims in southern Thailand has increased in daily life. For example, there is increasing attention given to Islamic Studies in both the traditional Islamic system and the national school system, and women wearing the veil are now a common sight. Yet the processes and consequences of marriages of Muslims in Thailand differ somewhat from those of Muslims in Malaysia and Indonesia in terms of the level of formal institutional control. In most cases of interfaith marriage in southern Thailand, the Buddhist partners convert to Islam. Only in a few cases do the Muslim partners become Buddhist, but even in these instances, religious conversion does not take place, but rather the Muslim partners lose their Muslim identity through a lengthy culturalization process.

While Muslim marriages in the southernmost provinces of Pattani, Yala, Narathiwat, and Satun are governed by Islamic family law and inheritance, marriage among Muslims in the rest of the country is governed by the civil law. Officially, however, the religious ideas, practices, and rituals of Muslims all over the country are determined through the mosque committee of each village, and this may include marriage. In practice, therefore, Islamic family law is extended to Muslims all over Thailand, although legally, Muslims outside of the four southernmost provinces may be married under civil law.

Islamic law regarding family and inheritance was formally adopted in 1946 with the application of the Islamic Law Act. It was recognized by the state for historical and political reasons (Metha Wadeecharoen 1995, pp. 11–12; Ismail Ali 1997: B; Funston 2006, p. 84). The dominant population in these areas is made up of ethnic Malay Muslims who have been struggling to retain their identity as a consequence of the intrusion of the Thai state and subsequent policies of cultural nationalism, especially during the eras of Field Marshal Phibulsongkram (Prime Minister 1938– 44 and 1948–57) and Field Marshal Sarit Thanarat (1958–63).

Currently, Thailand's Muslim population numbers about three million out of a total Thai population of about 62 million, the majority of whom are Buddhists (National Statistical Office, Thailand 2000). Muslims are, therefore, a minority in the country. However, most Muslims live in the four southern border provinces of Pattani, Yala, Narathiwat, and Satun while the rest are scattered throughout the country, though with a heavier concentration in

the mid-south than in the rest of the country. The number of
Muslims in Thailand has long been contested. The Islamic
Committee Office of Thailand put the number of Muslims at
7,391,235,[1] while the 2000 official census revealed a number at
2,815,900 or 4.6 per cent of the total population of 60,617,200,
up from 4.1 per cent in 1990.[2]

Gilquin argues that mixed marriage is an important factor
related to the number of Muslims in Thailand since most Buddhists
have to convert. It is, therefore, likely that the minority Muslim
population will exceed 10 per cent of the total population in
time (Gilquin 2005, pp. 41–42). However, Farouk is convinced
that the Muslim population is at least 5 per cent of the total
population and could very well be as large as 8 per cent now
(Omar Farouk Bajunid 2005, p. 17).

The Thai census appears to provide a more objective measure
of the number of Muslims in Thailand. According to the 2000
census, Muslims in Pattani comprise 80.7 per cent of the total
population of the province, while in Yala, Narathiwat, and Satun,
the Muslim population officially stands at 68.9 per cent, 82 per
cent, and 67.8 per cent respectively of the total population of
these provinces (National Statistical Office Thailand 2000). Satun,
in fact, differs considerably from the other three provinces in its
manifestation of ethnic Malay identity. It has a history separate
from that of Pattani. While Pattani, Yala, and Narathiwat were
once part of the Malay sultanate of Patani, Satun was part of
the sultanate of Kedah. However, when it comes to its religious
identity, Satun very much belongs with the three Muslim
provinces (Arin Sa-idee et al. 2002, p. 2).

Marriage between Muslims and non-Muslims in these four
border provinces has thus taken place in different circumstances
compared with other types of interfaith marriages in the rest of

the country. At the same time, Satun represents the southernmost limit of Thai ethnographical expansion on the western seaboard (Kobkua Suwannathat-Pian 2000, pp. 162–79; Nakamura et al. 2001, pp. 77, 80). Chavivun Pracuabmoh reported in the early 1980s that there are few cases of intermarriage in Pattani, on the east coast of southern Thailand (Chavivun Pracuabmoh 1982, pp. 79–80). However, there is no definite number showing that conversion on the western side of the peninsula is higher than on the east. This can be estimated from the socio-cultural and religious contexts of these two different sites. The western coast is a place where socio-religious, economic, and political factors have led Muslims and non-Muslims to interact with each other more than those on the east coast. Religious conversion can thus take place in either direction or not at all (Guelden 2005, pp. 160–61; Amornsakdi Ragsatipaya 2005, pp. 147–49).

Historically, intermarriage among people in southern Thailand, especially on the east coast, has taken place since the early fifteenth century. In 1457, the Kingdom of Pattani embraced Islam and most of the inhabitants adopted the faith of the princely courts. Thai-speaking Muslim communities are found in other southern Thai provinces such as Songkhla, Trang, Krabi, and Phang-nga. They are known among scholars and the locals as Sam Sam.[3] From various reports from the second half of the nineteenth century, it is clear that intermarriage is not well regarded. For instance,

> In most cases, the so-called Muslims cared very little and knew nothing about religion...An incident concerned two young people — the man, a Muslim Sam-Sam, and the girl, a Thai Buddhist. They were intent on getting married, and the man was prepared to give up his religion for the girl he loved...Then, in desperation, I asked him to consider the Holy Prophet

Mohammad, and what he said shocked me — "Why should I
consider Mohammad, he has never been in my kampong (village)
to see me, not even once?" (Rahman 1978, pp. 24–26, cited in
Kobkua Suwannathat-Pian 2000, p. 170).

There is no hard data on religious conversion by marriage.[4]
Scholars of Muslim organizations cannot verify the proportion of
men and women who convert to Islam in Thailand because
conversion can take place at any time just by invoking the *kalima
shahadah*, the pledge of conviction of faith, in front of at least
two adult Muslim witnesses.[5] Traditionally, conversion, as well as
intermarriage, takes place in front of the community leaders at
the mosque, or in the house of the woman who is getting
married. Generally, there are two or three converts in each Muslim
village of Pattani, Yala and Narathiwat, while the figure in the
mid-south and Bangkok is closer to twenty to thirty conversions
in a village.[6] The smaller number of conversions in the
southernmost provinces is presumably because they have a Muslim
majority. Language, belief system, ethnic, and cultural differences
between Muslims and Buddhists do not allow for regular
interaction and close relationships.[7] Moreover, the attitudes of
the Thai-speaking Muslims in the south including Satun, and the
Malay-speaking Muslims of the three provinces which were
formerly parts of the Patani Sultanate, are markedly different.
Thai-speaking Muslims live among their Thai-speaking Buddhist
neighbours and their mother tongue is Thai. Thus, language is
another factor related to levels of coexistence and plurality as
well as a key to the socio-cultural and demographic setting of
interfaith marriage.

Intermarriage interacts with the political sphere, since Islamic
family law and inheritance are applicable to Muslim and non-
Muslim couples in every part of the country. There are, however,
different ways in which this regulation is enforced. The Central

Islamic Committee of Thailand, as well as the forty-eight provincial councils of Islamic affairs, together with the country's 3,295 mosque committees (Department of Religious Affairs website, accessed 10 August 2007),[8] have the official authority to rule on Islamic family law and inheritance. Such a system supported by the state thus brings the Islamic worldview, as interpreted through mainstream Muslim scholars' interpretation, into legal culture and traditional practices related to marriage, family, and divorce. It has been noted that Thailand is predominantly Buddhist and historically has been more assimilationist as opposed to multicultural vis-à-vis non-Thai minority groups (Thompson et al. 2007, pp. 268–88). The Central Thai Government has attempted to assimilate culturally its minorities, including Muslims in the south. One important issue is religious observance which encourages and moulds Muslim identity. The ongoing practice of Muslim-non-Muslim marriage in Thailand then has led the authorities and institutions to call for the implementation of Islamic education in the Muslim community. The religious authorities have made it obligatory for the non-Muslim partner, who plans to marry a Muslim and who must therefore convert, to have basic knowledge of Islam before marriage. Those who do not want to go for the course are sanctioned; for example Muslim committee members will not conduct funeral or other merit-making ceremonies for the non-converts and their family members. Consequently, this makes it obligatory for the non-Muslim partner to have a basic knowledge of Islam before marriage.

CONCEPTUAL BACKGROUND

The concept of marriage in Islam is considered a religious matter, although there are different interpretations on the basic requirement for interfaith marriage. In some conditions it is considered permissible for a Muslim to marry a non-Muslim. For example, Muslim men may marry Jewish and Christian women, who are referred to as "*ahlul kitab*" or "People of the Book". This comes from the understanding that Jews and Christians share similar religious outlooks — a belief in One God, following the commandments of God, a belief in revealed scripture, and so on.[9] However marriage between a Muslim woman and a non-Muslim man is a more difficult issue. It can lead to the lack of acceptance and social space for them to live in the Muslim community. Many of them are requested by religious leaders to return to their communities. In addition, in the current era, people may choose to live in urban settings. Thus, the pressure to conform would decrease, but their parents living in the Muslim community continue to face the pressure to conform.

Muslim scholars stress that a Muslim woman is not permitted to marry anyone but a Muslim man. There is no exception allowing women to marry Jews and Christians. These ideas have been interpreted by mainstream Muslim scholars and jurisprudents as being based on the recognition that the head of the household is the man or husband who provides leadership for the family. Therefore, a Muslim woman cannot follow the leadership of someone who does not share her faith and values. Ali argues that there are two kinds of hierarchies: Muslims are to dominate over non-Muslims, and husbands over wives (Kecia Ali 2006, p. 1).

Essentially, the general idea of intermarriage is, in fact, permitted in the Muslim community. In this chapter I will examine the role and interaction of interfaith marriage in Muslim social contexts, rather than scrutinize Islamic theology and the traditions of Islamic legal thought, which have mostly been developed by Muslim male jurists and have been upheld in every school of Islamic law, including the codified elements of Islamic family law and inheritance. However, I will not discuss issues of gender justice through the different regulations on intermarriage and the possibility of alternative interpretations. Instead, the chapter stresses the need to understand the impact of socio-political constructions of ethnicity and religion on the lives and relationships in interfaith marriages. It is also based on observations and descriptions of the life experiences of some interfaith marriage couples and their relatives from Phuket and Nakhon Si Thammarat in the mid-southern region of Thailand. The Islamic family law and inheritance does not apply in these two provinces, and therefore, in general, Muslims here are more flexible than Muslims in the deep South in applying, or not applying, certain regulations of the Islamic family law and inheritance.

The emergence of Muslims in Phuket and Nakhon Si Thammarat has to be understood in relation to the interaction between Buddhists in Siam and Malay Muslims from Sai Buri, state of Kedah. Kobkua Suwannathat-Pian states that the Siamese Muslims were naturally attracted to the Kedah socio-religious centre. Intermarriage with Malay-speaking Muslims and other socio-economic and political factors have led to the migration of Thai-speaking Muslims to Phuket (Kobkua Suwannathat-Pian 2000, p. 169). This has led to the general belief that Muslims had settled in Phuket before the establishment of Mueang Thalang in the seventeenth century. The local story of two heroines, Jan and her sister Mook, who came from an interfaith family, reflects considerable religious integration in Phuket (Panya Srinaka 2003, pp. 15–47). Moreover, the *Baba* and *Yaya*, terms used to refer to the male and female descendants of mixed marriages between Chinese immigrants and locals (who may be Malay Muslims or non-Muslims in Phuket) is another reflection of the plural past.

Intermarriage without conversion was formerly frequent, but this has been very rare since the last three decades of Islamic revivalism.[10]

In Nakhon Si Thammarat, the majority of Muslims were descended from war captives taken by Siamese armies during the nineteenth-century wars between Siam and Sai Buri, Kelantan, and Pattani (Amornsakdi Ragsatipaya 2005, pp. 84–90). Nevertheless, Muslims ostensibly have a good relationship with Buddhists. The Central Thai Government in Bangkok aims at the integration rather than the assimilation of Muslims in this area. The concept of a unified Thai nation is based on the economic, political, and socio-cultural plurality of Phuket and Nakhon Si Thammarat. One can easily find an environment of religious tolerance in these areas, and there are numerous examples of intermarriage among the Thai-speaking Buddhists, Thai-speaking Muslims, and Sino-Thais in Nakhon Si Thammarat.

NOTIONS OF KHAEK

The term *khaek* literally means guest(s). It is used to refer broadly to Muslims, Malays, Indians, Middle Easterners, and foreigners in general, and also persons who phenotypically appear dark. Historically, Thailand was host to trade flowing from two major directions, with the Chinese from the north and east, and with traders from the south and west. These people became collectively referred to as *khaek* (Dirake Kulsirisawat 2002; Glowing 1975). On the other hand, Omar Bajunid observes that *khaek* is often used in popular parlance as a pejorative label meaning guest or dark-skinned visitor, to which people strongly object (Omar Farouk Bajunid 2005, p. 4).

Khaek is also commonly used as a racial-cum-religious description encompassing Muslims. The language for describing the Muslim inhabitants of southern Thailand is highly politicized.

In the eyes of the Thai state they are Thai-Muslims with the emphasis on Thai. Many Thai-Muslims see themselves as Malay or Malay-Muslims and only secondarily as Thai citizens. Jory argues that the Thai Government has attempted to replace Malay ethnic identity with the religious label in the hope that these linguistic changes would contribute to the overall goal of assimilation (Jory 2007).

Islam arrived in Thailand with different groups, but particularly through merchants of the Muslim-controlled Indian Ocean trade route near the end of the thirteenth century. However, ethnically and culturally, Muslims in Thailand are by no means a monolithic group, although officially they are labelled by the Thai state as Thai-Muslim or Thai-Islam. To distinguish Muslims in Thailand from *khaek* is, then, not easy and also paradoxical, because they have more than one identity. For Muslims in Thailand, the concept of being "Thai" varies. However, in the general ideology established over several centuries, to be Thai usually implies declaring Buddhism and going to the temple. Practically, being Thai is more complicated than this, especially when one takes into consideration the nationalist formulations of Thainess since the era of Field Marshal Phibulsongkram. Meanwhile to be *khaek*, by its etymology, excludes one from being considered as native. Language is an important element in differentiating *khaek* from Thai. I still vividly remember my grandmother who spoke in southern Thai dialect saying, "Even though we, *khon khaek* (*khaek* people), and our neighbours, *khon Thai* (Thai people), are different because we are not *khon phasa diow kan* (people who use the same language), we can be friends."

The idea of *khon phasa diow kan* implies a group of people who have the same path in faith. Over the past two centuries, Muslims in Phuket and Nakhon Si Thammarat spoke in Kedah Malay and southern Thai dialects in their daily lives. Some standard Malay words are picked up to add to their speech.

However, there are some Muslims who are Kedah Malay-speaking, which is similar to modern central Malay language, who reside in Nakhon Si Thammarat, especially in Tha Sala District.[11] Muslims in Phuket generally use Malay terms for personal pronouns and for kinship terms, for example, elder sister is *kak* or *jah*, elder brother is *bang*, and *paklang* and *maklang* or *maksu* which mean uncle and aunt respectively. Meanwhile, Buddhists, including those who convert to Islam, are referred to using Thai terms.

Consequently, the notion of *khaek* in southern Thailand precisely means Muslims. However, it is also used with some other terms to specify other groups of *khaek*, for example *khaek* Melayu refers to Malay-speaking Muslim. Nevertheless, Muslims in this area live in harmony with Buddhists and other foreign nationals. Many Muslim villages are located separately from Buddhist areas, such as the Muslim villages in Tha Sala of Nakhon Si Thammarat. But there are several mixed Buddhist-Muslim villages. Muslims in the mid-southern region of Thailand accept their own identity as *khaek* and are unaware of its connotations. It is acceptable to call themselves and be called by Muslims *khon khaek*, but if people of other faiths call them such, the meaning becomes derogative as it marks them out as an exclusive community. This concept is more insulting in the three border provinces as it infers that Muslims living in the region of the former Patani Sultanate are not native (and, therefore, do not belong) to those geographical areas (Thomas Parks 2005, p. 15). To be *khaek* is hence an ethnic category that can be regarded as a representation in Thai ideology on religion, race, national identity, and culture.

ON THE ROAD TO *KHAO KHAEK*

Khaek has implications at the cultural, ethnic, and religious levels. The term *khao* literally means to step in or come in. When these two words are joined as in *khao khaek*, it can be understood as converting to become Muslim. According to Islamic principles, being a Muslim begins when one is born of Muslim parents.[12] However, there is no coercion in matters of faith.[13] Another route to becoming a Muslim is *khao khaek* by marriage. The general perception and situation regarding marriage with non-Muslims in Thailand are related to Buddhist-Muslim relations because most interfaith marriages among Muslims are with Buddhists.

Indeed, interfaith marriages in the south are rising, leading to concerns in Muslim communities regarding how to follow Islamic principles correctly, e.g. the dietary restrictions. One villager expressed the following concern to me:

> Don't you observe the increase in intermarriage between *khon khaek* and *khon* Thai. Our Imam also worries about the food that we buy from those *khon thai pen khaek* (Thai Buddhists who convert to Islam) vendors. We are not sure about the way they wash those utensils, fish, meat and vegetables[14] (Sharifah, a thirty-three-year-old villager from Phuket).

Muslims in the mid-southern region of Thailand call themselves *"khon khaek"*,[15] where Muslim religious identity is distinct from the Buddhists. *Khon* Thai in this sense means the people of the *de facto* Thai state religion. Buddhism is actually not *de jure* the state religion.[16] However, by designating and differentiating these identities, it has not led to an antagonistic religious landscape. According to Sharifah, the dominant identity categories are religion and state embedded in the southern Thai Muslim community. This signals that the proclamation of religious identity is intertwined with and interacts with the official identity promoted by the state. The existing power of perception in state identity is still largely based on the assumption that the Thais are unified as Buddhists. Moreover, attitudes related to Islamic norms and cultural negotiation that seek Muslim space in a Buddhist country, as in the above-mentioned interviewee's concern about food, reaffirm Muslim identity. The identity of Muslims in Thailand thus directly relates to perceptions of "the other". Therefore, the process of national unification, underlined by concerted efforts by the state to define and promote a Thai culture and identity, has recreated or rediscovered perceptions of "the other" as well.

This is reflected by the fact that Buddhists who convert to Islam are referred to using Thai terms, such as *phi Dang* (elder sister and/or brother Dang) and *na Pen* (aunt Pen), even though non-Muslims take Arabic names when they convert to Islam. Changing names after conversion is not required by religion, but the Prophet encouraged Muslims to have good names.[17] Islam in Thailand became the context for the prevalence of Arabic and Malay cultures, Arabic and Malay names became Islamic names, and those who converted to Islam automatically adopted Arab and Malay culture in an attempt to become more Islamic. Muslim scholars insist that a name is associated with religion, such as Abdullah which means "the servant of God or Allah". When one has an Arabic name, people suddenly recognize that she/he is a Muslim. In the case of Aunt Loi, for instance, she converted to Islam thirty years ago. Aunt Loi met Ahmad in Bangkok when they were supplying goods from their hometowns, Chiang Rai and Phuket. She received a new name, which is Hasnah, but people in the village prefer to call her *kak* Loi.

Another issue relates to the notion of "*ahlul kitab*". As explained earlier, such marriages are restricted to a Muslim man contracting a marriage with a woman of the "People of the Book".[18] Buddhists are generally recognized not as people of the scripture, but as *mushrik* or idolaters.[19] Muslim scholars emphasize that matrimonial relations with *mushrik* are forbidden. From Qur'anic interpretations and the rulings of mainstream scholars, from which Muslims in Thailand take their guidance, Buddhists are identified as people who do not believe in God and Prophethood. As stated earlier, marriage with polytheists is prohibited. The only case in which marriage with Buddhists can be contracted is when the Muslim has been found guilty of *zina*, adultery, or fornication.[20]

Interfaith marriage in Muslim community is gendered, in that Buddhist women are more likely than men to convert into Islam through marriage according to the Islamic ritual, *nikah*. Furthermore, Muslim parents and relatives feel easier to accept Buddhist women rather than men into their families. Many villagers link this acceptance with the idea of men being the leader of the family. Women are more protected within the family, while men have more freedom to mingle outside the religious community. Buddhist women who marry Muslim men are usually requested to live in the Muslim community and the families will teach them religious regulations and practices after *nikah*. Similarly, non-Muslim men are required to embrace Islam before *nikah* and to undergo circumcision after conversion. I have heard many groups of Muslim leaders complain that the male converts hardly attend religious education at the mosque, "… so how can they lead their families?"[21]

In the religious wedding ritual, the wedding contract has to be signed by the man. Therefore, the man has to at least know the basics of this sacred legal contract which is conducted between the ritual guardian of the bride in the paternal line, called *wali*, and the groom through a legalization process, termed *nikah*. If the woman is the convert, the *imam* or other religious official will preside over the marriage contract ceremony. The concept of marriage itself is associated with the dichotomous concepts of *halal*, meaning permitted, and *haram*, meaning forbidden, because sexual relations outside of marriage is forbidden. Many cases of interfaith marriage in southern Thailand are allowed by the parents and the religious authority because they consider it to be the only way to avoid being held accountable for any extramarital sexual relationship that may otherwise occur.[22] Basically, the ceremony is carried out at the mosque of the village or the bride's home. The groom is seated on a specially-made cushion with the *wali* or *imam* seated in front of him. Before the citing of the *akad nikah* or sacred legal contract, the *imam* will read out and advise the groom on the duties of a husband, and the consequences if he leaves his wife. Normally the advice given is meant to ensure that he becomes a good husband and performs his responsibility as husband and head of a family properly.

Generally, the process and places to perform religious wedding contracts are similar for Muslims all over the country, but the ceremony after *nikah* will be different for each local tradition. In the deep south, the Malay wedding tradition usually follows. In the case of a Muslim-non-Muslim marriage, the parents of the couple, particularly the Muslim parents, will normally not hold a typically luxurious Malay wedding ceremony because the partner of their child is not of the same faith. While the wedding ceremonies of Muslims in the mid-southern provinces and around Bangkok have been modified to be more modern in terms of costume and style of celebration, there are also elements of the local tradition of the southern or central Thai. Having undergone democratization and capitalist development processes for several decades,[23] people in southern Thailand have been exposed to a more diverse lifestyle and socio-economic and religio-cultural patterns. The transformation has had a significant impact on the experiences of Muslims in the south, despite their reputation as the group most resistant to change. Visibly, Muslims have participated in the new economic activities, such as shopping for all sorts of consumer goods and delivering services to foreigners and tourists.

Historically, it was Islam that had created new respect for people in this region and intermarriage had enabled the spread of Islam.[24] The current global Islamic revival that is infused by the politicization of the religious arena has also "awakened" a large number of the locals in Thailand. The phenomenon brings an increased emphasis on Islamic values, practices, and institutions into the lives of Muslims. The resurgence emphasizes Islamic identity and stricter adherence to belief and practice. There are some movements towards searching for the true Islam in recent decades and the cleansing away of traditions of non-Islamic elements. This process has been accompanied by a genuine drive to become good Muslims. Also, as a minority people in Thai society, Muslims have strived to preserve their own identity through the Islamic faith. In the matter of interfaith marriage, involving asking non-Muslim partners to be *khon khaek*, family and community have been pushed to deal with the prohibition on intermarriage without conversion. Nevertheless, the means to become *khaek* or *khao khaek* by marriage is still related to the idea and image of being Muslim in Thailand.

EXPERIENCES OF CHANGE

The annual number of converts who participate in the short course on Islamic Studies for *muallaf* (converts) organized by the Santichon Muslim Foundation, Bangkok, has remained constant, at about 100 converts, since five years ago.[25] The converts were mainly women who married Muslim partners. They include university graduates and middle-class citizens. The increase in intermarriage indicates that Buddhists and Muslims in Thailand have more social interaction now than in the past. This is likely to result in a steady increase of Buddhist-Muslims of mixed origins.[26] Many Buddhists, in fact, live together with their Muslim lovers before marriage. This does not mean they are unaware of

Islamic sexual norms or do not fear the sin of adultery, but Muslim ideas and state institutions are regarded as too rigid and intolerant. In the case of Amran, for example, his father, the former *imam* of a mosque in Phuket, cannot accept that his first-born son who graduated from an Islamic school has a relationship with a non-Muslim woman working at the same place. After Amran unsuccessfully asked his parents to conduct *nikah* for them, he decided to run away from home and has not returned for almost two years. However, he is still in contact with some of his relatives who respect his decision.

The non-Muslim woman with whom Amran plans to marry (*nikah*) is a Sino-Thai, referred to by southern Thai Muslims as *sa-jeen*. The notion of *sa-jeen* among Muslims relates to a group of "unclean" people who eat unlawful food (especially pork) and have different (implying lower) hygiene standards compared with "us", *khaek*. Among many in the Muslim communities there is a popular joke with negative connotations regarding Sino-Thai, that they are "*sa-jeen khi mai lang*", meaning people who do not cleanse themselves after defecating. The image of *sa-jeen* has been constructed for a long time and makes *khaek* feel uncomfortable to enter into close relationships with them, especially in marriage. This is not only indicated by the physical, but also a spiritual dimension. The rituals prescribed to the Muslim community regarding the act of spiritual purification are more important than physical cleanliness, even though Islamic scholars insist that the latter is part and parcel of their faith. *Sa-jeen* and/or *khon* Thai, therefore have to believe and act as *khaek* if they marry Muslims, and this type of marriage implies that the couple cannot only focus on their own relationship, but they also have a relationship with the community as well.

The responsibility for the process of converting to Islam, or *khao khaek*, in southern Thailand as well as all over the country, lies with the authorities in charge of each community, the *imam*, and the mosque council committee. Faith is the first consideration of the Muslim community. People recognize that marriage and family life will be much more worry-free and harmonious if both spouses share the same ideas, especially the same belief system. The Muslim authorities always introduce Islam and encourage *khon* Thai and *sa-jeen* to become Muslims before *nikah*. This process will not be successful if their Muslim partners do not cooperate with the Muslim institutions.

Many Muslim-non-Muslim couples in Thailand get through this first step fairly quickly although this depends on the authorities as well. In some cases, after the non-Muslims have been taught the fundamentals of Islam, they are already allowed to invoke the *kalima shahadah*. After the invocation, Muslims believe that the convert not only attains the status of a Muslim, but he or she also becomes a purified person with his or her past sins forgiven by God. In the case of the conversion of a man (but not a woman), the authorities will also ask him to undergo the circumcision rite,[27] in order to become a Muslim.

Female circumcision is not a religious obligation for Muslim women. However, one can find this popular idea and practice among Muslims in southern Thailand. A few religious scholars assume this custom is accepted as part of Muslim women's tradition before the era of the Islamic revival in this country. This rite of passage is recognized by the local Muslims as a *sunnah* tradition. Describing a practice as *sunnah* essentially makes it equivalent to a religious principle, since Muslims in this region are adherents of the Sunni branch of Islam, that is, those who follow the *sunnah*. The term *sunnah* and Sunni have become ideologically linked, in spite of the fact that *sunnah* circumcision does not literally imply linkage to Sunni Islam. One young man discussed his views on the practice:

My mom asked Salma to undergo circumcision. She [my mom] has very strong ideas and refers this act to Islam. It was very surprising to me when she said that our *nikah* is not yet completed. I know, this is not our rite. She relies on my uncle who claims that he knows Islam. But I won't let my wife undergo such a thing. This is the practice from ancient Arabia done by primitive people who forced their women to do so (Isa, a 27-year-old villager from Nakhon Si Thammarat).

Isa informed me of this issue three months after beginning his matrimonial relationship. He is an educated Muslim man who chose to marry a *khon thai pen khaek*. Salma left her community as well as Thai Buddhist culture to live with Isa at Ban Kra (pseudonym), a Muslim village in Tha Sala district of Nakhon Si Thammarat. After marriage, it is difficult to find converts who live with their parents who are of a different religion. This religious-ethnic boundary limits the flexibility of cognate kinship relations. Certain situations that arise when dealing with persons who claim to be authorities on Islam can bring about misunderstandings for the newcomer. In this case, Salma insisted that as an adult Muslim woman, she has rights over her own body. Religious authority in this case is claimed by a man who identifies himself as a scholar, and the *khon Thai pen khaek* should therefore comply.

SUFFERING IN INTERFAITH MARRIAGES?

In marrying a non-Muslim man or woman, the Muslim partner realizes that she/he has already agreed to live with a non-believer. Meanwhile, the expectation of the Muslim community is that a man/woman should convert to Islam and behave like a Muslim in order to marry a Muslim. Such is the case of Fatin, a Muslim woman in Nakhon Si Thammarat married by common law marriage to a non-convert, a Buddhist man who is a local government official. Fatin grew up in a Muslim community and had to marry her husband because of an "accident". She uses the term, "accidental marriage", instead of premarital sex. Fatin tried to convince her husband to learn about Islam and to convert, but she was unsuccessful. Now Fatin admits that after almost twenty years of marriage life, with two daughters, living in her husband's village, she does not practise Islam, but still identifies herself as a Muslim. However, an often-felt agony in Fatin's life is the effect of her deeds on her parents. She does not want her non-Islamic marriage, living without *nikah*, to be a sinful burden on her parents.

This example shows a pattern of elopement which is different from Amran's case. That is, Fatin's marriage took place under secular law, while Amran used Islamic marriage law, *nikah*. Both cases have to overcome barriers to intermarriage. After the couple's elopement, their parents when faced with a *fait accompli*, usually recognize their marriages. They are already mated, so there is no way to prohibit their union. In regard to Fatin's married life, the religious differences under this environment have not damaged the relationship between her and her parents, nor the local Muslim and Buddhist communities, especially after she had her first child. That is because the grandparents and relatives from both sides have to visit each other.

Within this decade, numerous Muslims in southern Thailand have married foreigners, especially Westerners, who are understood by local people to be Christians. Muslim religious leaders and the local people recognize these married couples as exotic and liberal. This is not only an issue of faith, but also of race and culture. The phenomenon of Muslims marrying foreigners has become a normal occurrence among Muslims in Phuket, particularly in the tourist areas where there are increasing numbers of foreigners.

Being married to foreigners forces Muslims to think more about their own religion in order to distinguish Islam from tradition and custom. Consequently, the path to be *khaek* in the Thai context does not only involve religion, but also ethnicity, economy, cultural values, race, and state authority. Southern Thai Muslims actually have different thoughts, feelings, and behaviours in both obvious and subtle ways, which play a major role in determining how people deal with changes in their lives. Ethnicity is a powerful influence in determining identity. However, one cannot ignore how the state and religious factors construct the lives of Muslim and non-Muslim couples.

CONCLUSION

Interfaith marriage thus not only changes people's individual lives, but also their identities, through the requirement of changes in name, actions, behaviour, and so on. But the community cannot reject the demands for adaptation and openness to new patterns of families in contemporary generations. Intermarriage challenges the boundaries of what is normal through a re-negotiation of cultural language and norms. The issues arise from the way in which Muslim-non-Muslim couples, as actors, respond to any perceived threat to the established order.

There is limited research and documentation of interfaith marriage in southern Thailand. Few scholars have shown interest in examining interreligious, interethnic, and intercultural coexistence. Much of the scholarly literature on southern Thailand presents Muslims as a homogeneous group. The dominant theme is the various degrees to which Muslims as minority communities were integrating successfully into the Thai-Buddhist dominant host society (Alexander Horstmann 2004). We cannot overlook the historical and contemporary phenomenon of interethnic marriage, the practices of conversion in Muslim-Buddhist co-residence, religious coexistence, and the religious and cultural complications that are the result of intermarriage.

Regarding intermarriage between Muslims and Buddhists in southern Thailand, it is evident that ethno-religious integration can effectively proceed. In the deep south, the couple's lives are governed by Islamic family law and practices of inheritance which are rooted in a very different ethnic and socio-political context in comparison to that of the mid-southern region. The latter group of people, including the west coasters, represents a more liberal social group when it comes to attitudes and practices involving religion. The relationship between Buddhists and Muslims has been influenced by the combined effect of socio-political, cultural, and administrative change.[28] The practice of intermarriage in two provinces — Phuket and Nakhon Si Thammarat — despite the fact that they are located on different sides of the peninsula, display similar patterns of religious integration. The religio-cultural amalgamation of interfaith marriage between Buddhists and Muslims can proceed according to the religious requirements of the Muslim community. Whether or not other processes of social integration and assimilation are occurring, the greatest requirement in intermarriage is tolerance and a willing acceptance of different belief systems and communities, which in intermarriage are united.

Notes

1. On the problem of Muslim statistics, see Michel Gilquin (2005), pp. 39–40; Omar Farouk Bajunid (1988).
2. Census details have been taken directly or calculated from <http://web.nso.go.th/pop2000/tables_e.htm>.
3. For more information, see Kobkua Suwannathat-Pian (2000), pp. 180–200.

4. From telephone interviews on 16 January 2007 with the staff of the Central Islamic Committee of Thailand and Banjong Binkasan, including the staff of Santichon Muslim Foundation, which is a pioneer and moderate Islamic organization based in Bangkok, which has been educating converts since 1986.

5. The utterance with which one declares his/her intention to become a Muslim.

6. The estimated number of converts in Nakhon Si Thammarat was 700. This number was reported by the President of the Islamic Committee of Nakhon Si Thammarat in October 2006. The President of the Islamic Committee of Phuket, however, informed me that there is no data available, unlike Nakhon Si Thammarat where there is a group of *muallaf* (converts) who regularly have activities. He can only estimate that the number of converts in Phuket is fewer than in Nakhon Si Thammarat. In the lower south, many scholars say there are very small numbers of converts in their community, especially in the remote areas.

7. Interviews with Muslim scholars from the deep south who currently live in Nakhon Si Thammarat and Phuket.

8. The Central Islamic Committee of Thailand website indicates that there are thirty-six provincial Islamic committees in addition to the country's 3,507 mosque committees (Department of Religious Affairs website, accessed 10 January 2007). Thailand has a highly centralized official Islamic administration, which is headed by the Chularajamontri or Syaikh al-Islam, who is elected by members of National Council of Islamic Affairs (NCIA) and heads of the Provincial Councils for Islamic Affairs (PCIAs). Both the Chularajamontri and the NCIA are part of the Thai bureaucratic system, belonging to the Islamic Centre of Thailand, which is administered by the Thai Government (Funston 2006, pp. 83–84).

9. "This day is all things good and pure made lawful to you.... Lawful to you in marriage are not only chaste women who are believers, but chaste women among the People of the Book, revealed before your time, when you give them their due dowers, and desire chastity not lewdness. If any one rejects faith, fruitless is his work, and in

the Hereafter he will be in the ranks of those who have lost."
(Al-Qur'an 5:5).

10. Interviews with Muslim and non-Muslim scholars in Nakhon Si Thammarat and Phuket in August 2006.

11. For more information, see Kitti Ali-ae and Tadsanai Nualvisai, "Panglimor Jekteh Cemetery: The Cemetery of Muslim Primogenitor in Tha Sala", in *Hundred Years of Tha Sala: Back to the Future* (in Thai), edited by Suebpong Thammachat (2000), p. 169; Amornsakdi Ragsatipaya (2005) and Abdul Razak Panaemalae (forthcoming), *Melayu Ligor* (Mimeograph).

12. The Prophet Muhammad had said, "No babe is born but upon *Fitra* (as a Muslim). It is his parents who make him a Jew or a Christian or a polytheist." (*Al Hadith, Sahih Muslim*, Book 033, No. 6426).

13. "There is no compulsion in religion." (Al-Qur'an 2:256).

14. In general, every food is considered permissible unless it is specially prohibited by the Qur'an and/or the hadith.

15. Except the Malay Muslims in Pattani, Yala, and Narathiwat, who call themselves *"Melayu"*.

16. The state religion in effect is Theravada Buddhism; however, it is not officially designated as such. When the previous Constitution was being drafted in 1997, the Constitutional Drafting Assembly rejected a proposal to have Theravada Buddhism named the official religion on the grounds that such an action would create social division and be offensive to other religious communities in the country. Recently, the 18th Thailand Constitution Drafting Committee rejected another proposal to enshrine Buddhism as the national religion in the aftermath of a military coup on 19 September 2006 that annulled the previous charter (*Bangkok Post*, 30 June 2007, "It's Official: No State Religion").

17. *Al Hadith, Sahih Muslim*, Book 033, No. 841 and 354.

18. "...Lawful to you and yours is lawful unto them. (Lawful unto you in marriage) are (not only) chaste women who are believers, but chaste women among the People of the Book, revealed before your time..." (Al-Qur'an 5:5).

19. Some Reformist Muslim scholars regard Buddhists and Hindus as

"People of the Book" because they follow religions based on scripture. However, this idea is not influential in southern Thailand.

20. "Let no man guilty of adultery or fornication marry but a woman similarly guilty, or an unbeliever: nor let any but such a man or an unbeliever marry such a woman: to the believers such a thing is forbidden." (Al-Qur'an 24:3).

21. I took down this statement made by a Muslim leader at a village in Phuket province while I was doing fieldwork there in August 2006.

22. Based on the saying of the imam of Ban Node (Synonym) in Nakhon Si Thammarat.

23. The first National Economic and Social Development Plan (NESDP) was implemented in 1961. The development strategy for the southern region involves a transportation system serving as an economic land bridge and gateway connecting the Gulf of Thailand to the Andaman Sea, as well as developing the deep sea harbour, marine commerce, gasoline, and petrochemical industries.

24. For more information, see Ibrahim Syukri, *History of the Malay Kingdom of Patani*, translated from Yawi by Conner Bailey and John Miksic (2005), pp. 20–24.

25. This course has changed into a programme for those who are interested in Islam.

26. The general view that intermarriage has increased comes from a telephone interview with the President of Islamic Committee of Nakhon Si Thammarat on 14 January 2007, and interviews with six Muslim religious leaders in Nakhon Si Thammarat between 7 September 2006 and 17–18 January 2007.

27. Circumcision for male Muslims is an important step in the transition from childhood to adulthood.

28. Omar Farouk Bajunid distinguished between two types of Muslims, namely the "assimilated" and the "unassimilated". The former constitutes a whole diversity of ethnic groups in Thailand, such as the Arabs, the Pathans, the Thai-speaking Muslims, etc. Meanwhile, the latter is predominantly Malays who reside in the tri-province area of Narathiwat, Pattani, and Yala, together with some parts of

neighbouring Songkhla. Imtiyaz Yusuf (2007) argues that the main factor responsible for this is the Malays' firm adherence to an ethnicized religious identity and their strong attachment to the concept of race, language, and Islam, which are largely shaped and inspired by an ethno-religious nationalism based on Malay ethnicity.

References

Abdul Razak Panaemalae (forthcoming). *Melayu Ligor* (Mimeograph).
Amornsakdi Ragsatipaya. "Ethnic Relations in Dynamic of Resource Management: A Case Study of Klai Community, Thasala, Nakorn Si Thammarat". M.A. thesis (in Thai). Thailand: Walailak University, 2005.
Arin Sa-idee et al. "Gender Issues Concerning Muslim Women in Thailand: Family Planning and Women's Political Participation". Paper presented at Short Course on Islam, Gender, and Reproductive Rights. Center for Women Studies (IAIN) Kalijaga State Institute of Islamic Studies, Yogyakarta, 14 July – 4 August 2002 (Mimeograph).
Chavivun Prachuabmoh. "Ethnic Relations among Thai, Thai Muslim and Chinese in South Thailand: Ethnicity and Interpersonal Interaction". In *Ethnicity and Interpersonal Integration*, edited by D.Y. H. Wu. Singapore: Maruzen Asia, 1982.
Department of Religious Affairs website. "Population in Thailand by Religious Belief". Available online at <http://www.moe.go.th/ webrad/ data/data_02.htm> (accessed 10 August 2007).
Dirake Kulsirisawat. *Khwam Sampan Khaung Muslim Thaang Prawadsart Lae Wannakhadii Thai (Muslim's Relationship in Thai History and Literature)*, in Thai. Bangkok: Matichon, 2002.
Funston, John. "Thailand". In *Voice of Islam in Southeast Asia: A Contemporary Sourcebook*, edited by Greg Fealy and Virginia Hooker. Singapore: Institute of Southeast Asian Studies, 2006.
Gilquin, Michel. *The Muslims of Thailand*, translated by Michael Smithies. Chiang Mai: Silkworm Books, 2005.
Glowing, Peter G. *Mooraa Lae Khaek: Thaana Khaung Chaaw Muslim Nai*

Philippines Lae Thai (Mora and Khaek: The Status of Muslims in the Philippines and Thailand). Bangkok: Mokemthong Foundation, 1975.

Guelden, Marlene. "Ancestral Spirit Mediumship in Southern Thailand: The Nora Performance as a Symbol of the South on the Periphery of a Buddhist Nation-state". Ph.D. thesis, University of Hawaii, 2005.

Horstmann, Alexander. *Ehnohistorical Perspectives on Buddhist-Muslim Relations and Coexistence in Southern Thailand: From Shared Cosmos to the Emergence of Hatred?* 2004. Available online at <http://goliath. ecnext.com/coms2/gi_0199-413371/Ethnohistorical-perspectives-on-Buddhist-Muslim.html> (accessed 1 September 2006).

Ibrahim Syukri. *History of The Malay Kingdom of Patani (Sejarah Kerajaan Melayu Patani)*, translated by Conner Bailey and John Miksic. Chiang Mai: Silkworm Books, 2005.

Imtiyaz Yusuf. "Faces of Islam in Southern Thailand". *East-West Center Washington Working Papers*, 7 March 2007. Available online at <http://www.eastwestcenter.org/fileadmin/stored/pdfs/EWCW wp007.pdf> (accessed 10 June 2007).

Ismail Ali. *Kodmai Krobkrua Islam (Family Law in Islam)*, in Thai. Pattani: College of Islamic Studies, Prince of Songkla University, 1997.

"It's Official: No State Religion". *Bangkok Post*, 30 June 2007.

Jory, Patrick. "From 'Melayu Patani' to 'Thai Muslims': The Spectre of Ethnic Identity in Southern Thailand". *ARI Working Paper* 84, 2007. Available online at <http://www.ari.nus.edu.sg/showfile.asp?pubid= 643&type=2> (accessed 3 July 2007).

Kecia Ali. *Sexual Ethics & Islam: Feminist Reflections on Qur'an, Hadith, and Jurisprudence*. Oxford: Oneworld, 2006.

Kitti Ali-ae and Tadsanai Nualvisai. "Panglimor Jekteh Cemetery: The Cemetery of Muslim Primogenitor in Tha Sala". In *Hundred Years of Tha Sala: Back to the Future*, in Thai, edited by Suebpong Thammachat. Nakhon Si Thammarat: Time Printing, 2000.

Kobkua Suwannathat-Pian. "The Historical Development of Thai-Speaking Muslim Communities in Southern Thailand and Northern Malaysia". In *Civility and Savagery: Social Identity in Tai States*, edited by Andrew Turton. Richmond: Curzon, 2000.

Metha Wadeecharoen. *Kodmai Islam Por Sor Song Ha Sam Ped (Islamic Law, BE 2538)*, in Thai. Bangkok: Sutra Phaisan, 1995.

Nakamura, Hisako et al. *Khaniyom Thang Sangkhom Sadsana Khong Satri Muslim Nai Paktai: Koranee Suksa Khon-ngan Nai Rong-ngan Auttasahakham Changwat Pattani (Socio-Religious Values of Muslim Women in Southern Thailand: A Case Study of Factory Workers in Pattani)*, in Thai. Pattani: Mitraphap, 2001.

National Statistical Office Thailand. Population and Housing Census 2000. Available online at <http://web.nso.go.th/pop2000/tables_e.htm> (accessed 15 July 2007).

————. Key Indicator and Important Tables from Final Report by Provinces, 2000. Available online at <http://web.nso.go.th/pop2000/pop_e2000.htm> (accessed 16 July 2007).

Omar Farouk Bajunid. "The Muslims of Thailand: A Survey". In *The Muslims of Thailand*, edited by Andrew D. W. Forbes. Gaya, India: Center For South East Asian Studies, 1988.

————. "Islam, Nationalism, and The Thai State". In *Dynamic Diversity in Southern Thailand*, edited by Wattana Sugunsil. Chiang Mai: Silkworm, 2005.

Panya Srinaka. *Thalang Phuket Lae Banmuaeng Fang Thale Tawan Tok (Thalang, Phuket and the West Coast Land)*, in Thai. Bangkok: Matichon, 2003 [in Thai].

Parks, Thomas. *Maintaining Peace in a Neighborhood Torn by Separatism: The Case of Satun Province in Southern Thailand*. Mimeograph, 2005.

Rahman S.A. *Punishment of Apostasy in Islam*. Lahore: Institute of Islamic Culture, 1972.

The Central Islamic Committee of Thailand (2006) Provincial Islamic Committees and Mosque in Thailand. Available from <http://www.cicot.or.th> (accessed 10 January 2007).

The World's Most Advance Hadith Search Engine. *Al Hadith, Sahih Muslim*, Book 033 The Book of Destiny (Kitab ul-Qadr), No. 6426. Available online at <http://www.guidedways.com/book_display-book-33-translator-2-start-30-number-6419.htm> (accessed 15 April 2008).

Thompson, Eric C., Chulanee Thianthai, and Irwan Hidayana. "Culture and International Imagination in Southeast Asia". In *Political Geography* 26 (2007): 268–88.

Acknowledgement

Dr Patrick Jory, Head of Regional Studies Program of Walailak University, provided valuable assistance in my writing this chapter.

Chapter 8

INTERETHNIC MARRIAGES AND CONVERSION TO ISLAM IN KOTA BHARU

Jolanda Lindenberg

INTRODUCTION

Malaysia is a multi-ethnic country of which the population is constitutionally divided in two large groups, namely the *bumiputera*, comprising Malays, Orang Asli, and indigenous groups in Sarawak and Sabah, with special rights;[1] and non-*bumiputera* encompassing other ethnic groups. In the negotiations leading to Independence, special privileges were granted to the first group in exchange for citizenship rights for the latter group. This has been enshrined in Article 153 of the Constitution, and can be seen as a social contract to maintain the delicate unity that the British colonial legacy left the independent post-colonial government. Ethnically based economic divisions, and the threat of a minority position for *bumiputera*, who were generally seen to be socio-economically deprived, contributed to a rather fragile unity (Andaya and Andaya 2001, pp. 273–87; Hitam 2001; Ling-Chien Neo 2006, p. 96).

Despite these preventive measures, twenty years later the multi-ethnic unity was threatened when ethnic riots broke out in the bigger cities, as a manifestation of socio-economic inequalities and the accompanying politicization.[2] In response, the government implemented the New Economic Policy (NEP) to reduce economic inequality and poverty and lessen the identification of ethnicity with economic function. After more than thirty years, this has created a more equalized socio-economic position of the ethnic groups, which is often seen as a prerequisite for intergroup contact.

Paradoxically, though, the constitutional definition of Malay in Article 160, as being someone who habitually speaks Malay, professes Islam, adheres to Malay customs, and is domiciled in Malaysia or Singapore, has resulted in a strong fusion of Malay with Muslim; subsequently Islam is seen as preordained for Malays. Accompanying measures to foster ethnic harmony, as in the case of the NEP, have, in addition to this religious ascription, resulted in a strengthened group feeling and competition, which can decrease intergroup contact. The different institutions that have been established to deal with the different ethnic backgrounds on social, economic, judicial, and educational matters have ensued in a stronger emphasis on group identity. Scholars have, therefore, referred to the country as plural (Fenton 2003), and the state as ethnocratic (Haque 2003) or based on a form of consociationalism (Brown 1994; Trezzini 2001).

To investigate this fascinating, complicated institutionalization for a country, and the resulting intergroup dynamics that take place in Malaysia, interethnic marriages were chosen for the study described in this chapter. A situation of interethnic contact can both illustrate the influence of this legal structure on daily life as well as trace the different kinds of relationships that exist between members of different ethnic backgrounds. Interethnic marriage is a domain that encompasses different aspects of interethnic contact in everyday life. It brings together social ties of varying degrees of intimacy between families, friends and colleagues. Furthermore, the ethnically different spouses are subjected to various religious, cultural, social, and legal (Maznah Mohamad et al. this volume) arrangements, which converge within this most intimate commitment.

Malaysia may have a long tradition of intermarriages, but few have studied marriages in contemporary society between the Malays who form the largest group of the *bumiputera*, and the Chinese who form the largest group of the non-*bumiputera*. Marriages between members of these two groups are central to this chapter. A marriage between a Malay and a Chinese is not only an interethnic marriage, but is, in most cases, an interreligious marriage between a Muslim and a non-Muslim, and this will be an important focus in this chapter. The term "Muslim-non-Muslim marriage" itself, however, might not be appropriate for these marriages in Malaysia since conversion to Islam by the Chinese spouse is required before marriage, thus the marriage itself is an Islamic marriage.

Religion is strongly identified with ethnicity in Malaysia and thus both play an important role in marriages between Malays and Chinese. Theories concerning ethnicity have given attention to the fact that people can emphasize or disguise ethnic markers, depending on the situation at hand. Scholars who voice such a conceptualization of ethnicity are often portrayed as instrumentalists or constructivists, although they can rarely be distinguished as purely instrumentalists or constructivists. Constructivists are often put in binary opposition with primordialists, who see ethnic markers as fixed and inevitable, although absolute primordialists are hard to find. In this discussion of ethnicity I agree with many other scholars, among them Barth (1969), Cohen (2000) and Schlee (2001) that primordialist/

constructivist cannot be seen as a dichotomy, but rather as a continuum. Even though certain primordial traits can have a limiting effect on people's options due to their ethnic identification, these identifying symbols can often be emphasized or veiled strategically to a certain extent to accommodate the situation and be used for the benefit of the person in question. For example, intermarried individuals can be observed to use the characteristics ascribed to them in a strategic manner, as shall be illustrated in this chapter.

The need to combine ethnic backgrounds is a prominent concern in intermarriages because of the direct intimacy of married life. In these marriages, certain group specific systems such as values, norms, status systems, and stereotypes come together and have to be combined, particularly if children are involved (Hassan 1974; Jager 1969; Lee 1988). This chapter focuses on how the couples within different contexts of religion, politics, and group identities, tried to merge their different backgrounds in married life. For this purpose, different reactions, tensions, negotiations, and coping mechanisms of the spouses and the people surrounding them are discussed. As background to this study, a brief overview of the position and policies of the Kelantan state on the Malaysian peninsula will be described, because, as I will try to demonstrate, it has a strong influence on the daily life of the interethnically married spouses.

BACKGROUND OF THE STUDY

The fieldwork for this study took place from June to November 2004 in Kota Bharu, the capital of the north-eastern state of Kelantan. In-depth interviews were held with ten intermarried couples involving five Chinese female converts and five Chinese male converts. Several other interethnically married couples were met for informal conversations. Each spouse was individually interviewed at least three times. Every interethnic couple was matched by profession[3] to a Chinese and a Malay intra-married couple.[4] The twenty intra-married couples each participated in one interview focused on a limited number of themes. All thirty couples participated in an indicative sorting test on stereotypes and a Likert-scale test on status symbols.[5] Besides this, the marriage register of the *Balai Islam* in Kota Bharu was drawn on to estimate the number of marriages between Chinese and Malays in the district.[6] Several spokespersons of organizations that provided assistance, education, or support for the prospective converts, such as the Malaysian Association of Chinese Muslims (MACMA), the Muslim welfare organization *Pertubuhan Kebajikan Islam Malaysia* (PERKIM), and the Muslim Youth Movement *Angkatan Belia Islam Malaysia* (ABIM),[7] were interviewed as part of this research.

Since independence, Malaysia has been governed by a coalition government led by the United Malays National Organisation (UMNO). The single real challenge to UMNO's overwhelming monopoly has been the Islamic Parti Islam Semalaysia (PAS). PAS derives its most important support from the northern and eastern states on the Malaysian peninsula and governed the Kelantan state from 1959 until an unsuccessful coalition with UMNO in 1977 probably caused its subsequent loss of the state. The party regained Kelantan in 1990 and has been governing it since. PAS has, since its establishment, moved from a defender of Malay rights to an Islam-centred party in the 1980s, and during the second half of the 1990s, to a more moderate Islamic agenda. The success of PAS in Malaysia has often been attributed to the Islamic resurgence, known as the *dakwah* movement, which began at the end of the 1970s, in which religious concerns became relatively more significant, although election results of the PAS do not directly support this hypothesis (Chin Yong Liow 2004*b*; Noor 2002). The more moderate agenda in combination with the incarceration of Anwar Ibrahim[8] presumably contributed significantly to the success of PAS in the elections of the 1990s.

In response to the PAS party renewal — focusing on Islam rather than Malay identity — and Islamic resurgence, the federal government felt it had come under the threat of losing its important electoral support of the Malays and started emphasizing the Islamic foundation of Malaysia in the 1980s by, among other things, establishing an Islamic university and installing a governmental agency which organizes pilgrimages to Mecca (*Tabung Haji*). This response has also been expressed in the enlargement of the competences and independence of the Islamic syariah courts by the federal government under former Prime Minister Mahathir Mohamad. These courts are the legislative body for matters that fall under the family law, such as marriage, divorce, and matters of Islamic conduct; only Muslims are subjected to these courts. To enable the increased competences, the Constitution was revised in 1988 (Hamayotsu 2003; Horowitz 1994) to state that the High Court of civil law have no jurisdiction in respect to the matters of the Syariah Court. As a result of these measures, the syariah courts have become more centralized. The syariah courts are nonetheless part of the authorities at state-level and have in the past evolved separately in each state.

The government by PAS and Malay demographic majority of 95 per cent (Population and Housing Census of Malaysia 2000) have led to several differences in the pervasiveness of Islam in Kelantan. The state was the first to introduce the Family Law Enactment of 1984 (Jones 1994, p. 53). Highly controversial was the attempt to introduce the Hudud Bill in 1992 (Kamali 1998) passed in 1993 as the syariah criminal code in which corporal punishments for different *hudud* offences[9] were to be legislated. The bill was condemned by former Prime Minister Mahathir Mohamad in 1994 as being "cruel" and "against the teachings of Islam", adding that it was only used for PAS's political gain. The dispute between UMNO and PAS continued under current legislation when Prime Minister Abdullah Badawi in December 2004 indirectly portrayed the party as a deviating movement and PAS politicians as Islamic extremists (Abu Bakar 1981; Camroux 1996; Malhi 2003).

Islamic policies of PAS have important effects on the everyday lives of intermarried couples. Expressions of this in daily life are (in contrast to the other states on the Malaysian peninsula) the designation of Friday and Saturday as the official weekend, gender segregation of aisles in shops, the restriction on entertainment, the control on female performers, and the control of the sale of pork and alcohol.

Locals and some scholars claim that the contentious relationship between the federal and state governments has led to a low socio- economic level in Kelantan as a result of decreasing investments from the federal level (Winzeler 1985, p. 123). In electoral competition with UMNO, PAS increasingly intertwines politics and religion in a move which Chin (2004*a*, p. 359) describes as a "politicisation of Islam". PAS claims to follow the correct Islamic way which in practice has led to increased social control and pressure on Muslims to follow PAS as a sign of being a righteous Muslim. Not only PAS, but also many Kelantanese in daily conversations, consider Islam to be not only a religion, but a way of life which should not only be followed in religious practice, but in every sphere of life, including politics. This also has effects at the federal level, as members of Parliament opposing PAS have been accused of being un-Islamic. The federal government on the other hand uses Kelantan as an example of "economic backwardness and excesses of Islamic practice" (Camroux 1996, p. 861) while claiming to strive for a civilized Islam under the name of *Islam Hadhari*. Both UMNO and PAS risk losing votes of non-Muslims with the increasing intertwining of Islam and politics, which is also seen as a sign of Malay dominance due to the conflation of Malay and Muslim. This may result in increasing tensions between Muslims and non-Muslims. Some non-Muslims may even experience this intertwinement as accompanied by xenophobic overtones due to the ethnic identification of Malay concurring with Islam in Malaysia (Peletz 1993, p. 81).

Within this context, Kelantan has important demographic characteristics given that it is the state with the highest percentage of Malays (93 per cent) and the lowest percentage of Chinese (3.8 per cent) in the Malay Peninsula. In the district of Kota Bharu where this research took place, Malays amounted to about 77 per cent and Chinese to almost 21 per cent (Population and Housing Census of Malaysia 2000). The Chinese in Kelantan form two distinctive groups of *Cina Kampung* and *Cina Bandar*. The first group grew up in rural areas , while the latter lived their childhood in the city. *Cina Kampung* are said to be better integrated with Malays and have more in-depth knowledge of Malay customs, Islamic practice, and the Kelantanese dialect. Both rural and urban Chinese, though, seem to dress more modestly than elsewhere in Malaysia, and speak the Kelantanese dialect rather well. Nonetheless, the marriage register of Kota Bharu and Winzeler (1985, p. 45) show that intermarriages between Malays and Chinese in urban and rural areas in the Kota Bharu district are rather limited. Regardless of this, the relatively strong emphasis on Islamic practice instilled in daily life has an important effect on the responses to the interethnic marriages and the relations between Malays and Chinese in the Kota Bharu district.

CONVERSION FOR MARRIAGE

The limited number of Chinese marrying Malays has been attributed to different factors. According to Hassan (1974) the compulsory conversion to Islam is an important deterrent to interethnic marriages between Malays and Chinese in Singapore. In Malaysia, a possible added difficulty could be the conflation of Muslim with Malay. The identification of Islam with a certain ethnic group has perhaps created a greater impediment for interethnic marriages with Chinese in view of the politicization of ethnicity. In Malaysia, 0.7 per cent of the more than 5 million Chinese follow Islam (Population and Housing Census "Population and Housing Census of Malaysia" 2000, p. 70).[10] The large majority of Chinese who convert to Islam mention marriage as the decisive factor for conversion (Ma 2005, p. 100). The Chinese spouses in my sample confirm this, though in two cases the marriages were actually arranged because of the conversion to Islam. In these cases, a Muslim husband was sought to guide the Chinese convert in Islam and as support against pressure from the Chinese family to revoke the conversion. This measure already signals that conversion itself, and not only interethnic marriage, is in general opposed by Chinese.

The Chinese spouses whom I interviewed all underwent a similar process of conversion. Most of them started to learn Islamic teachings through books and courses at PERKIM, sometimes assisted by their spouses. When the teachers at PERKIM felt that the convert was ready to register at the religious department, the Chinese spouse and two witnesses (usually from PERKIM or members of a Malay foster family chosen to support the conversion process) went to the *Balai Islam* to undergo a test of Islamic knowledge. The spouses described that they had to prove their sincerity in converting; they had to answer questions about Islam and show that they knew how to pray correctly. Converts were urged to change their surname to an Islamic name[11] which was *bin* or *binti Abdullah*. Several informants describe how the changing of the surname was an important barrier and cause for discussions with the functionary who deemed that a change of surname was compulsory, although based on an official statement of Jabatan Agama Kemajuan Islam Malaysia in 1999, one is free to either change or retain the original name in Malaysia (Ma 2005, p. 105).[12] Chinese informants refer to the changing of the family name as one of the most drastic changes.

Conversion signals a decisive break from the former lives of the Chinese spouses. Crucial to understanding the problems faced by Chinese converts during and after the process of conversion is the intertwinement of Islam with the Malay ethnic identity. This is well illustrated by the phrase used to describe conversion to Islam, which is *masuk Melayu*, meaning entering the Malay ethnic group, or becoming a Malay. Hence not only marrying a person of different ethnicity gave reasons for tensions, but the compulsory conversion into a Muslim which is synonymous with being Malay increased the antagonism experienced by the spouses.

REACTIONS: TENSIONS AND HOSTILITIES

The idea then was that when you become a Muslim, you become Malay, you could not be different, you were expected to be a Malay, you had to talk like a Malay, dress like a Malay, walk like a Malay, speak like a Malay, and all this straight away.[13]

The principle of *masuk Melayu* leads to pressure on the Chinese spouses to follow not only Islamic practices, but also Malay customs. This is even more the case in Kelantan as religion and Malay practices are highly visible in daily life. Moreover the PAS government has increased official and social control over religiosity. Chinese spouses said they felt that they were expected to change immediately after their conversion to Islam, whereas they themselves felt more comfortable with a slower pace of change. Not only Malay family members, but also Chinese family members, expected the Chinese converts to "become Malay" and this understanding of the consequences of conversion led to a variety of reactions to the conversion and subsequent marriage. Reactions varied according to degree of intimacy of the relationship; in this chapter a general categorization is made according to relationship with family, friends, and acquaintances. These groupings should be considered ideal-typical and in reality might overlap.

Chinese relatives generally responded negatively to the conversion of the Chinese spouse. Prominent in their objections was the required name change on conversion. The Chinese name is seen as a symbolic connection to the forefathers, the family, and the future generations. It is thus also a symbol for the continuation of the family and the family history. Changing the family name is seen as betrayal of one's own history, family, and ethnic group.

Other objections from both relatives and friends were voiced in relation to the fact that a conversion meant that the Chinese converts were no longer able to return home because of Islamic prohibitions. Chinese Muslims were no longer considered able to take part in Chinese community life. The conversion was seen as detrimental to the success and size of the Chinese ethnic group in Malaysian society as Chinese converts *masuk Melayu*. The rhetoric of group competition was considered even more valid because of the interconnectedness of Islam and politics. The group size is, according to some Chinese, vital to the competition with Malays as Chinese are a small minority in Kelantan. This was emphasized because the Chinese had to "withstand the Malay threat" of PAS in Kelantan.

For parents, the conversion felt like a loss of their credibility and they thought that people would accuse them of being unable to take care of their children. Nevertheless, a few Chinese relatives and friends were supportive of conversion and said that they had no objections to conversion as long as the convert would become a good Muslim. However when it came to marrying a Malay spouse, they did not give their approval as illustrated by the following statement made by a Chinese female who converted to Islam before marriage:

> Actually my family did not have many objections that I wanted to embrace Islam, but when I told them I wanted to marry a Malay, the first thing my auntie said was, "You know they can marry four wives?" They had expected me to marry a Chinese Muslim and thus objected to my marriage.

Disapproval of Chinese acquaintances was also related to the incongruity of group values and norms of the Chinese with Islamic and Malay practices. For instance, a symbolic connection to family history is expressed by the Chinese in forefather remembrance in rituals, but this is forbidden in Islam. Furthermore several customs, such as keeping long fingernails to symbolize wealth[14] and the consumption of pork, are forbidden in Islam or are considered inappropriate by Malays. The participation in Chinese community life was thus severely restricted by the conversion to Islam and this non-attendance was seen as a sign of disrespect.

The negative reactions varied from verbal disputes to physical violence. Some Chinese spouses found that their friends did not want to meet them anymore, while others had continuous verbal conflicts with friends and relatives. In other cases, they were threatened, and in two cases, the family members tried to kidnap the Chinese spouse to prevent a conversion. As such, some couples decided not to tell their parents about the conversion or their marriage, or told them only after the marriage had taken place. Those who did confide in their Chinese family members and friends also tried to invite them to the marriage ceremony, but the invitation was turned down. Social requirements for the legitimation of the conversion and the marriage were as a consequence often not met (cf. Nagata 1986) and the marriage was in some cases seen as illegitimate. This was especially visible in attempts of both Chinese and Malay relatives to try to match make one of the partners with someone from their own ethnic group even after marriage.

Reactions of Malay acquaintances were less opposing and numerous Malays encourage Muslims to marry non-Muslims as playing a role in conversion is seen as a good deed in Islam. In addition, the intermarriage was seen as a positive sign of harmonious relations between the different ethnic groups. This acceptance was not unconditional, as Ma (2005) observed. In several cases Malay relatives changed their attitude after a while because the Chinese spouse did not adapt fast enough. Furthermore contact between the Malay spouse and the Chinese relatives was sometimes limited because of the fear of encountering *haram* things. As one of the Malay husbands told me:

> After several months, four months or so, it became difficult. The parents-in-law, the mental picture they have of Chinese is still different, they think that their hands are still full of … impurity (*haram*) with pork, they will not let their daughter-in-law cook. My mother was checking her, she felt uncomfortable when she prepared the food.

The disapproval of some Malays was uttered in accusations that the Chinese spouse strategically changed religion to fulfil the constitutional requirements for being Malay to gain the special rights of *bumiputera*. Although religion alone is *de jure* insufficient to fulfil requirements of being a Malay, this, in effect, could *de facto* be claimed by a Chinese convert. Malay friends of the Malay spouse warned that their Chinese partner was only in the marriage to profit. Some converts felt that Malays looked down on them because they were not born Muslims. The conversion of one of the Chinese females in my sample even led to a heated quarrel with her boss because she was "just a Chinese anyway and not a born Muslim or Malay and she was not to aspire to become one".

While on the one hand, Malays expected Chinese converts to acquire the Malay lifestyle, on the other hand, they did not fully accept them because they would always remain Chinese. This complicated the position of the Chinese spouse. Both the Chinese and the Malay sides presume that after conversion, Islam would become a way of life and they would thus become Malay, especially with the salience of Islam in Kelantanese life. Paradoxically they were not fully accepted by Malays and, in most cases, rejected by Chinese, leaving their ethnic identity ambiguous. Adjustment problems to this Malay lifestyle were consequently a major concern between the two spouses in their private life that is aggravated by external pressure. Loneliness was often a result, as one Chinese female told me:

> My mother couldn't accept it, my brothers and other relatives couldn't, and actually all couldn't accept it. It was hard for me, really hard, because I am the only daughter. My mother didn't agree and my father had already passed away. It was like I was alone, no one to talk to. I couldn't talk to my friends at the office, because they were Malays, I couldn't talk to my former schoolmates, because they were all Chinese. I was just alone, literally, and utterly alone.

NEGOTIATION STRATEGIES

The couples used different negotiation strategies to increase contact with their family, friends, and acquaintances. The most important negotiation strategy to cause no offence to those involved was the strategic use of ascribed characteristics through emphasizing or disguising certain ethnic or religious markers. This was done in different domains. I will discuss four different strategies, although this is not an exhaustive list.

Integration

> Of course, we had to have the religious, the Islamic ceremony, but we also wanted to add some Chinese elements. We wanted to have the Chinese tea ceremony, but his Chinese family refused. I wanted to have Chinese and Malay dresses, so we did, although his family didn't show up. We also had the pictures taken before the actual marriage, to show them, as is usually done in Chinese families. We even wanted to pick the wedding date according to tradition and have the dinner with several courses, but none of it happened, because his family refused.[15]

One of the frequently applied strategies to gain acceptance was the integration of Malay and Chinese customs. However, as the above interview excerpt shows, the success of the strategy was limited, because of resistance from Chinese as well as Malay family members. The performance of the ceremonies of both traditions, as far as possible within Islam, and the attendance of life cycle events, were done with a dual purpose; first of all to show the Chinese family that Islam is not as strict and intolerant as perceived, and secondly to fulfil the wishes and requirements of both families.

The integration of customs began with the organization of the marriage ceremony. All couples followed Islamic wedding traditions and tried to add Chinese elements to it. This rarely succeeded because, with the exception of one couple, all couples got married without the attendance of the Chinese family and without Chinese customs. Besides being a direct consequence of the family's refusal to attend, this absence was also due to the barring of non-Muslims from the mosque where the *akad nikah*[16] takes place; or to the requirement to be dressed according to Islamic rules, which Chinese family members in general refused to comply with. Furthermore integrating Chinese elements into the marriage ceremony was seen as inappropriate because of religious concerns by Malay relatives.

Besides the wedding celebration, they also attempted to integrate and attend certain celebrations such as Chinese New Year, the mooncake festival, and Hari Raya. During those occasions Chinese and Malay acquaintances were invited, although not many of them turned up. Later on in their marriage some couples did combine celebrations by, for example, celebrating the Malay *aqiqah*[17] ceremony together with the name-giving ceremony among Chinese. In the integration of ceremonies and celebrations the couples tried to show their goodwill to both cultural traditions, to participate in both ethnic communities, and to get both families acquainted with each other to decrease prejudices and stereotyping.

In married life, intermarried couples continued to merge ethnic traditions, despite the opposition, and insofar as these were tolerated by Islamic rules. In daily life, this was done, for example, in combinations of food, such as *kai lan*[18] with Malay curry dishes. The intermarried also tried to combine dressing styles, literally in combining the different styles in a *baju kebaya* with a long slit as Chinese wear in traditional dresses. In addition, they used clothing intentionally, for instance, wearing traditional Malay clothing such as a *baju kurong* or *baju kebaya* while visiting Malay acquaintances. When visiting Chinese friends and relatives they often wore western clothing, and some of the women even left their headscarves in the car, because it might be considered offensive. Decoration was also an area in which different cultural backgrounds were combined. Some informants decorated their homes with red lanterns, while a picture of Mecca was rarely missing. In terms of language, most couples spoke Malay at home, but others spoke English as a neutral language. Some couples tried to teach their children Chinese, but considering that most of them, especially in the early period of their marriage, did not have much contact with Chinese relatives, this was hard to sustain. Again in all these combinations, the different Chinese elements were emphasized and Malay elements were veiled when a Chinese visited, or the other way around when a Malay visited.

In some domains, the combining of Chinese as well as Malay aspects was possible. In informal conversations and in response to the status symbol test, three symbols were consistently mentioned as being important; successful children, following the religion truthfully, and attaining higher education. These status symbols were the only coinciding status symbols which were stated as highly valued by Chinese as well as Malay intra-married couples. It seems that these matching symbols are emphasized by the couples, thus accommodating Chinese as well as Malay status systems. With this the intermarried couples find a place within both ethnic groups and can manoeuvre in both groups.

The usage of integration strategies enabled the couples to participate in the social and cultural life of both groups. The integration of different domains gained approval at times, but were sometimes met with resistance. Nevertheless the attempts showed family members and friends that they did respect and cherish their ethnic backgrounds, while simultaneously increasing contact opportunities.

Contact Measures

> We actually moved to Kelantan to improve the relationship with his Chinese family. It worked! Now our mums go shopping together. My mom was very nervous to meet his mum, and finally after two years she came, and after that they just went shopping; now they often go shopping.[19]

A second important way to gain acceptance was through changes in the extent of interaction. The amount of contact between the spouses and their family members and friends was either increased or decreased, depending on which was considered the more appropriate.

A common strategy to increase the contact between the spouses and family members was to live with the opposing family member to "get to know the partner". Sometimes, after enduring a long period of silence even when living in the house, this worked. Others used less confrontational measures and increased contact by visiting the neighbourhood or places frequently visited by the family members, even if the targeted family members refused to talk to them.

Others resorted to a decrease in contact with acquaintances to prevent any hostilities, especially at the beginning of the marriage as the spouses expected adjustment problems from the conversion to Islam and the interethnic marriage itself. Thus, going against Kelantanese tradition, a number of couples started to live independently immediately after marriage. There were three cases in which family members were not informed of the official marriage and were told that "they were just friends" until the relatives began to take a liking to the spouse and a marriage might be less disapproved, after which their matrimony was revealed.

In some cases both strategies of increasing and decreasing contact did not work because family members just refused any contact. Spouses then resorted to remaining in contact by other means without having to have actual face-to-face contact. This, for example, was done by sending money monthly to one of the parents, by helping out through influential contacts, or by sending gifts. With these measures, contact remained, only more indirectly, in order to avoid complete loss of contact. The assistance given created a situation of dependency and reciprocity, and for some couples, this in the end resulted in a slow increase in contact until normal contact was restored.

Markers of Success in Life

> I had to show my [Chinese] family, my father, that even though I left my family, and I was not able to further my studies and I converted, I could still be successful, in all ways, in bringing up the children, in everything.[20]

Doing well was a central approach to gaining approval and acceptance of disapproving relatives. This meant that couples strove to excel in several aspects which were valued by objecting relatives. This entailed succeeding in domains which were valued by the Chinese and those which were valued by the Malays.

Professional success and participating in a number of charity organizations were often mentioned as means of gaining respect. The success and resulting social network was also a resource for assisting relatives in different ways in order to win their approval; one example is a Malay anaesthetist in a hospital who used his position to get his Chinese father-in-law into a better ward:

My relationship with her [Chinese] family took a couple of
years. Only after her father had an operation and I helped to get
him into a better room did it improve. This was a couple of
years after marriage, the first year I did not see her family. I was
surprised that they could accept me.

To seek approval for their marriage, the couples often
emphasized the strong influence of Islam in their marriage in the
presence of Malay family members and friends. Chinese spouses
tried to gain understanding of Islam to show that they were
knowledgeable, righteous Muslims. In contrast, they strategically
downplayed the influence of Islam as a distinctive religion in the
presence of Chinese acquaintances and stressed the universal
and coinciding values found in Chinese culture and in Islam.
Malay spouses meanwhile tried to gain knowledge of Chinese
traditions and customs to be able to participate in those permitted
by Islam. As with other strategies, this can be seen as either
highlighting or veiling certain group characteristics to accommodate
and gain acceptance.

The achievements of children were emphasized to show that
their conversion and marriage was a good choice. Children were
usually sent to a prestigious school such as an international
school, an Arabic school, or a Chinese school. Efforts were made
to send their children to different tuition schools and Islamic
classes after school. Children were also taught Chinese customs
such as eating with chopsticks and Chinese cooking to show that
Chinese culture was well respected in their family.

The markers of success in life were not only used to show
their well-being to their family, but also to gain a higher status in
society and to gain the respect of friends, colleagues, and outsiders.
This higher standing was sometimes used to emphasize another
social identity in social interactions. In this way they distanced
themselves from their ethnic identity to give another identification
salience (cf. Goffman 1972).

HAVING CHILDREN

I did not have any contact with my [Chinese] family in the
following years, but then my son was born, and I guess a
mother's heart, my mother softened up and after he turned six
or seven months I could go back home.[21]

Having children was often seen as an important strategy to
convince their acquaintances that their marriage was a sustainable
marriage, and worth their appreciation. Small children were
brought to their family houses, even if they were not welcome.
Some couples visited a public place in the neighbourhood visible
from their parents' house and played with their children there.
Most of the couples who tried to gain acceptance in this way
succeeded in their efforts. Only two couples did not restore
contact with their families after their first child was born. One
couple is still childless, but is already considering having children
as an important strategy to "win their hearts".

The belief prevalent among Malays and Chinese that mixed
children are genetically more intelligent was cherished by the
parents. Children were told that they would have "the better of
both worlds" and parents would stress positive stereotypes
attached to their respective ethnic groups such as Chinese
"business-mindedness" and "hard-working" with Malay "good
heartedness" and "soft-spoken nature". Initially though, children
were often bullied by classmates because of their mixed
background. This might stem from the limited contact children
have with children from other ethnic groups as a result of
vernacular education. At a later age most children of the couples
I spoke to emphasized being, and were proud to be, the "true
Malaysians, being a mix of the two largest groups". The state
advertisement promoting "Malaysia, truly Asia" confirmed this
epitome and the harmony attached to it made them feel like a
living symbol of this state slogan. In contrast to being positive

about being "mixed", the children also encountered negative feelings and were victims of the surrounding ethnic tensions and antagonism, as this statement of a Chinese woman clearly demonstrates:

> If one of my children marries a Malay, I would be very sad, very sad indeed. But what can you do? If they have fallen in love, one can not do anything, but I think…even my grandchildren, the mixed ones then, I would love them less than my other grandchildren.

Despite these negative feelings of people, parents often tried to teach their children about their Chinese and Malay backgrounds. Some send their children to Chinese school.[22] Vernacular education is, in this sense, both a positive and negative factor. On the one hand, it offers the possibility of getting children with different mother tongues acquainted with one another. On the other hand, it also decreases contact between groups, because these schools seem to encourage ethnic segregation. Parents who did send their children to a Chinese school or taught them Chinese often had the hope that the children would virtually function as a bridge to get in touch with family members.

The foremost purpose of using these different negotiation strategies for most of the couples was to regain or improve contact with family members. For nine out of the ten couples involved in this research, contact was indeed restored or improved. The duration and the intensity of the deterioration of contact varied from a decrease in contact for several months to a complete loss of contact for twenty-three years. The success of the negotiation strategies is rather situational and dependent on many factors. It seems though that the couples managed to maintain ethnic practices of both groups in their personal life and were sometimes able to do so in other spheres as well. Most of all the negotiation strategies show how the spouses tried to merge and keep in touch with their different ethnic backgrounds, within the legitimacy of Islamic practice. It reveals how they tried to combine and merge their backgrounds, and with this, also attempted to show that being Muslim does not make one ethnically Malay.

COPING MECHANISMS

As is obvious from the above examples, these intermarried spouses were subjected to a lot of distress as a consequence of their choice of each other. Not only did they have to face challenges within their marriages, but they were also negatively regarded by family members, friends, colleagues, and even strangers. These tension factors were dealt with in several ways[23] which I call "coping mechanisms".

First of all the interethnically married couples considered themselves better prepared for possible problems than others because they were constantly reminded by people that problems were due to arise as a result of their different ethnic and religious backgrounds. Indeed this was confirmed after interviews with intra-married couples. As argued by intermarried individuals, the problems faced by intra-married couples were quite similar to those of intermarried couples. The difference between intermarried and intra-married couples lay in the fact that, these problems were unexpected by the intra-married couples. Nonetheless, the interethnic spouses experienced these problems on a larger and more intense scale. This was due to the fact that negative reactions were magnified as a result of their choice of a spouse of different ethnicity and religious background, but also due to the fact that, as a result of this choice, they often lacked the social support available to other couples. Although this loneliness is often considered a source of distress within the marriage, this is also a strain that actually causes the couples to grow closer to each other. The disapproving reactions to their marriage not only made them resolute to make the marriage succeed, but also made the intermarried dependent on each other, as they had no one else to turn to. The isolation from others actually caused the couple to grow closer together. Several spouses even maintained that this was the reason their marriage was "very strong".

Another method of dealing with possible dispute factors was extensive communication about divergent issues. Interethnic married couples claimed that they emphasized communication in their marriage because they knew of the claim that conflicts often arise because of different ethnic backgrounds (this is also mentioned in academic works e.g. Collins & Coltrane 2001; Cramer 1998; Heijdt 1995). Interethnic couples reasoned that they were so aware of this that they discussed issues often left unspoken by intra-married couples, resulting, according to them, in a more open relationship and fewer unexpected problems. Furthermore, some spouses noted that they had to learn and ask everything about each other's habits as they had little personal contact with people from another ethnic origin before their marriage in consequence of, for example, vernacular education, living in a Chinese neighbourhood, or working in a Chinese company. Conflicts were seldom discussed with others, as outsiders might see it as a sign of failure of their marriage. Instead they talked directly to their partner. This also created an image of a balanced marriage for friends and family members.

A third method of dealing with tension was through mutual understanding of religion as a result of the conversion process of the Chinese partner. Due to the change of faith, questions were asked about the religious foundation of the Malay spouse, while at the same time a new, combined, understanding evolved. Islam, besides creating a mutual understanding, also formed the primary source for solving issues concerning raising children, disputes, and worldviews.

Another way to deal with the hostilities to which their marriage and conversion was subjected to was to emphasize their incorporation into a superordinate category of *Bangsa Malaysia*, the ethnic group of Malaysians. With this move, they could overcome their religious and ethnic identity. With this category they also created a sense of belonging, which Chinese spouses especially missed out on due to their ambiguous status as Chinese Muslim.

These coping mechanisms seemed to work for these couples. In general the couples felt that the tensions in their marriage did make their lives difficult, but simultaneously, they claimed that the ways of dealing with these tensions made their relationships stronger. The mechanisms show how the hostilities created an increased awareness of prospective problems. Difficulties were resolved with a strong reliance on each other and the employment of the superordinate category.

CONCLUSION

The joining of two ethnically different people in marriage does not only relate to two individuals, but involves two families, two groups of friends, two ethnic groups, and in Malaysia, even different legal arrangements. In this in-depth case study, the demographic and political context of Kelantan exacerbated the tensions and hostilities. Group feelings to be steadfast in the face of the perceived threat of PAS and the increasing fusion of politics with Islam were projected on the conversion of the Chinese spouse who was accused of betrayal and disrespect in many cases.

The intermarried couples I spoke to tried to combine their ethnic backgrounds in several domains. In this chapter I have tried to demonstrate a number of combinations made in the personal, educational, and social domains to accommodate wishes of outsiders and to seek approval from family members and friends. Within these negotiation strategies, the spouses seemed to use different ethnic and religious attributions strategically to suit the situation at hand and emphasize the common ground the different ethnic groups have. By combining distinctive ethnic elements they succeeded in finding a place in the Malay as well as the Chinese society. The different ethnic characteristics that were stressed were often the ones that were expressed in Chinese and Malay culture, for instance, as is illustrated by status symbols and stress on (universal) mutual values.

Nonetheless they did not succeed in integrating their backgrounds in every way the spouses themselves had intended to. Integration of different ethnic characteristics turned out to be limited because they had to be careful not to offend anyone. Furthermore their attempts were restricted by macro influences such as religious rules and ethnic group ascriptions. Their efforts were met with rejection from family members and friends. The negative reactions towards the interethnically married can be seen as a reaction to the ambiguous position of these intermediary persons within Malaysian society.

Chinese Muslims are especially difficult to place in the prevailing structure provided by the legal arrangements, such as the Constitution, in which being Muslim strongly correlates with being Malay. Governmental policies and politics in which ethnic groups are clearly delineated increased these difficulties. As there is no fitting, existing framework, difficulty in interaction and identification is a consequence (Ellemers and Knippenberg 1997; Fein & Spencer 1997; Oakes & Reynolds 1997; Stangor 2000). This is especially apparent in the loss of contact, the feelings of loneliness, and the ambiguous position of the Chinese spouse, who, on the one hand, will be seen as a Chinese and not a born Muslim like Malays, and, on the other hand, as a Malay because of the conversion to Islam.

Tensions and hostilities were directed not only towards their interethnic marriage, but also to the fact that the Chinese spouse converted to Islam. The conversion had a profound two-sided impact on the marriage. On the one hand, the religion provided a mutual basis for dealing with hostilities and an important coping mechanism. On the other hand, it caused more distress in the marriage, since conversion itself was often opposed by Chinese acquaintances and, furthermore, required a profound change in the habits of the Chinese spouse, who was often judged by Malay acquaintances on whether he/she was behaving as a Muslim, and concurrently Malay. If conversion was not required, perhaps these last two problems would not be so prominent, and in addition, the ambiguous position of the Chinese spouse would be less conspicuous. However the conversion to Islam also provided a mutual starting-point, which perhaps decreased problems within the marriage itself. The impact of conversion by itself is thus hard to judge since being Malay cannot be separated from being Muslim in the Malaysian context.

Regardless of these barriers and paradoxes, couples in interethnic marriages I studied seem to pursue a combined ethnic lifestyle, and at the individual level, they seem to cross ethnic group boundaries and embody and propagate a superordinate category in which Islam is their mutual basis. With their conversion and marriage they increase interethnic interaction and reduce ethnic antagonism. Within their marriage they do seem to bridge the interethnic gap in different ways and are connected religiously. Ironically, they seem to strengthen group boundaries at the same time. This is illustrated by the disapproving reactions from outsiders. The intermarriage seems to increase awareness of the importance of ethnicity and the focus on ascribed group characteristics. The (strongly) negative reactions of relatives and friends and the resulting loss of contact illustrate that interethnic marriage is still considered an anomaly. In this case one can agree with Dea (2005) that "religions seem to connect believers across ethnic boundaries, but simultaneously, it paradoxically divides neighbours and relatives".

Notes

1. Special rights concern, for example, quotas for entry in civil service, public scholarships, and public education. See Article 153 of the Malaysian Constitution.
2. The riots followed the elections of 10 May 1969 which focused on the sensitive issues of education and language. The People's Action Party — later Democratic Action Party — a party opposing the special position of the *bumiputera*, acquired substantial gains in votes in these elections.
3. In consideration of the small sample, a match by profession was made in order to increase the likelihood of concurrence of socio-economic factors. In this sample, two teachers, two civil servants, two entrepeneurs, two nurses, a doctor, and a student were matched according to correlation in gender and profession of the Chinese spouse to one Malay and one Chinese intra-married couple.
4. Intra-married couple: a female married to a male from the same ethnic background.
5. Due to the small sample this test was not representative and only indicative and used to evoke further information. Statistical results of the tests will not be discussed in this chapter.
6. Over the years 1999–2003, these accounted for less than 1 per cent of the marriages in the district of Kota Bharu according to the registers of the *Balai Islam*. The registers were manually registered and were used because of a lack of other sources.
7. MACMA is a welfare organization for Chinese Muslims although, at

the time, still in a starting phase in Kelantan. PERKIM is a welfare organization working in line with Islam. In this context it provided assistance and education for several converts in this research. ABIM was established in 1971 as a youth movement propagating a Malaysia based on Islamic principles (Qur'an and Sunnah) and scientific and technological knowledge. Until 1982 it was led by Anwar Ibrahim and, although non-political, it is an influential organization (Abu Bakar 1981; Chin Yong Liow 2004a). Volunteers of ABIM were especially important in marriage counselling and helping converts as well as prospective converts.

8. In 1998, former ABIM leader and popular politician, Anwar Ibrahim, was arrested and incarcerated for sexual misconduct and corruption, causing widespread discontent with the ruling UMNO party (Chin Yong Liow 2004a; Noor 2002; Hitam 2001).

9. These are theft, robbery, slanderous accusation, unlawful carnal intercourse, wine consumption, and apostasy.

10. In 1999, forty-eight Chinese converted to Islam in Kelantan, in 2000 this number dropped to twenty-five, and in 2001, increased again to forty-five (MACMA Department of Kelantan, Berita MACMA, 2 (1) 2004).

11. In Islamic practice, the "surname" is the name of the father.

12. See also the National Fatwa Committee on the case of Ahmad Chong Ah Kaw on 28 January 1981 and the National Fatwa Committee, available online at <http://infad.kuim.edu.my/>. Changing names upon conversion is also debated in the news by, among others, Mufti Dr Mohd Asri Zainul Abidin (*New Straits Times*, 11 March 2007) and PAS (*New Straits Times*, 12 March 2007).

13. This statement by a male informant, and other citations that follow, is drawn from the in-depth interviews conducted by the author.

14. Long fingernails used to signal that the person involved did not have to do manual labour and was seen as a social status symbol. Chinese nowadays consider it a symbol of richness and intelligence, but some also grow long fingernails out of convenience.

15. Excerpt of an interview with a Malay female.

16. The solemnization of the marriage by the Islamic official.
17. An Islamic tradition in which the baby's head is shaved and the *azan* (call to prayer) is whispered into the baby's ear to thank Allah, to bless the baby, to bring the child close to Allah, and to gather relatives and friends (see also National Fatwa Committee, available online at <http://infad.kuim.edu.my>).
18. A vegetable which is considered "Chinese".
19. Statement made by a female Malay informant during informal conversations.
20. Interview statement by a Chinese female, who left her family due to the threat of physical violence towards her when she converted.
21. Interview statement by a Chinese female.
22. As the children follow Islam, they are considered Malays by the law and in society.
23. The effectiveness of these coping mechanisms cannot be determined in this research as only married couples were involved and no divorced couples were included. The mechanisms are drawn from interview excerpts with the ten intermarried couples.

References

Abu Bakar, M. "Islamic Revivalism and the Political Process in Malaysia". *Asian Survey* 21, no. 10 (1981): 1040–59.

Andaya, L.Y., and Andaya, B.W. *A History of Malaysia*. 2nd ed. Hampshire: Palgrave, 2001.

Barth, F. *Ethnic Groups and Boundaries: The Social Organization of Cultural Difference*. Bergen, London: Universitetsforlaget, Allen & Unwin, 1969.

Brown, D., ed. "Class, State and Ethnic Politics in Peninsular Malaysia". In *The State and Ethnic Politics in Southeast Asia*. London, New York: Routledge, 1994.

Camroux, D. "State Responses to Islamic Resurgence in Malaysia: Accomodation, Co-option and Confrontation". *Asian Survey* 36, no. 9 (1996): 852–68.

Chin Yong Liow, J. "Exigency or Expediency? Contextualising Political Islam and the PAS Challenge in Malaysian Politics". *Third World Quarterly* 25, no. 2 (2004a): 359–72.

————. "Political Islam in Malaysia: Problematising Discourse and Practice in the UMNO-PAS 'Islamisation race' ". *Commonwealth & Comparative Politics* 42, no. 2 (2004b): 184–205.

Cohen, A.P. *Signifying Identities: Anthropological Perspectives on Boundaries and Contested Values*. London, New York: Routledge, 2000.

Collins, R. and S. Coltrane. *Sociology of Marriage and the Family: Gender, Love and Property*. Belmont, Singapore: Wadsworth, 2001.

Cramer, D. *Close Relationships: The Study of Love and Friendship*. London, New York: Arnold, 1998.

Dea, D. "Christianity and Spirit Mediums: Experiencing Postsocialist Religious Freedom in Southern Ethopia". Max Planck Institute for Social Anthropology Working Papers (75), 2005.

Ellemers, N. and A. Knippenberg. "Stereotyping in Social Context". In *The Social Psychology of Stereotyping and Group Life*, edited by R. Spears. Oxford, Cambridge: Blackwell, 1997.

Fein, S. and S.J. Spencer. "Prejudice as Self-image Maintenance: Affirming the Self through Derogating Others". In *The Social Psychology of Stereotyping and Group Life*, edited by R. Spears. Oxford, Cambridge: Blackwell, 1997.

Fenton, S. "Malaysia and Capitalist Modernisation: Plural and Multicultural Models". *International Journal on Multicultural Societies* 5, no. 2 (2003): 135–47.

Goffman, E. *Encounters: Two Studies in the Sociology of Interaction*. Harmondsworth: Penguin, 1972.

Hamayotsu, K. "Politics of Syariah Reform: The Making of the State Religio-legal Apparatus". In *Malaysia: Islam, Society and Politics*, edited by V.M. Hooker and N. Othman. Singapore: Institute of Southeast Asian Studies, 2003.

Haque, M.S. "The Role of the State in Managing Ethnic Tensions in Malaysia: A Critical Discourse". *American Behavioral Scientist* 47, no. 3 (2003): 240–66.

Hassan, R. *Interethnic Marriage in Singapore: A Study in Interethnic Relations*. Singapore: Institute of Southeast Asian Studies, 1974.

Heijdt, v.d., J. "Gemengde Huwelijken Lopen Vaker Stuk (Mixed Marriages End up in Divorce More Often). *Maandstatistiek Bevolking* 44, no. 6 (1995): 6.

Hitam, T.S.M. "Islam and the State in Malaysia". *Paper Series of the Institute of Southeast Asian Studies* 9 (2001): 1–27.

Horowitz, D.L. "The Qur'an and the Common Law: Islamic Reform and the Theory of Legal Change". *The American Journal of Comparative Law* 42, no. 2 (1994): 233–93.

Jager, d., H. *Het Sociaal-gemengde Huwelijk (The Socially Mixed Marriage)*. Leiden: H.E. Stenfert Kroes, 1969.

Jones, G.W. *Marriage and Divorce in Islamic South-East Asia*. Kuala Lumpur; New York: Oxford University Press, 1994.

Kamali, M.H. "Punishment in Islamic Law: A Critique of the Hudud Bill of Kelantan, Malaysia". *Arab Law Quarterly* 13, no. 3 (1998): 203–34.

Lee, S.M. "Intermarriage and Ethnic Relations in Singapore". *Journal of Marriage and the Family* 50, no. 1 (1988): 255–65.

Ling-Chien Neo, J. "Malay Nationalism, Islamic Supremacy and the Constitutional Bargain in the Multi-ethnic Composition of Malaysia". *International Journal on Minority and Group Rights* 13 (2006): 95–118.

Ma, R.W. "Shifting Identities: Chinese Muslims in Malaysia". *Asian Ethnicity* 6, no. 1 (2005): 89–107.

Malhi, A. "The PAS-BN Conflict in the 1990s: Islamism and Modernity". In *Malaysia: Islam, Society and Politics*, edited by V.M. Hooker and N. Othman. Singapore: Institute of Southeast Asian Studies, 2003.

Nagata, J. "The Impact of Islamic Revival (Dakwah) on the Religious Culture of Malaysia". In *Religion, Values and Development*, edited by J. Nagata and B. Matthews. Singapore: Institute of Southeast Asian Studies, 1986.

Noor, F.A. "PAS Post-Fadzil Noor: Future Directions and Prospects". *Paper Series of the Institute of Southeast Asian Studies* 8, 2002.

Oakes, P.J., and Reynolds, K.J. "Asking the Accuracy Question". In *The Social Psychology of Stereotyping and Group Life*, edited by R. Spears. Oxford, Cambridge: Blackwell, 1997.

Peletz, M.G. "Sacred Texts and Dangerous Words: The Politics of Law and Cultural Rationalization in Malaysia". *Comparative Studies in Society and History* 35, no. 1 (1993): 66–109.

Population and Housing Census of Malaysia. In t. 4.1, ed., p. 70. Kuala Lumpur: Department of Statistics, 2000.

Schlee, G. Einleitung. "Introduction". In *Integration Durch Verschiedenheit: Lokale und Globale Formen Interkultureller Kommunikation (Integration Through Diversity: Local and Global Forms of Intercultural Communication)*, edited by G. Schlee and A. Horstmann. Bielefeld: Transcript, 2001.

Stangor, C., ed. "Conceptualizing Stereotypes and Prejudice". In *Stereotypes and Prejudice: Essential Readings*. Philadelphia: Psychology Press, 2000.

Trezzini, B. "Embedded State Autonomy and Legitimacy: Piecing Together the Malaysian Development Puzzle (Review)". *Economy & Society* 30, no. 3 (2001): 324–53.

World Fatwa Management and Research Institute (2007) National Fatwa Committee. Available online at <http://infad.kuim.edu.my/>.

SECTION III

PERSPECTIVES

Chapter 9

PROMOTING GENDER EQUITY THROUGH INTERRELIGIOUS MARRIAGE
Empowering Indonesian Women
Siti Musdah Mulia

INTRODUCTION

The Compilation of Islamic Law in Indonesia was promulgated on 10 June 1991 through Presidential Instruction No. 1/1991. Comprising regulations on marriage, inheritance, and religious donation, it is the official legal guidance for judges in religious courts all over Indonesia. The Law consists of three books: Book I on marriage, Book II on inheritance, and Book III on religious donation. With 229 articles, the biggest portion is on marital law (170 articles).

The Law was the government's response to the "social unrest" arising from different verdicts issued by the religious court on similar cases. The diversity is actually a logical consequence of the various jurisprudential references of the judges. However, instead of perceiving the diversity of views as a treasure of legal sources, the government responded by homogenizing the law.

On the one hand, the Compilation made it easier for judges to issue a verdict and for other parties looking for legal references. On the other hand, it restricted the creativity and *ijtihad* (independent judgement, based on recognized sources of Islam, on a legal or theological question) efforts in the legal field.

When analysed carefully, the Compilation of Islamic Law contains no less than nineteen crucial issues including, among others, the definition of marriage, marriage representatives, marriage registration, stipulation of marriageable age, dowry, interfaith marriage, polygamy, the right of the wife to divorce her husband and to return to her husband after reconciliation, love token given by a man to a woman at a betrothal or at the beginning of a sexual liaison (*idah*), mourning upon the death of one's husband (*ihdah*), the earning of a living, marriage vow, the wife's refusal to obey or follow what her husband asks her to do (*nusyuz*), rights and responsibilities, issues of inheritances involving different faiths, portion of inheritance for sons and daughters, religious donation involving different faiths, illegitimate children, and methods/formulae for calculating the different portions of inheritances (*aul* and *radd*).

In 2004, as Special Assistant to the Minister for Religion, I led a team of Islamic legal scholars in the preparation of the Counter Legal Draft (CLD), which was to be submitted for legislative approval to replace the Compilation of Islamic Law (Compilation). The thinking behind this move was that the Compilation, which has been very influential in guiding legal judgements, is grounded in a worldview in which women are presumed to be inferior to men and is inconsistent with a number of binding national and international laws (Musdah Mulia and Cammack 2007, pp. 128–45).

The Counter Legal Draft (CLD), when made public in September 2004, provoked strong responses, both pro and contra, from Indonesia's Muslim community. It was denounced in some quarters as secular and un-Islamic, or as affording too broad a scope for reason and considerations of public interest (Yanggo 2005). Because of the strong reactions provoked by the draft, the Indonesian government withdrew the CLD from consideration.[1] One of the features of the Compilation on which it takes a narrower approach than the majority opinion within Islamic jurisprudence is the rule regarding marriage across religious lines. The CLD, by contrast, takes a very liberal position on interreligious marriage. In this chapter, I elaborate on the philosophical and theological considerations that guided the CLD team in formulating its position on interreligious marriage. Towards the end of the chapter, I present some of my own thinking.

WHAT IS RELIGION?

Social injustice and gender discrimination in today's world is frequently laid at the feet of religion. One type of injustice and gender discrimination that is very often blamed on Islam is the rule regarding marriages across religious lines or interreligious marriage. What interreligious marriage refers to in this chapter is a marriage that takes place between a Muslim and non-Muslim. The generally accepted view within the schools of Islamic law permits a Muslim man to marry a Christian or a Jewish woman, but disallows marriages between Muslim men and other non-Muslim women, as well as all marriages between Muslim women and non-Muslim men.

The Compilation of Islamic Law in Indonesia takes the restriction on interreligious marriage a step further, prohibiting all marriages between Muslims and non-Muslims. Because religion deals with fundamental beliefs, values, and world views, false religious legitimation of unjust social practices is particularly dangerous. The question arises, however, whether injustices that have been attributed to religion are the result of religion itself, or whether these social inequalities arise from conceptions and interpretations of religion that are influenced by the culture and tradition of patriarchy, capitalist ideology, and the influence of Arabic cultural practices.

With regard to the matter of interreligious marriage or marriage between Muslims and non-Muslims, a fundamental question arises, not only regarding the basic rights of women, but of the crucial role of religion itself. For, in the face of the controversial view in religion regarding interreligious marriage, the question that crosses our minds is: Do we still need religion? To be honest, this question often irks me these days. How can it be otherwise when people of different religions or faiths entering into a marriage are often treated in a discriminatory and unfair manner? Again, the victims in such cases are the women and the offsprings of such a union. But before we can answer this question, we need to ask the more fundamental question of what religion is.

The essence of religion lies in the spirit of humanistic values contained therein, and one form of humanistic values is a sincere recognition of the equality and unity of mankind. Human beings are equal and come from the same source, namely God. Therefore, every religion sets forth two aspects in their teachings: the teaching about God and about human beings. The first one concerns a vertical relationship, while the latter concerns a horizontal one. The vertical aspect in Islam talks about man's duty to God, while the horizontal aspect contains a set of conventions regarding human relationships as well as the relationship between humans and the environment. So, I firmly believe that, viewed from any perspective, religion is very much needed in human life.

PROMOTING ISLAM AS A HUMANE RELIGION

Islam stipulates that a person is judged by his/her achievement and the quality of his/her faith, and when it comes to faith, only God has the right to pass judgement. The principal purpose of every religion is to instil in its followers the essence of goodness in all aspects: physical, mental, moral, spiritual, and social. One of the principal teachings of religion is respect for every person regardless of gender, race, ethnic background, and religion.

According to Ibn 'Arabi, a famous Muslim Sufi, the humanistic dimension in Islam is given more concrete attention at the *tasawuf* (mysticism) level, as reflected in the concept of love. A passage in his famous poem states: "...the religion that I profess is a religion of love *(udinu bidin al-hubb)*". This *tasawuf* teaching asserts that human beings exist because of God's love, and therefore human beings are obliged to practise in their lives the spirit of God's love. Islam teaches the concept of love not only for God, the Creator, in the form of sincere and unreserved devotion, but also love for fellow human beings, reflected by a willingness to maintain harmony with every human being, regardless of differences in gender, language, ethnic background, race, colour, culture, and even religion. Human beings are required to treat not only fellow humans, but every living creature with kindness.

Unfortunately, this holy and noble mission of Islam is not properly practised by its followers. In practising their religion, humans tend to focus more on building a good relationship with God. It means they desire to "satisfy" God rather than to maintain a peaceful and harmonious relationship with fellow human beings, which in actuality is the real essence of Islamic teaching. As a result, conflicts, exploitation, violence, and discrimination, including gender discrimination that causes misery to women, are practised in the name of Islamic teachings.

Al-Ghazali, one of the greatest reformers of the "Islamic Middle Ages" asserts that the fundamental purpose of Islamic teachings is to uphold the five basic human rights, which is the right to live, the right to practise a religion, the right of opinion and speech, the right to procreate, and the right to property. These five basic rights are known in *fiqh* (Islamic jurisprudence) as *"al-kulliyyat al-khams"*. Therefore all Islamic teachings must be focused on safeguarding and enforcing these five basic rights. Our biggest challenge is to formulate and spread the teachings of Islam that accommodate and appreciate humanistic values, in order to ensure that its followers are more humane. This is the topic that will be addressed here.

ISLAM'S RESPECT FOR INTERRELIGIOUS MARRIAGE

Islam teaches that human beings are superior and, at the same time, unique — thus distinguishing them from other living creatures in the sense that they are appointed as *khalifah fi al-ardh* (God's vice-regent on earth), whose duty and responsibility is to manage life on earth. To accomplish this task, human beings are permitted and even encouraged to marry so that human existence is ensured until the end of time. It should be noted, however, that in Islam, reproduction is not the only purpose of marriage. The other purpose is recreation.

Marriage in Islam is a contract or transaction. This is reflected in the fact that there is an *ijab* (offer) and a *qabul* (acceptance). A contract or transaction should involve two equal parties who shall come to a consensus. Thus it is correct to define marriage as a contract that binds two equal parties, a man and a woman, each fulfilling the requirements according to the law, both willing and consenting, to form a family together.

It is interesting to note that Al-Qur'an addresses marriage in detail, as there are no less than 104 verses on the subject, using the word *nikah*, which means to unite, or the word *zauj*, which means to pair. The word *nikah* (marry) is mentioned twenty-three times, while the word *zauj* is mentioned eighty-one times. Thus, in order to understand the true meaning of marriage fully, we must study all the verses on marriage thoroughly and link each verse with the others. By doing so, we will have a clear understanding of the moral implications of marriage in Al-Qur'an. A thorough study of verses dealing with marriage will sum up some basic principles that form the foundation of marriage (Siti Musdah Mulia 2000, p. 9). The first one is monogamy, the second is *mawaddah wa rahmah* (love and affection), the third is complementing and protecting each other, the fourth, *mu'asyarah bi al ma'ruf* (politeness and good manners), and the fifth is the freedom to choose one's life partner, both for men and women.

In marriage, Muslims tend to regard men as the active party, particularly in choosing a mate and proposing, while women are positioned as the passive party, waiting to be married off. Therefore every instruction on marriage is directed to men. Consequently, it is the man who becomes the actor, the initiator or the one who proposes, while women wait to be proposed to. This practice reflects the ways of the community to which Al-Qur'an was first revealed, namely the Arab community with their entrenched culture of patriarchy. The women of that time were not regarded as independent subjects with rights of opinion and expression. However, with the passage of time, many changes have taken place within Muslim society in line with the demands of the times, and also as a result of advances in technology and information. Women have become more independent and are not afraid to express their opinions and needs, so it is only natural that the rules that do not accommodate women's interests and aspirations are reviewed.

Pertaining to the interreligious marriage issue, Al-Qur'an categorizes non-Muslims into three groups: the *musyrik*, *kafir*, and the *ahlul kitab* (*kitabiyah*) (Al-Qur'an 98:1). However, it is interesting to note that Muslims have never come to an agreement on which group belongs to the *musyrik, kafir,* and *ahlul kitab* categories. In general, the word *musyrik* usually refers to those who believe in more than one God other than Allah, such as idolaters and fire-worshippers (Al-Qur'an 29:61–63; Al-Qur'an 31:25; Al-Qur'an 43:9 & 87).[2] *Kafir* (infidels) refers to non-Muslims, while *ahlul kitab* are those who embrace the *samawi* (revealed) religion, namely the Jews and Christians.

The issue of interreligious marriage has always been a controversial issue in the history of Islam. In principle, Muslims have three views on this issue. In the first view, interreligious marriage is completely forbidden. Some Muslims, especially conservative ones, totally oppose marriage between Muslims and non-Muslims who are *musyrik* or *ahlul kitab*. This prohibition applies to both men and women.[3] In the second view, marriage between a Muslim man and a non-Muslim woman is allowed on condition that the non-Muslim woman belongs to *ahlul kitab* (*kitabiyah*). In the third view, marriage between Muslims and non-Muslims is permissible for both men and women. Let us now analyse the arguments that support each of these three opinions.

First Opinion: Forbid Interreligious Marriage Entirely

This opinion is based on the verse Al-Qur'an 2:221: "Do not marry idolatrous women unless they join the faith. A maid servant who is a believer is better than an idolatress even though you may like her. And do not marry your daughters to idolaters until they accept the faith. A servant who is a believer is better than an idolater even though you may like him. They invite you to Hell, but God calls you to paradise and pardon by His grace. And He makes His signs manifest that man may happily take heed." Those that hold this opinion do not distinguish between the *musyrik* and the *ahlul kitab* as these two groups are in reality the same, as is stated by Abdullah ibn Umar, one of the companions of the Prophet. He argues: "I know not of any *musyrik* deeds that are worse than one who believes that his God is Isa (Jesus), one of God's servants." (Al-Bukhari 1987, *juz* 5, p. 2024). The words "one who believes that his God is Isa or one of God's servants" refer to Christians. Thus, according to this group, Christians belong to the *musyrik*, and not *ahlul kitab*, as in practice, they worship one other than Allah.

Another argument put forth by this group is that although there is a verse in the Al-Qur'an that allows a Muslim man to marry a woman of the *ahlul kitab*, namely Al-Qur'an 5:5, this verse is nullified by Al-Qur'an 2:221, as mentioned above (Quraish Shihab 1996, p. 196). Another argument is based on the interpretation of Al-Qur'an 6:10: "People of faith, when faithful women come to you, you shall test their faith. Allah already knows their faithfulness; if you are sure about their faithfulness do not return them to their husbands who are infidels. They (women) are not meant for infidels, and these infidels are also not meant for them. And return the *mahar* to their husbands And you shall not sin, if you pay them the *mahar*. And do not marry *kafir* women, and you shall demand your *mahar*, and they should ask their *mahar* to be returned. This is the law of Allah, and Allah is the source of knowledge and wisdom."

In view of such reasoning, conservative Muslims have agreed to forbid such marriage, and this agreement is considered "*ijma*" (social consensus). "*Ijma*", in their opinion, can be used as one of the bases for Islamic law. The absolute ban on interreligious marriage has become the view of the mainstream Islamic community in Indonesia, the majority of whom are the followers of Al-Shafi, the founder of one of the legal schools in Islam. This view was then legalized by the Indonesian state through the Compilation of Islamic Law.

As a result, the state provides no possibility whatsoever for interreligious marriage in Indonesia. Hence, couples of different religions or faiths entering into a marriage are unable to register their marriage at the Religious Civil Registry Office of the Ministry of Religious Affairs (*Kantor Urusan Agama* or KUA), or at the National Civil Registry Office (*Kantor Catatan Sipil* or KCS) of the Ministry of Home Affairs.[4] Consequently, those who have been denied recognition of their marital status cannot acquire a marriage certificate as legal proof of their union. The absence of a marriage certificate will prevent them from getting their civil rights as citizens, and the most likely to fall victim are the women and their children.

The Council of Indonesian Ulama (Majelis Ulama Indonesia)[5] is outspoken on this matter. Through its *fatwa* (religious decree) issued on 1 June 1980, the Council forbids any form of interreligious marriage, including the marriage between a Muslim man and a non-Muslim woman, albeit from the *ahlul kitab* group. The reason given is that the *mafsadah* (damage) caused by this marriage is greater than the *mashlahah* (benefit), especially for the Muslims. In this context, the basis for the *fiqh* that the *ulama* uphold is the avoidance of peril, and this is preferred over obtaining goodness (*dar' al-mafasid muqaddam 'ala jalb al-mashalih*), a sort of preventive measure.

From the above mentioned explanation it is clear that the school of thought that forbids interreligious marriage comes from the desire to build a happy family, one that lives in harmony within the community. This is possible if husband and wife share common views and principles, especially the same religion.

Logically, the more differences there are between the husband and the wife, particularly difference in religion, the more vulnerable the marriage will be. In short, it is believed that being of different faiths or religion will affect the solidity and happiness of a marriage as well as the harmony between families.

Although prevailing rules and regulations do not accommodate them, the number of couples entering into interreligious marriage appears to keep growing.[6] It is important to note that to acquire a marriage certificate as legal proof of their marriage, Indonesians from the middle and upper classes have to resort to going abroad to countries such as Singapore and Australia to get married. Strangely enough, the certificates issued by a marriage institution abroad will be used as a basis by the National Civil Registry Office in Indonesia to register the marriage without even questioning the form of the union.

Another strategy commonly used is where one of the couple will pretend to convert, and thus the couple will be able to register at the authorized institution. Afterwards the person who converted will return to his or her original religion. The conversion is only a means to fulfil the administrative requirements. Another alternative is to marry according to their beliefs and not bother with registration. Consequently if a marital problem arises, the wife and children will be the victims. Since no marriage certificate is available, the wife will find it difficult to obtain what is rightfully hers, such as alimony and inheritance.

Second Opinion: Allow Interreligious Marriage if the Non-Muslim Woman is a Kitabiyah

Now let us examine the theological argumentations of the second group,[7] the one that allows a marriage between a Muslim man and a non-Muslim woman from the *ahlul kitab* group by referring to Al-Qur'an 5:5: "...And you are allowed to marry respected women from the *ahlul kitab* if you have given them their right with the intention to marry them and not with the intention of adultery, and also not to make a mistress of them...." According to those who support this opinion, the above verse affirms that a marriage between a Muslim man and a non-Muslim woman of the *ahlul kitab* is allowed, while the marriage of a Muslim woman and a non-Muslim man of *ahlul kitab* is not explicitly mentioned. This leads to the conclusion that a marriage between a Muslim woman and a non-Muslim man of *ahlul kitab* is forbidden. If it were allowed, it would surely be mentioned in this verse.

The group of Muslims who allow a marriage between a Muslim man and a non-Muslim woman from the *ahlul kitab* group are still at odds over the definition of *ahlul kitab* mentioned in the verse. Some Muslims confine the term *ahlul kitab* to Jews and Christians who lived during the time of the Prophet, while other Muslims, including Quraish Shihab, believe that the term *ahlul kitab* refers to all Jews and Christians up to the present (Al-Juzairy 2000, p. 198). However there is one requirement that must be fulfilled, that the woman of *ahlul kitab* should be virtuous as defined in the verse, namely respectable women who preserve their purity as accorded by the holy book (*wal-muhshanat minallazina utul-kitab*). This means that not all women of *ahlul kitab* may be taken as wives, but only those who satisfy the requirements stated in the aforementioned verse.

Mahmud Syaltut, the prominent *ulama* from Egypt has yet a different opinion. According to him, permitting a marriage between a Muslim man and a non-Muslim woman of *ahlul kitab* is a strategy for *dakwah* (proselytization). In his position as a husband, the man has the right to educate his family, his wife, and children on Islamic morals. It is hoped that the marriage will eliminate non-Muslims' hatred and vendetta towards Islam, especially in the wife's heart. Likewise, the wife, being well-treated by her husband, will get to know the beauty and goodness of Islam, and realize that Islam provides absolute rights to the wife. However if circumstances are not such, then it is better to disallow the marriage (Mahmud Syaltut 1959, p. 253). Responding to Syaltut's opinion, Quraish Shihab, a Muslim scholar from Indonesia, says if the marriage is forbidden for fear of the wife being influenced by the husband's religion, then a marriage between a Muslim man and a woman of *ahlul kitab* should also not be tolerated, if it is feared that the husband or his children will be influenced by values contradictory to Islamic values (Quraish Shihab 1996, p. 199).

Another opinion is that of Maulana Muhammad Ali. He says that although it has not been firmly stipulated in the divine revelation, the majority of Muslims have always been opposed to marriage between Muslim women and non-Muslim men. This opposition is purely based on the *ijtihad* (independent legal reasoning) that a Muslim woman who is married to a non-Muslim man will feel miserable because she will be deprived of the rights she would otherwise enjoy if she were to live amongst Muslims. A wife will follow her husband's tradition and this will impact on her faith as a Muslim (Maulana Muhammad 'Ali 1993, p. 119).

Another reason interreligious marriage is frowned on is the fear of the possibility of conversion to another faith. On the other hand, a Muslim man is allowed to marry an *ahlul kitab* woman on the assumption that men are usually stronger in their faith and are thus able to convince wife and children to embrace Islam.

There is an impression that Muslim men are permitted to wed non-Muslim women because they are devout and strong in their faith, whereas a Muslim woman is not allowed to marry a

non-Muslim man, including an *ahlul kitab* man, because it is
feared the woman and her children will be tempted to convert
to her husband's religion. Unlike men, all women are assumed
to be weak in their faith. This view is clearly biased in terms of
gender and patriarchal values as it is based on stereotyping a
woman as a weak being whose belief is easily shaken. So,
according to the logic of this stereotyping, Muslim women are
advised not to marry non-Muslim men, including those from
the *ahlul kitab*.

On the other hand, the notion of forbidding Muslim men
from marrying women of *ahlul kitab* also stems from the stereotype
that women are seductive and the source of slander. Marrying a
woman of *ahlul kitab* will cause a negative impact because it is
feared that the husband and all their offsprings will convert to
the woman's religion. For this reason some Muslims assert that
such a marriage will cause the husband and children to fall
victim to slander, thus marriage to an *ahlul kitab* woman is
strictly forbidden (Ali al-Shabuni, p. 537).

Third Opinion: Muslims, Both Men and Women, Should Be Allowed to Marry Non-Muslims

The argumentation of the third school of thought[8] is also based
on the three verses that were used by the two earlier groups,
namely Al-Qur'an 2:221; Al-Qur'an 60:10; and Al-Qur'an 5:5, but
differences lie in the interpretation. This group has presented
several arguments. First, Al-Qur'an 2:221 only forbids marriage
between a Muslim and a *musyrik*. Muhammad Abduh and Rasyid
Ridha explain that the *musyrik* women mentioned in this line are
Arab *musyrik* women of the time of the Prophet (Muhammad
Abduh & Rasyid Ridha, p. 193). This is indicated by the fact that
the verse which forbids Muslims from marrying a *musyrik* also

suggests that they marry a Muslim slave instead. It is clear from the context that the *musyrik* indicates those who lived during the time of the Prophet, and they no longer exist. Another opinion regarding Al-Qur'an 2:221 is that this verse has actually been annulled by Al-Qur'an 5:5 because the latter verse was revealed after the former (Al-Thabari, p. 390).

Second, the verse Al-Qur'an 5:5 can be interpreted as saying that a Muslim man can marry a woman of *ahlul kitab*, and consent is given to Muslim women, as well, to marry *ahlul kitab* men. In the Arabic language there is a literary style called *al-iktifa*, where we need only to state a particular part (of a writing), from whence we may understand the other parts. For example this verse asserts that a Muslim man may marry a woman of *ahlul kitab*, so logically a Muslim woman may marry a man of *ahlul kitab*.

Third, Al-Qur'an 60:10 gives the only explicit prohibition of marriage with infidel women (Al-Qur'an 7:190; Al-Qur'an 4:12; Al-Qur'an 43:39). If we understand the context of the revelation of this verse, this ban is only natural as the infidel people of the Arab Quraisy tribe were very hostile to the Prophet and his followers. At that time, there was also war between Muslims and the infidels. This ban was imposed in order to clearly distinguish friends from enemies and when the war ended, the ban was naturally lifted. Al-Qur'an 60:10 is also considered to have been revised by Al-Qur'an 5:5.

DISCUSSION

It may be concluded that the problem of interreligious marriage in Islam lies in defining who exactly fits in the category of *musyrik, ahlul kitab*, and *kafir* in the context of Al-Qur'an and the difference between these three groups. *Musyrik* can be defined as a person who worships gods or entities other than Allah, such as humans, objects, power, wealth (Al-Qur'an 2:264). A question arises: Is it impossible for a Muslim to be a *musyrik*?[9] In the interpretation of a majority of Muslims, the definition of *musyrik* is always limited to non-Muslims who worship idols, fire, or other entities. The fact is that in our community, including the Muslim community, it is common to find people who worship power, wealth, position, and living creatures. So labelling only non-Muslims as *musyrik* is immensely misleading, and this is why Muslims in this country lose the ability to examine their own morals and guard themselves against the danger of *syirk* (polytheism). Raghib al-Asfahani, a prominent scholar, stated that from the perspective of law, there are two kinds of *syirk*: minor *syirk* and major *syirk*. The first occurs when one worships another god other than Allah for the purpose of *riya* or for receiving a compliment (Al-Qur'an 12:106; Al-Qur'an 3:36), while the second occurs when one equates Allah with one of his creations in terms of divinity (Ibnu Katsir; Muhammad Abduh and Ridha, vol. 4:, pp. 185, 193). This ambiguity indicates how difficult it is to determine whether a person is a *musyrik*, as it concerns a very personal issue related to a person's faith.

Similar to the term musyrik, the term *ahlul kitab* is also prone to diverse interpretations. A number of Muslims restrict the term *ahlul kitab* to the Jews and Christians who lived at the time of the Prophet, whereas a majority of Muslims are of the opinion that *ahlul kitab* are simply Jews and Christians, regardless of the period they live in. On the other hand, some Muslims suggest that the term *ahlul kitab* is not restricted to Jews and Christians, but includes Buddhists and Hindus, and yet other Muslims include in this category, the followers of other religions such as those of the ancient Persians, Indians, Chinese, and Japanese (Quraish Shihab 1997, p. 189).

The term *kafir* (infidels) is also ambiguous. In general, Muslims define *kafir* as the renunciation of God, the prophets and their teachings, and doomsday. Al-Qur'an itself uses the term *kafir* to describe various groups, namely the *kafir* who lived before the period of the Prophet, the Arab Quraisy people who renounced God and denounced the Prophet, those who reject God's benevolence, those who seek help and protection from a god other than Allah, and hypocrites (Quraish Shihab 1997, pp. 189–92). With such a broad meaning, the term *kafir* can even apply to many Muslims.

However, it should be noted that the Council of Indonesian Ulama in Jakarta (MUI of Jakarta Province) issued a *fatwa* on 30 September 1986 adhering to the third school of thought which allows interreligious marriage (Ichiyanto 2003, pp. 143–44, fn. 164 and 167). This *fatwa* evidently contradicts the *fatwa* of the Central Board of the Council of Indonesian Ulama (*fatwa* MUI Pusat) which forbids interreligious marriage. Basically, the *fatwas* of MUI of Jakarta adopts the view of Muhammad Abduh and Rasyid Ridha, and some *ulama* of India and Pakistan. This view is in accordance with the characteristics and attitudes of Islam as portrayed in Al-Qur'an, and appropriate for Indonesia as a pluralistic society and country based on *Pancasila* and UUD 1945 (State Constitution). It is not inappropriate to say that this *fatwa* is based on the law and policy of Indonesia, although it conforms to the situation in the country, and enforces unity. The data issued by the MUI Jakarta shows that between April 1985 and 10 July 1986, there were 239 cases of interreligious marriage and 117 among them were marriages between non-Muslim men and Muslim women. Based on this *fatwa*, the KUA in Jakarta was also permitted to register marriages between Muslim men and women of *ahlul kitab*, and the Civil Registry Office, too, was allowed to process and record interreligious marriages.

In this matter, it is interesting to take note of the decree issued by the Supreme Justice. In its decree No. 1400 K/Pdt/1986, the Supreme Justice granted an appeal by Andi Vony, a Muslim woman, to marry Adrianus Petrus, a Christian Protestant man, and nullified the verdict of the Central Jakarta State Court, dated 11 April 1986, No. 382/PDT/P/1986/PN JKT.PST, which supported the refusal of the Extraordinary Official of the Civil Registry in Jakarta to officiate the marriage.

According to the Supreme Justice's decree, the Indonesian Marriage Law No. 1 1974 does not contain any stipulation that bans interreligious marriage, and this is in accordance with Article 27 of the Constitution of 1945 which stipulates that all citizens are equal before the law, granting every citizen his/her right to marry a fellow citizen regardless of religion. The lack of the existence of a law forbidding marriage between people of different religions or faiths is in accordance with the spirit of Article 29 of the Constitution regarding the state's guarantee of freedom for every citizen to profess his/her religion. Furthermore, this decree states that there is a shortcoming in the Marriage Law. In reality and based on jurisprudence, there are two systems of law that govern a mixed marriage, and it must be decided which system is to be applied in cases of mixed marriage. Yet Paragraph 2 of Article 1 of the Marriage Law No. 1 1974, and Paragraph 10 of Article 2 of Government Regulation on Marriage Law No. 9 1975 state that only marriage between people of the same religion or faith is permitted.

Besides the lack of legal surety, Indonesia is, in reality, a country with a pluralistic community and, therefore, interreligious marriages are likely to occur. Taking note of these factors, the Supreme Justice decided to allow Andi Vony's marriage and ordered the Civil Registry Office to register it. The verdict issued by the Supreme Justice also refused to accept the reasons given by the KUA and the KCS not to record the marriage of Andi Vony on the grounds of paragraph 60 of the Marriage Law. According to the Supreme Justice, this Article must be linked to Articles 57, 58, 59 of the Marriage Law, which state that mixed marriages are defined as marriage between those with different nationalities and not different religions.[10]

Unfortunately, in 2000, the MUI Jakarta launched a new *fatwa* contradicting the previous one. Similar to the policy of the MUI Pusat, this *fatwa* prohibited marriage between Muslims and non-Muslims. Clearly, from studying these *fatwa*, it can be concluded that the *fatwa* of MUI changed legal opinions from one school of thought to another.

MY PERSPECTIVE ON INTERRELIGIOUS MARRIAGE

The majority of Muslims tend to position women as objects. Women are labelled as inferior beings, weak and easily convinced to convert to another faith. In addition, they are stigmatized as the root of vicious slander. Thus Muslim men are forbidden to marry non-Muslim women as it is feared that these men will renounce their faith.

Even though Muslim men are allowed to marry non-Muslim women of *ahlul kitab*, there is a hope that they will be able to convince their wife and children to embrace Islam, a hope that sometimes proves to be unfounded. A survey on interreligious marriage shows that in mixed marriages between Muslim men and non-Muslim women, 50 per cent of couples raise their children according to the Islamic faith, while in mixed marriages between Muslim women and non-Muslim men, 80 per cent of couples raise their children to follow their mother's religion (Nuryamin 1990). This indicates that in interreligious marriages, women have a greater influence than men in deciding their children's religion, contradicting the belief that women are weak and easily tempted.

In my opinion, the fear that the Muslim spouse will convert to another religion if married to a non-Muslim is an apprehension based on a psychological syndrome. Muslims often lack confidence in themselves and suffer excessive and unjustified fear. Muslims in Indonesia make up the majority of the population, but often have the mentality of minority groups. One indication of this is that even when Muslim Indonesians do tolerate interreligious marriage, it is always in the hope that the Muslim spouse will be able to influence his/her partner to convert to Islam, but if he/she is unable to do so, we get angry and condemn the marriage. In other words, Muslims celebrate if a non-Muslim converts to Islam, but when a Muslim leaves the religion, they get outraged. In short, they only accept winning, while losing is intolerable. In this context they should be honest and admit that such thought is unreasonable and petty. To make matters worse, such a mindset can be found among non-Muslims too. I am saddened and concerned that this pettiness is a part of our religious outlook.

I am in favour of forbidding interreligious marriage on more objective grounds, such as proof that interreligious marriage has become one of the causes of a high rate of divorce or domestic violence, or that interreligious marriage is a cause of trafficking of women and children that has become rampant in Indonesia. The reason for forbidding interreligious marriage would then be the prevention of the spread of social disease in society (*sadd al-dzara'i*).

If interreligious marriage does, in fact, cause domestic violence or trafficking of women and children, and it is allowed in Indonesia, I would suggest that the community make a strong effort to communicate to the public about these social problems. Thus women will be able to make wiser choices in choosing a life partner and protect themselves from exploitation and violence in marriage.

Based on the above analysis it can be concluded that all the opinions on marriage between a Muslim and a non-Muslim are merely a matter of *ijtihad* (process of critical reasoning). There is no verse in Al-Qur'an that firmly and resolutely forbids or allows interreligious marriage. According to *fiqh*, this absence of reasoning is in itself an argumentation (*adam al-dalil huwa al-dalil*). This means that if there is no text that clearly forbids or commands, then the matter is resolved by referring the case to the original law. One of the *fiqh* norms asserts that in matters regarding *muamalah* such as marriage, the original law is considered *mubah* or permitted (*al-ashl fi al-asyya al-ibahah*).

A law that results from *ijtihad* is then called *fiqh*. *Fiqh* is a formulation of Islamic concepts taken from the Al-Qur'an and Sunnah (the Prophet's tradition), which is why it is not absolute or certain (*qath'i*). Being the result of the human mind's rumination, this conclusion is not guaranteed to be error-free. The conclusion of *ijtihad* is subject to the influence of the socio-cultural and socio-historical context of the surrounding community, or of the period in which the *ulama* lives. Therefore, a conclusion of *ijtihad* cannot be valid for all people and all times. It might be suitable for a certain period of time, but not others, or for a certain society, but not another. In other words, we might accept an *ijtihad*, but this acceptance should not deter us from being critical, or prevent us from accepting a different *ijtihad* conclusion, which turns out to be better for our well-being.

However, in reality, Muslims mostly understand *fiqh* as a religious teaching that is absolute and unconditional. Thus, any effort to change the view of *fiqh* is regarded as a denial of Islamic teaching. This line of thinking is the result of the incapability to distinguish between a religious teaching and its interpretation. Religious teaching comes from a divine revelation and is, therefore, absolute and cannot be changed, while *fiqh* is a result of human logic of the divine revelation, which is relative and can be changed for the good of mankind.

As a believing Muslim woman, I firmly believe that the religious texts contained in Al-Qur'an and Sunnah possess noble and idealistic values. The problem is that when these values interact with the various human cultures, distortions are created in their implementation. These distortions are caused by the difference in the level of intellectuality and the socio-cultural and socio-historical background of each individual. Aside from that, the texts in Al-Qur'an consist of literal and symbolic meanings. The Arabic vocabulary is known to be rich in meaning. A single word can have several meanings, depending on the context.

Multiple interpretations of religious teaching are a certainty to which the Prophet affirmed: *"Ikhtilaf ummati rahmah"* (difference of views among my followers is a blessing). Therefore we must read religious teachings, including those on the issue of interreligious marriage, with wisdom, deep understanding, and an open mind. In other words, new interpretation of religious teaching is encouraged in order to uncover its universal spirit such as the values of fairness, equality, brotherhood, and peace.

In this respect, some Muslims suggest the need for criticisms of the various interpretations of Al-Qur'an, because each explanation is a reflection of the social condition and progress of the society during a certain phase, the level of education, and a vested interest in the interpretation process. Thus the re-actualization and renewal of the interpretation of Islamic teachings must begin from this phase. Basically, the purpose is to obtain a deep understanding of the Islamic texts and not merely to read and explain them repetitively in the same old way.

In the context of re-actualization and renewal of Islamic teachings, we can learn from the experience of a female exegete named A'isyah binti Abdurahman, who was born in Egypt in 1913. She uses the name Binti al-Syathi in her works. For re-interpretation, she developed a method based on theme (*maudu' al-wahid*), which is popularly known as *al-tafsir al-mawdu'iy*. It is known that Muslim exegesis seldom used an inductive method in interpreting Al-Qur'an. This inspired Binti al-Syathi to conduct a re-interpretation of Al-Qur'an. Conducting the interpretation with full responsibility and objectivity, she criticized the traditional method of interpreting Al-Qur'an in her book, *Al-Qur'an wa Tafsir Ashr.*

According to her, there are at least five flaws in the conventional method of interpreting. First, the interpretation of Al-Qur'an is strongly influenced by sectarian views (*al-ta'milah al-ashabiyyah*). Second, the concept produced by the conventional interpretation method seems to be exaggerated. Third, the conventional interpretation is largely influenced by non-Islamic teachings, such as the *Isra'iliyat* point of view. Fourth, Al-Qur'an's miracle or *i'jaz* is seemingly neglected in the conventional method of interpretation. Lastly, the uniqueness and power of Al-Qur'an's rhetoric have escaped the attention of traditional *mufasir* or interpreters of the Al-Qur'an (A'isyah 'Abd al-Rahman binti al-Syati' 1970, p. 24). Besides criticizing, she offers a concrete alternative to the conventional method. An attractive solution in response to contemporary issues such as interfaith marriage is called the cross-referential method, or integral method, which is also called the inductive method. This method is developed based on the theory that asserts that the content of Al-Qur'an is integrated and its parts are inseparable. One part of Al-Qur'an explains another part (*Al-Qur'an yufassiru ba'dhuhu ba'dhan*).

Finally, Binti al-Syathi recommended that the exegesis must understand Al-Qur'an based on the information contained in the holy book itself. This is why, in her interpretation, she emphasized the importance of understanding the words, sentences, and structure of Al-Qur'an. She explained her method in detail using three approaches. First is the emphasis on the importance of understanding the lexical meaning of words in Al-Qur'an. An understanding of the original meaning of the contents of Al-Qur'an can be very helpful to the exegesis in understanding the purpose of the meaning (*al-ma'na al-murad*). Second is the need to study and select all the verses that are related to the subject being discussed. Using this method, Al-Qur'an can freely speak for itself, and this results in an objective interpretation, instead of a subjective one that is laden with vested interest. Third, to master the words, sentences, and structure of Al-Qur'an, we must be aware that some religious texts were revealed in a particular context (*al-siyaq al-khash*), while other texts were revealed in normal circumstances (*al-siyaq al-'am*) (Quraish Shihab 1992, pp. 3–5). In other words, an interpretation must be based on textual and contextual approaches.

From the various views in interpreting Islamic teachings, I come to the conclusion that one must be open-minded in understanding a text, and this includes understanding texts which address interreligious marriage. We must also be aware that these texts were meant for the interest and well-being of human beings, male and female, so that we can benefit from these religious teachings in accordance with the universal mission of Islam as *rahmat lil-alamin*, blessing and love for the entire universe.

CONCLUSION

Interreligious marriage is a logical consequence of the pluralistic society in Indonesia. In dealing with this reality, I recommend that the state make a regulation that can accommodate the aspiration of every party in the community. The Indonesian government must immediately make three changes, namely: change the current Compilation of Islamic Law, revise the current Marriage Law No. 1 1974, and immediately adopt a reformed Law on Civil Registry. Last but not least, several *fatwa* of the Council (MUI) regarding interreligious marriage should be revoked.

As a Muslim woman, I am absolutely convinced that the struggle for social justice did not end with the Prophet or the generation of his companions, but is the common heritage and continuing duty of Muslims of every era. It is in the tradition and spirit of that struggle that I proposed the Counter Legal Draft to the Indonesian people. The proposed draft is a new Islamic Family Law model for Indonesian Muslims and was launched in 2004 by the Team of Gender Mainstreaming in the Ministry of Religious Affairs, which is under my coordination. Articles 52–55 of the draft state that: marriage between a Muslim and a non-Muslim person or interreligious marriage is unconditionally allowed; marriage between a Muslim and a non-Muslim shall be conducted based on the principle of mutual respect and appreciation of rights of freedom to perform their respective religious teachings and belief; before the marriage is performed, the Government shall provide explanation to the groom and bride concerning issues that arise in marriages between a Muslim and non-Muslim so that each party is aware of these issues; in a marriage between Muslim and non-Muslim, children have the right to choose their desired religion and adhere to it; and in the event that the children have not been capable of determining their religion of choice, their religion should be decided by their parents, with mutual consent of parents and children.

Basically, the draft is based on the framework of equality and justice, and it is also grounded in Al-Qur'an and Sunnah, and it proposes a number of novel interpretations of Islamic law on marriage and divorce. The proposed changes, however, are greater than the sum of the parts. Taken together the proposals contained in the draft reflect a fundamentally different conception of marriage and the rights of men and women within marriage than that embodied in the current Compilation. *In uriidu illa al-ishlah mastatha'tu. Wa ma tawfiqy illa billah. Wa Allah a'lam bi al-shawab* (I want nothing but feasible reform. There is no success except with God. And God knows best).

Notes

1. Suhadi Cholil, chapter 5 of this volume, situates the Compilation and the CLD in a political analysis.
2. In these verses, Al-Qur'an states that the *musyrik* are those who worship not only God as the Creator of the earth and the universe, but also worship idols.
3. The *ulama* that fall into this first category are, among others, Umar ibn al-Khaththab, Atha', 'Abdullah ibn Umar, and Muhammad ibn al-Hanafiyah. A more extensive discussion on this matter can be found in Fakhr al-Din al-Razi, *Tafsir Fakhr al-Razi* (Beirut: Dar al-Fakhr, 1995), *juz* 3, p. 62 and *juz* 6, p. 150.
4. However, in reality some cases of interreligious marriage can be registered at the National Civil Registry Office on approval of the National Court.
5. Majelis Ulama Indonesia (MUI) was established on 26 July 1975. MUI is a vehicle for the deliberations of *ulama, umara*, and Muslim intellectuals. The vision of this institution is the creation of healthy and sound condition for social and national life by garnering the participation of Indonesian Muslims and actualizing the potentialities of ulama, *zua'ma*, and Muslim intellectuals for the sake of the glory and prosperity of Islam and Muslims (*izzu al-Islam wa al-Muslimin*). This undertaking is carried out by, among others, providing advice and Islamic legal pronouncement to the government and society on matters pertaining to religious and social issues. This organization has its board of management from

central to village level throughout Indonesia. MUI's central board of management oversees ten committees, one of which is the Committee on *Fatwa*. This Committee is responsible for conducting studies on various religious and social issues emerging within the Muslim community at national or international level, the results of which are then formulated into, and issued in the form of, *fatwa*.

6. Maria Ulfah Anshor dan Martin Sinaga, *Tafsir Ulang Perkawinan Lintas Agama: Perspektif Perempuan dan Pluralisme* (Jakarta: Kapal Perempuan, 2004), pp. 3–19.

7. The *ulama* who fall into this second category are, among others, Said ibn al-Musayyab, ibn 'Abbas, and the Hanabilah people, although there are different opinions among them as to who fits in the category of the *ahlul kitab* mentioned in the verse. See Al-Juzairy *Al-Fiqh ala Al-Madzahib Al-Arba'ah* (Cairo: al-Maktab al-Tsaqafi, 2000), *juz* 4, p. 64.

8. The *ulama* who fall in the third category are, among others, Muhammad Abduh and Rasyid Ridha.

9. Any Muslim, man or woman, who intentionally does not pay *zakat* can be categorized as *musyrik*. See Al-Qur'an 41:7.

10. The complete verdict of the Supreme Justice can be found in S.H. Soedharyo Soimin, *The Law of People and Families: The Perspective of Western Civil Laws/BW, Islamic Laws and Custom Laws*, 2nd ed. (Jakarta: Sinar Grafika, 2004), pp. 98–105.

References

A'isyah 'Abd al-Rahman bint al-Syati'. *Al-Qur'an wa Tafsir Ashr*. Cairo: Dar al-Ma'arif, 1970.

Al-Bukhari. *Al-Jami' Al-Shahih, juz* 5. Beirut: Dar ibn Katsir al-Yamamah, 1987.

Al-Juzairy. *Al-Fiqh ala Al-Madzahib Al-Arba'ah, juz* 4. Cairo: al-Maktab al-Tsaqafi, 2000.

Al-Thabari. *Jami al-Bayan fi Ta'wil Al-Qur'an* vol. 2, p. 390.

Ali al-Shabuni. *Rawa'i Al-Bayan: Tafsir Ayat al-Ahkam*. Mecca: Dar Al-Qur'an al-Karim, t.t., p. 537.

Fakhr al-Din al-Razi. *Tafsir Fakhr al-Razi, juz* 3 & *juz* 6. Beirut: Dar al-Fakhr, 1995.

Ibnu Katsir. *Tafsir Ibn Katsir.*

Ichiyanto. *Mixed Marriages in the Republic of Indonesia.* Jakarta: The Agency for Research and Development of the Ministry of Religious Affairs, 2003.

Mahmud Syaltut. *Min Taujihat Al-Islam.* Cairo: al-Idarah al-'Ammah li al-Azhar, 1959.

Maulana Muhammad 'Ali. *The Holy Qur'an: The Translation and Interpretation of the Arabic Texts* (translation). Jakarta: Dar al-Kutub al-Islamiyah, 1993.

Muhammad Abduh and Rasyid Ridha. *Tafsir Al-Manar.* Beirut: Dar al-Fikr, t.t., p. 193.

Musdah Mulia, Siti. *Polygamy in Islam's Views.* Jakarta: LKAJ, Solidaritas Perempuan and The Asia Foundation, 2000.

Musdah Mulia, Siti with Mark E. Cammack. "Toward a Just Marriage Law: Empowering Indonesian Women through a Counter Legal Draft to the Indonesian Compilation of Islamic Law". In *Islamic Law in Contemporary Indonesia: Ideas and Institutions*, edited by R. Michael Feener and Mark E. Cammack. Cambridge, Mass.: ISLP/Harvard University Press, 2007.

Nuryamin. A Study on the Implementation of the Marriage Law (unpublished). Jakarta: Pusat Studi Wanita, IAIN, 1990.

Quraish Shihab. "The Implementation of the Laws Textually and Contextually: A Musafir's View". *Dialog* 35 (Year 16) (1992): 3–5.

———. *The Scope of the Al-Qur'an.* Bandung: Mizan, 1996.

———. *The Qur'an Encyclopedia: Studies of Vocabulary and the Interpretations.* Jakarta: Bimantara, 1997.

Soedharyo Soimin, S.H. *The Law of People and Families: The Perspective of Western Civil Laws/BW, Islamic Laws and Custom Laws.* 2nd ed. Jakarta: Sinar Grafika, 2004.

Yanggo, Huzaemah Tahido. *Kontroversi Revisi Kompilasi Hukum Islam.* Jakarta: Adelina, 2005.

Chapter 10

MUSLIM-NON-MUSLIM MARRIAGE IN SINGAPORE

Noor Aisha Abdul Rahman

Marriages between Muslims and non-Muslims have attracted little research attention in Singapore. The few studies that exist focus essentially on legal issues within the conflict of law perspective.[1] This chapter seeks to provide another dimension to the study of the phenomenon by examining the dominant *style of thought* of groups who select, interpret, and administer the Muslim personal law bearing on the problem. It also discusses the implications of this mode of thinking on the status and rights of parties and children of such unions. Some plausible measures in alleviating problems arising from the operation of the style of thought will also be discussed.

LAWS GOVERNING MARRIAGE INVOLVING MUSLIMS

Unlike the other religious communities in Singapore, Muslims are bound by a system of personal law which defines their legal rights and obligations in specific areas such as marriage, divorce,

and matters of intestacy. In effect this means that they are subject
to the operation of the Muslim law on these matters, regardless
of their choice and which they cannot relinquish. This position
of Muslims at law in contemporary Singapore reflects continuity
from the colonial era. As early as 1823, Raffles, in laying down
rules for Singapore, had provided that "in all cases regarding the
ceremonies of religion and marriage and rules of inheritance, the
laws and customs of the Malays will be respected where they
shall not be contrary to reason, justice or humanity". Though
the introduction of the Charters of Justice in 1826 and 1855
made the English law and its administration the only applicable
law in Singapore, Muslim personal law was observed via the
Muhammedan Ordinances.[2] This position persisted after
independence with the enactment of the Administration of the
Muslim Law Act (AMLA) in 1966. The AMLA applies to all Muslims
and presumably ceases to have application only in the event of
the Muslim abjuring Islam. It would be erroneous to assume that
the AMLA was a State imposed legislation on the Muslim
community. Select Committee representations to the Bill capture
the consensual sentiments and contributions of prominent
Muslim personalities and groups within the community towards
the substance of the enactment.[3] This indissoluble link between
a Singaporean Muslim and the system of personal law is reinforced
by the existence of provisions within specific national legislation
touching on these areas, which have the effect of expressly
excluding or exempting Muslims from their purview.

By virtue of the operation of the Muslim personal law,
marriages between Muslims are excluded from the purview of the
civil law. The Women's Charter which regulates civil marriages
expressly provides in section 3(4) that no marriage between
persons who are Muslims shall be solemnized or registered under
the Act. Marriages involving Muslims, or in which one of the

parties is a Muslim and solemnized in accordance with the Muslim law, falls under Part 1V of the AMLA.[4] The AMLA empowers the *wali* (guardian) of the women to be wedded or *kadi* (a judge of the religious court) appointed as Registrar of Muslim marriages to solemnize such marriages in accordance with the Muslim law. The *kadi* is directed to satisfy himself that there is no lawful obstacle to the marriage under both Muslim law and the AMLA. It is pertinent to note that what constitutes the "Muslim law" is not defined in that part of the statute. Disputes pertaining to Muslim marriages and divorce are heard and determined by the Syariah Court (SYC) constituted by the AMLA. By virtue of section 35 of the AMLA, the Syariah Court is accorded the jurisdiction to hear disputes pertaining to marriage, nullity, separation, divorce, and ancillary issues arising from divorce where all the parties are Muslims, or where the marriage was contracted under Muslim law.

Muslims, however, may avail themselves to the civil court on certain issues specifically spelt out in the AMLA and the Women's Charter (WC), namely maintenance of wives and children during the subsistence of a marriage, and issues ancillary to divorce, such as custody and division and disposition of matrimonial property. Section 35A(1) and (2) of the AMLA allow Muslim parties and those married under the provisions of the Muslim law, who have commenced divorce proceedings or obtained a divorce order in the SYC, the choice of commencing or continuing proceedings in any court pertaining to the ancillary matters above. The jurisdiction of the High Court, however, is not automatic. For instance, civil proceedings relating to custody which have commenced prior to a divorce proceeding in the Syariah Court may not continue except with leave from the Court or the consent of both parties. Parties who obtained a divorce by mutual consent (*kadi* divorce) can also refer to the civil court for resolution of matters ancillary to divorce. Although the Syariah Court is empowered to declare rights of kin to inheritance of deceased Muslims, jurisdiction to hear and determine disputes pertaining to distribution of estate lies with the civil court. Apart from the Syariah Court, the role of the Legal Committee of the Muslim Religious Council of Singapore (MUIS) is relevant to the discussion. Chaired by the *Mufti*, the Committee's role is to issue legal opinion *(fatwa)* on any point of Muslim law in response to requests by any person or court including the civil court.[5] *Fatwa* on marriages involving Muslims and non-Muslims and related issues have been pronounced by the Committee. Unlike judgements of the Syariah Court, they are only persuasive, but are nevertheless legally binding if accepted by a court as basis for legal judgement.

Civil law, however, does not exclude marriages in which one of the parties is a Muslim. Such a marriage is recognized within the meaning of section 3(4) of the WC. While the marriage is valid under the Charter, it has repercussions on the Muslim party who continues to be bound as a Muslim to some aspects of his personal law. This gives rise to a number of pertinent issues with serious implications for individuals and their families. Major issues of concern include the status of the marriage, determination of law governing distribution of property of the Muslim spouse upon death, legal status of children born out of such unions, and the rights of non-Muslim spouses and children to the estate of the deceased Muslim.

It is pertinent to reiterate that the AMLA, as its title conveys, does not generally lay down the substantive Muslim law in the areas defined under its purview. While the Act essentially regulates and administers the Muslim law, what constitutes the substantive Muslim law that is selected and applied by the relevant groups within the Registry of Muslim Marriage (ROMM), Syariah Court, and the Legal Committee are largely undefined within it. As with other aspects of the Muslim personal law, the Muslim law upheld and applied to interreligious marriage or marriage involving a non-Muslim, is based on selected sources formulated by jurists of the past believed to have been derived from opinions and interpretations of relevant verses of the Qur'an and *Hadith* or Traditions of the Prophet Muhammad and his Companions. Positive law, based on the historical legacy of diverse Muslim societies, constitutes another source of the Muslim law. It is the style of thought expressed in the selection, construction, and application of the Muslim law on mixed marriage involving a Muslim, and their impact, that we seek to examine.

TRADITIONALISM AS STYLE OF THOUGHT

The concept of style of thought has been utilized by Mannheim to analyse the manner in which groups think. Each style of thought is characterized by its value premises, assumptions, and basic categories of thought around which ideas are organized in response to problems that confront the group. A group's style of thought is reflected in its main concepts utilized, the absence of counter concepts, the level of concreteness and abstractness attained by particular ideas, the angle with which particular problems are approached, identification of the problem itself, and the assumptions contained in its ideas. It has been observed that each style of thought has its basic intention, be it to maintain certain conditions, or to destroy, change, adapt, or reform them.[6]

A group's style of thought is conditioned by the philosophy and social position of the bearers. As Mannheim says, "It is never an accident when a certain theory, wholly or in part, fails to develop beyond a given stage of relative abstractness and offers resistance to further tendencies towards becoming more concrete, either by frowning upon this tendency towards concreteness or declaring it to be irrelevant. Here too, the social position of the thinker is significant." (Manheim 1946, p. 248).

Focusing on style of thought as expressed in problems raised or neglected — in responses to, and judgement on, issues pertaining to marriages between Muslims and non-Muslims — contributes to avoiding the common pitfall of according overriding significance to Islam or the Muslim law in diagnosing problems. Such a tendency often misses the crux of the problem, namely the orientations of specific social groups who attempt to make sense of religious values, injunctions, and teachings embodied in religious sources. By focusing on the groups' mode of thinking, we are able not only to identify the source of problems more objectively, but also to avoid entanglement with theological debates that delve into the correctness of theological viewpoints, while allowing for assessment of ramification of ideas of its bearers. In my earlier writings, I have utilized the concept of traditionalism as a style of thought in attempting to grapple with the problems of the Muslim law in various domains (Noor Aisha Abdul Rahman 2004, 2007). The mode of conceiving law affecting Muslim-non-Muslim marriages provides yet another dimension in which traditionalism is by no means insignificant.

In order to avoid confusion, it must be reiterated that the concept of traditionalism differs from tradition. While tradition refers to the corpus of values and principles that shape the world view of a people for a significant period of their cultural history, giving them their sense of identity as a distinct group and providing them the basis for response to future challenges, traditionalism refers to a particular mode of thinking. It is characterized by a dogmatic attitude that clings firmly to old ways, resisting innovation or accepting them only unwillingly (Shaharuddin 1992, pp. 242–43).

As a mode of conceiving and experiencing religion, traditionalism, as Towler explicates, is characterized by a striking sense of obligatoriness, distinguished by the necessity of believing rather than what is believed. This cognitive style reveals uncritical and dogmatic reliance on traditions perceived as holistic, complete, and immutable, the products of pious savants of the past. As Towler noted, its essence is to cherish the entire tradition received as sacred, such that if any part is threatened or called into question, it is the whole pattern which is put at risk. Traditionalism is distinguished by the attitude of unquestioning acceptance of religious traditions that has no place for doubt or uncertainty. Since its main thrust is to keep a whole tradition intact, it is necessarily opposed to any change and is always alert to press attempts at innovation into the established mould.[7]

Perceptions of, and judgement on, Muslim personal law bearing on issues relating to marriages between Muslims and non-Muslims by those who pronounce and administer them, reveal traits of traditionalism in many respects. In their discourse, traditions which are in fact selected from the vast and rich legacy of Muslim legal heritage, assume certainty, finality, and absoluteness. They are upheld without need for justification of the basis of selection amidst other conflicting traditions on similar issues, or differing constructions of similar traditions. This mode of thought is distinguished by a strong tendency to remain bound to specific interpretations or sources in spite of the existence of others that may contradict or undermine its authority. In fact, traditionalists do not even care for the existence or relevance of other authorities as a basis for evaluation or comparisons since overriding importance is given to the application of selective sources. Neither are there attempts at distinguishing the socio-historical basis of traditions from the moral eternal principles and values underlying them. The quest for principles in justifying precepts is at odds with traditionalism whose very essence is unquestioning acceptance. Traditionalism is also unconcerned with the implications and consequences of traditions selected and upheld on the actual lives of people. In applying or appropriating selections of these traditions, traditionalism is revealed in the highly rigid and dogmatic way of conceiving them. Although traditionalists may accommodate change, these are usually imposed on them rather than arising from within its cognitive mould. It is the dominance of traditionalism that conditions problems raised or neglected, the level of abstraction of problems perceived, and the existence of alternative ideas and views in the domain of marriages involving Muslims and non-Muslims.

Certain developments in the legal history of the Singapore Muslim community common to the experience of other previously colonized Muslim societies have reinforced the predominance of traditionalism within the domain of the Muslim personal law. A major factor is the institutionalization of the personal law isolated from the English law that regulated all other aspects of life during the colonial period. This arrangement reinforced traditionalism as it arrested the evolution of the Muslim personal law, insulating it from the dynamism of contemporary life and conditions. While innovation, modification, and reform to the English law in response to radical socio-economic transformations brought about by industrialization and capitalism were evident, the Muslim personal law remains embedded in archaic social relations and concepts. It is also pertinent to add that the law came to be enforced under the centralized authority of the state while remaining immune to the constitutional and other requirements of the rest of the apparatus of the state that had been introduced since then. Thus while the Constitution enshrines fundamental liberties accorded to the individual, he remains bound to a system of personal law, even if it means the curtailment of the right of choice of law within the State. An-Naim (2005, pp. 24–25) maintains that the process is incongruent with the early development of the formation of the Muslim law, which occurred in informal settings of mosques and homes and which had interacted dynamically with the ethnic and cultural affiliations, historical experiences, economic relations, political and security concerns among Muslims, and between them and non-Muslims. The Muslim law characterized then by vast jurisprudential diversity in schools of thought, as well as a variety of opinions within the same school, gained acceptance in the early period over time, rather than by way of enforcement as positive law emanating from a centrally organized political organ.

Traditionalism expressed in the unchanging perception of personal law was also reinforced by the fact that the modernization of the Malays was thrust upon them by an external authority. It was not preceded by internal democratization and reform, which would have ushered a philosophical revision of values emerging from forces within. Thus it is not unjustified to say that for the Malay society, to a large extent, the world view of the past survives intact with repercussions in the domain of religion. It continued to be shielded from the influence of capitalism and industrialization and their accompanying structural and philosophical revision of values, which placed importance on reason, individualism and democracy.[8] The absence of these precipitating elements, which would have contributed to the development of intellectual and humanistic tradition, left its impact in the domain of Muslim personal law. It impeded the development of a systematic legal methodology that involved the process of weighing and balancing the core values of syariah in pursuit of a moral life (El Fadl 2001, p. 268). Attitude to religious traditions is generally marked by what Fadl refers to as authoritarian hermeneutics, characterized by a dominant group assuming finality of their views, which are upheld as representing the authentic Islamic tradition. These are pronounced as "self evident" truths based on the overriding assumption that God's words are clear and the guardians of religion hold the key to these truths. In this mode of thinking, legal methodological approaches that place significance on rational discourse by developing arguments, justifying standpoints, examining socio-historical bases, reconciling or rejecting sources based on clear guiding principles in the light of present dilemmas and conflicts, are underdeveloped.

TRADITIONALISM AND ITS OPERATION IN INTERRELIGIOUS MARRIAGE

Marriage as Sacrament

A major manifestation of traditionalism bearing on Muslim-non-Muslim marriage is the notion that in Islam marriage is a sacrament, an act of worship, which requires both parties to proclaim their common faith. Hence it is more than a mere legal contract that binds consenting parties.[9] This standpoint applies without distinction to civil marriages in which only one of the parties is a Muslim, and those in which both are Muslims. Such a dominant perception is reflected, for instance, in a legal opinion (*fatwa*) enunciated by MUIS in response to a question by a member of the public who wished to know whether a Muslim married under the civil law falls outside the fold of Islam (MUIS 1991, p. 17). (Issued by the highest official representatives of Islam in the State, *fatwa* are powerful instruments in shaping opinions, perceptions, and even law.) The *fatwa* declared to the effect that though a civil marriage is a valid marriage in accordance with the law of the State, it is inadmissible in Islam. Hence it is deemed *haram* (sinful). Relations arising from such unions are considered adulterous. Similarly the offspring of such marriages are deemed to have been born out of wedlock. If a party, though aware of this law, chooses to enter into a civil marriage based on the belief that the marriage is permissible, then it follows that that party falls outside the fold of Islam. This is because whosoever permits what has been prohibited falls outside the fold of Islam. However, if a party who contracts a civil marriage continues to regard the marriage as forbidden, he/she commits a grave sin of adultery, but remains within the fold of Islam. Invoking the notion of "consensus of legal scholars" the *fatwa* adds that whosoever commits a grave sin is not deemed an apostate, but will be punished as *fasik* (*one who ignores what is revealed*) and will die in a sinful state.[10]

Though alternative perceptions of marriage as a contract bound by conditions and principles that bind consenting parties exist in Muslim juristic thought, these are ignored in the *fatwa* which makes no distinction between civil marriages in which only one of the parties is a Muslim, and those in which both are Muslims. The selective interpretation is portrayed as if the law on this issue is absolute and final. An interview with officials from the Office of the Mufti reveals that the possibility of rethinking on the status of civil marriage is remote, because in Islam, marriage is a religious matter.[11] It can be argued that the style of thought discerned reveals the characteristics of traditionalism manifested in the absence of systematic and rational justifications for the position upheld on the basis of clear principles and values of Islam. What is pronounced as law assumes a position of finality and immutability. Consistent with the traits of traditionalism, the pronouncement also reveals the absence of consideration for the implications of the *fatwa* on the status of multitudes of Muslims who are subjected to an inclusive civil legal system governing marriages. By implication these marriages are unlawful.

The traditionalistic response lies in advocating re-solemnization according to Islamic rites after the civil marriage has been performed to confer validity on the marriage.

Traditionalism is further manifested in the lack of consideration for contrary opinions on the matter at issue. Several prominent Muslim scholars are known to uphold the view that such marriages are indeed valid from the point of view of religious teachings. For instance, Faiz Badruddin Tyabji, the prominent Indian judge, in his book *Principles of Muhammedan Law*, submits that marriage in Muhammedan law is purely a civil contract (Tyabji 1919, p. 94). That the civil law on marriage does not violate religious tenets of Islam has also been opined by several other Indian scholars who had advocated for the operation of the Special Marriage Act (1954) in India, a secular piece of legislation for Indian Muslims as an alternative to the Muslim personal law. Essentially their views convey the argument that the procedure of civil marriage is no different from *nikah* (solemnization) except that there is no *khutbah* (sermon) in a civil marriage, which they submit, is in any case, not obligatory in Islam. Tahir Mahmood, for instance, maintained that "the Islamic law of marriage, devoid of customary rituals and interpreted in its true spirit, will not find itself violated by the Special Marriage Act".[12] Islam, according to the jurist, does not treat marriage as a sacrament. On the contrary it has always considered marriage a secular activity. Justification for this principle is also found in the argument that the Muslim law of marriage allows parties the freedom to choose their own marriage conditions. Furthermore, it is maintained that some schools of law do not require a religious ceremony as only free consent of both parties (under Hanafi law, to be exchanged in the presence of witnesses) and the dower is necessary. Although in civil marriages, polygamy and extrajudicial divorce are not permissible, unlike Muslim marriage law, it has been argued that neither of these is a "must" in Islam. On the contrary both are discouraged in Islam.[13] The dominance of traditionalism on the perception of civil marriage is marked by the conclusion made in advance of what are perceived as "self-evident truths without need for rationalizing or justifying one's position in relation to other views advanced on the issue". Marriage under civil law, whether interreligious or otherwise, is simply not permissible to Muslims.

The overriding emphasis on application of selective traditions circumscribes the level of abstraction of problems. An instance is provided in the approach adopted by the ROMM in cases of conversion to Islam after parties had entered into a civil marriage. In such cases parties were made to re-solemnize, this time according to Islamic rites, without due consideration for implications on the subsisting marriage. It is clear that since the first marriage has not been terminated, the issue of which system of law should apply in case of disputes remained. The cases of Noor Azizan bte. Colony (alias Noor Azizan bte. Mohamed Noor) v Tan Lip Chin (alias Izak Tan) [2006] SGHC 121 and Rosenah bte. Ahmad v Mitsuru Sakano [Divorce Petition No. 602424 of 2001] highlight the problem. In both these cases, the Muslim wives had married non-Muslims under the WC. Subsequently their husbands converted to Islam. The couples then went through Muslim marriages at the ROMM, and in Rosenah's case, the marriage was registered by the *kadi*. Unfortunately in both these cases, the marriages broke down and the Syariah Court issued decrees dissolving their marriages. However, the marriages contracted under civil law remain. Although in both these cases the High Court judges resolved the matter by affirming the ruling of the Syariah Court as that of a court of competent jurisdiction which had, by virtue of section 35 of the AMLA, the right to "hear and determine all matters of marriage in which all the parties are Muslims or where the parties were married under the provisions of the Muslim law", the issue of concern to us is the decision of ROMM to allow parties to solemnize and register the marriage whilst the one contracted under the civil law subsisted. Characteristic of traditionalism, the decisions of the *kadi* reveal an overriding concern with implementing selected religious sources without much consideration for deliberation about their implications for the legalities of the first marriage.

DEFINITION OF *KITABIYAH* (PEOPLE OF THE BOOK)

An extension of traditionalism lies in the selection and application of a restrictive interpretation of a *kitabiyah* as evident in the judgement by consent of the Singapore Syariah Court in the case of Abdul Razak vs Lisia binte Mandagie alias Maria Mernado (SYC No. 42/1964). In that case, the Syariah Court declared that the marriage between the couple was void as the wife was, at the time of marriage, a Christian whose ancestors had converted to Christianity after the coming of the Prophet Muhammad.[14]

The fact that the court subscribed to an opinion which contradicts dominant rulings on the issue without providing any justification illustrates the persistence of traditionalism. Generally, scholars maintain that according to the Sunni school of law, a Muslim man may marry a Muslim woman or a *kitabiyah*; a *kitabiyah* being defined as a woman who believes in a heavenly or revealed religion. Under both the Sunni and Shiite schools, a Muslim man is prohibited from marrying a non-*kitabiyah*. These include those who do not believe in any prophets or holy scriptures, the atheists, the idolators, and the worshippers of the sun or stars. Contrary opinions exist between the Sunnis and Shiite on marriages to Magians. According to some Shiite jurists, a Magi woman falls into the category of the people of the Book, while dominant Sunni juristic opinion deems her otherwise.

The general opinion of the permissibility of a marriage between a Muslim male and a *kitabiyah* is based on a number of apparently categorical verses and traditions ascribed to the Prophet Muhammad. The Qur'anic Sura Maida, verse 5, is often cited in support for this view. It stipulates, "This day are all good things made lawful for you. The food of those who have received the scripture is lawful to you and your food is lawful to them. And so are the virtuous women of the believers and the virtuous women of those who received the scripture before you (lawful to you) when you give them their marriage portion and live with them in honor, not in fornication, nor taking them as secret concubines." The general opinion is reflected in the legal codes of many contemporary Muslim states.

Traditionalism is also manifested in the lack of significance accorded to socio-historical conditions in which rulings were formulated that would have provided an evaluation of the law in context. This is indeed an important principle in Muslim legal methodology since "Muslim law seeks to serve the needs of men and not for the glorification of the Lawgiver" (Abdur Rahim 1963, p. 43). Muslim law is thus not a mechanical bundle of decrees administered without relation to its purpose and effects in society. Thus the Caliph Ali in his instruction to his judge, Abu Musa al-Ashari, emphasized the importance of reasoning in seeking judgement that is just (Ramadan 1970, p. 25). To a large extent, legal opinions on marriages to non-Muslims espoused by Muslim jurists were conditioned by socio-political conditions. However, the judgement in Razak's case mirrors the perception that law is absolute and cannot be changed, without relation to the conditions and problems of society. As the then Attorney General, Ahmad Ibrahim, in responding to the judgement above conveyed:

> it is undoubtedly true that marriage with a non-Muslim is frowned upon in Muslim law. The reasons for this as pointed out by Syed Ameer Ali are largely historical. Difference of religion implied in earlier times hostility to the commonwealth of Islam and apostasy was regarded as tantamount to treason. In modern society in which Muslims and non-Muslims live together in fraternity as fellow citizens of the state with equal rights and responsibilities it seems fair and equitable that men and women of full age should have the right to marry and have a family without any limitation due to race, nationality or religion; and so it is provided in the universal declaration of human rights. It is perhaps a matter of regret that the Shariah Court in Singapore has sanctioned rather arbitrarily, a view on this matter which is even more restrictive than is generally believed to be the case under the Muslim law (Ahmad Ibrahim 1965, p. 68).

Traditionalism is also evident in the lack of reflection on the implications of judgements arising from overriding importance accorded to the letter of the law. This occurs with respect to the matter of proof. The ruling suggests strongly that the Christian wife is in a position to be able to prove whether her ancestors were Christians before the arrival of Islam, with a presumption in favour of those who fall into this category as against those who do not. Yet, how the party is to satisfy the burden of proof imposed upon her in those circumstances was not considered. As Hickling rightly observed, "it is one thing to prove that one's ancestors have not embraced a particular religion say after 622AD and another thing to prove that they have done so before that date but in each case the burden seems so impossible as to be almost incredible" (Hickling 1979, p. 68).

The *fatwa* and Syariah Court ruling on the validity of a marriage between a Muslim and a *kitabiyah* in the above case does not provide principles that justify departures from contrary opinions. Such a view, however, is reflective of influential theological opinions, such as that espoused by the prominent theologian Yusuf Qardawi. Qardawi opined that in order of preference, a Muslim woman regardless of her merits, is better suited to a Muslim man than a woman of Christian or Jewish faith. If a Muslim man suspects that a non-Muslim wife might affect the beliefs and attitudes of his children, it becomes obligatory on him to exercise caution. Furthermore, Qardawi is also of the view that if the number of Muslims in a country is small — such as in the case of Muslim migrants residing in a non-Muslim country — their men ought to be prohibited from marrying non-Muslim women because, since Muslim women are prohibited from marrying non-Muslim men, marriages occurring between Muslim men and non-Muslim women will mean that many Muslim women will remain unmarried. This situation, deemed disadvantageous to Muslim society, can be avoided by temporarily suspending the permission for Muslim men to marry non-Muslim women (Qardawi 1980, pp. 250–52).[15] That a marriage to a *kitabiyah* is not deemed valid in Singapore, in which the Muslim community is a minority, may be due to the influence of such theological opinions. The adherence to a highly circumscribed definition of a *kitabiyah* at the expense of others, without justification on the basis of religious values, manifests the traits of traditionalism. This position reveals a belief that presupposes undisclosed assumptions about the "other" from which conclusions are then made in advance about their ability to achieve objectives of a marriage in Islam. The logic in this style of thought is thus based on "self-evident" truths instead of attempting to develop principles in support of the ruling. There is certainly an absence of attempts to reconcile the rather exclusive attitude towards the "other" with the universal values of Islam. The ruling also stands in contrast to existing laws and practices of many Muslim states, past and present, without justifications.

This absence of clear guiding principles limits the ability to conceive implications of views upheld. For instance, prohibiting Muslim-non-Muslim marriage will not stop those who, for a variety of reasons, take on spouses from outside their religious community in violation of such prescriptions. The problem then is the legal alternative available to couples in such circumstances. Grappling with these problems does not feature in traditionalism in which there are no alternatives except, presumably, severance of relations or excommunication. Efforts at providing measures to alleviate problems arising from the occurrences of such marriages do not arise from within this mode of thought. Although an amendment to the WC 1961 was made to allow for the recognition of marriages in which one of the parties is a Muslim, this was not spearheaded by the traditionalists. The framers of the AMLA itself had incorporated section 89 which presumably contemplated marriages between a Muslim male and a *kitabiyah* (broader concept) under Muslim law. This section stipulates that the provisions of the Act shall apply to marriages in which one or both of the parties profess the Muslim religion and which have been solemnized in accordance with the Muslim law. Although implied recognition was accorded to such unions, it has been noted by the Attorney General, Ahmad Ibrahim, that the *kadi* had refused to solemnize these marriages, a position reinforced by the Syariah Court ruling in Abdul Razak's case. The example provides an instance in which the law, even if clearly formulated, could not achieve its intent in the hands of the traditionalists. Thus in addressing the problem, the Attorney-General advocated that the WC be amended to include such marriages, adding that such a provision in the Charter would also allow for marriages between Muslim men and non-Muslim women who are not *kitabiyah*.[16]

Yet another manifestation of traditionalism is evident in the basis of the theological view that it is *haram* (not permissible) for females to contract a marriage with a *kitabi*, an inference from selected Quranic verses (Al-Qur'an 2:221; Al-Qur'an 60:10). Argument utilized for the prohibition rests strongly on the assumption that a man has guardianship over the woman, thereby the husband over his wife in marital relations. This doctrine is also believed to follow necessarily from the general verses that establish the guardianship of Muslims over non-Muslims, which is taken to mean that a non-Muslim man should not have guardianship over a Muslim woman, which would necessarily be the case when he marries her. Such basis reflects traditional sex role differentiation which may not necessarily mirror dynamic changes in family relations and expectations of marital life today. Furthermore, it is also based on the assumption that a wife is more susceptible to influence by her husband than *vice versa*. This rationale, as Naim maintains, is part of a wider sociological phenomenon, namely, the lack of confidence in a woman's integrity and good judgement (An-Naim 1998, p. 235). As Tahir Mahmood submits, although Islam has made an improvement by allowing its followers to seek marriage partners among scriptural (*kitabiyah*) communities, the traditionalistic interpretation under which the concept of *kitabiyah* was greatly restricted, denied women the freedom to marry even those men whose religions were recognized as *kitabi* (Mahmood 1978, pp. 62–63). It is without doubt that while there have been reforms in the personal laws of Muslims, the influence of traditionalism remains significant in perceptions of women's rights in marriage.

EFFECT OF CIVIL MARRIAGE AND CONVERSION ON STATUS OF SPOUSES AND CHILDREN AND THEIR RIGHTS TO INHERITANCE

Traditionalism is also evident in *fatwa* and judgement passed on the rights of non-Muslim family members to the estate of a deceased Muslim. Problems arise in cases involving marriages solemnized under the Muslim law where the surviving spouse had renounced Islam during the subsistence of a marriage. It can also occur in cases where the deceased Muslim had married under the WC. Section 112(1) of the AMLA states that in the case of any Muslim domiciled in Singapore dying intestate, the estate and effects shall be distributed according to the Muslim law as modified, where applicable, by Malay custom. The question at issue, therefore, is whether Muslim law allows a non-Muslim spouse the right to inherit the property of a deceased Muslim. Dominant religious opinion on this issue is in the negative, unless the testator left a will in favour of the surviving beneficiary. According to this view, the Muslim law allows a person to will away one-third of his property to whosoever he wishes, a position recognized in Singapore (Ahmad Ibrahim 1976, p. 15).

An interview with officials of the office of the Mufti reveals that the issue of concern is whether the surviving relatives were Muslims at the time of death of the Muslim party.[17] Non-Muslim kin will not be able to inherit the deceased Muslim's property except that which has been willed to them. If a Muslim dies without a will in favour of his non-Muslim beneficiaries, his property reverts to the *baitul mal* or public fund administered by MUIS. The application of selective rules at the expense of underlying principles, characteristic of traditionalism, clouds inconsistencies in judgement. Two relevant *fatwa* passed by the Legal Committee, based on traditions ascribed to the Prophet

Muhammad, are overlooked in determining the issue. The first pronounces that a non-Muslim cannot inherit the property of a Muslim, likewise a Muslim, the property of a non-Muslim (MUIS 1991, p. 16). The *fatwa* was enunciated in response to the question as to whether a non-Muslim wife married to a Muslim under civil law can inherit her husband's property. The other *fatwa*, discussed earlier, relates to the position that a Muslim who willingly contracts a marriage with a non-Muslim under the civil law is outside the fold of Islam. Logically it should then follow that no Muslim person or organization (including MUIS) should have any claims over the property of one who has contracted a civil marriage as that person is deemed to have fallen outside the fold of Islam. The property belonging to him/her should revert to the surviving non-Muslim spouse and children. However, the emphasis on application of specific rules at the expense of their full implications in relation to other rulings creates unwarranted inconsistencies. It also conditions the neglect of principles prescribed by the religion, such as justice and compassion and its consequences on the lives of those involved.

In Singapore the legal forum for disputes pertaining to matters of inheritance is the High Court since the Syariah Court is not accorded jurisdiction to preside over the matter. Where it involves a Muslim, the law that will be applied by the Court is presumably the Muslim law by virtue of section 112(1) AMLA. Within this domain, it is not unlikely that the dominant opinion in Muslim law discussed above will hold sway in the event of a dispute.

An extension of the implication of this mode of thinking is also revealed in the perception of rights of children born in a civil marriage to inherit their Muslim father's estate. Dominant views express the position that such children cannot inherit the property of their Muslim father according to the *faraid* (injunction, statutory portion, lawful share). This stems from the view pertaining to the status and validity of a civil marriage. Children born out of such perceived unlawful union are deemed illegitimate. This opinion is expounded without attempts at evaluating its repercussions on fundamental ethical values of compassion to orphans and human welfare generally prescribed by Islam.

The matter is complicated by the influence of traditionalism in perceptions of paternity and matter of proof. Paternity is denied since the union was created outside the bounds of a valid marriage recognized in Islam. Furthermore, proof of paternity by admitting modern evidence such as DNA does not feature in this style of thought. Thus while the adoption of new scientific procedures have been widely accepted, it remains questionable within the mode of traditionalism. Equally pertinent is the lack of consideration for the implications of the judgement on the child and mother. The opinion is at odds with the principle of justice since it has the effect of limiting the responsibility for the child to the mother while the father is absolved from duties and obligations. Such implications do not fall within the radius of vision of traditionalists. Even worse, the opinion can logically result in bizarre consequences as it implies that a father can marry his daughter borne from his union with the child's mother since paternity cannot be ascertained. The possibility of incest following from this reasoning is conditioned by the overriding tendency to cherish the letter of selected traditions at the expense of deliberating upon principles and effects of rulings on human lives.

Within this mode of thought, legitimacy of a child is deemed to be dependent solely on the mother. The biological link with the mother, it has been argued, is indisputable since it is the mother who has given birth to the child and nourishes him/her through breastfeeding, for instance. Thus, if the mother is a non-Muslim so would the child be until such time when the latter can make a rational choice pertaining to his or her religious preference. The situation is the reverse if the mother is a Muslim, in which case the child would automatically be a Muslim. However since a civil law marriage is deemed invalid in the eyes of the traditionalists, the status of the child is put to question.

The problem of non-recognition of civil marriages and its impact on paternity gives rise to other related concerns. A Muslim father who is not considered the lawful father is prohibited from being the *wali* (guardian) for his daughter. In cases where the father as *wali*, solemnizes his daughter's marriage, the marriage has been declared as void. The daughter is then made to undergo another marriage ceremony, this time with the *kadi* as *wali*. Repercussions arising out of this traditionalistic orientation on the issue of paternity can be serious if, for instance, the daughter had given birth to a child without having gone through a remarriage. The marriage, deemed void, gives rise to problems pertaining to the status of her child.

It is pertinent to note that while upholding the letter of selected laws regardless of their implications, in practice, traditionalists have in most cases been forthcoming in granting property of deceased Muslims to their non-Muslim surviving spouses and children. Children of parties who remain in the civil marriage after converting to Islam have also benefited from their parents' estate as have non-Muslim parents and siblings of a deceased Muslim convert.[18] Thus, although traditionalists uphold these laws and will not call for their modification or change, they tamper with their harsh effects in actual cases that come before them. However, traits of traditionalism remain as rights of beneficiaries are not deduced from rethinking of the law in which clear, guiding principles are formulated, but are accorded based on a sense of sympathy and compassion for those affected by the operative rulings.

Though honourable, the attitude is, nonetheless, a reflection of traditionalism. It reveals unquestioning acceptance of selective legal authorites which, applied literally, can undermine humanitarian values prescribed by Islam, particularly the emphasis on justice to widows and orphans, irrespective of religious affiliations. Despite consistent efforts at overriding the literal effect of the law and tampering with its harshness, the dominance of traditionalism weighs heavily against proactive change involving a review of the laws as selected and applied. Hence, though extra-legal means can be adopted to deal with the effects of selective authorities, these are deemed immutable and not subject to reform.

APPROACHES TO REMEDIAL MEASURES

Traditionalism is also manifested in the approach adopted by MUIS in the resolution of appeals by non-Muslim surviving spouses/children of civil marriages or those who have converted to Islam upon marriage, but subsequently abjure the religion. Such appeals are usually heard and deliberated by the Office of the Mufti.[19] While emphasis is given to humane principles and compassion in arriving at decisions, there is a lack of systematic guiding principles that are institutionalized as bases for allowing or rejecting appeals. This reflects a traditionalist mode of administration.

Advice dispensed to couples married or intending to enter into civil marriages provides another manifestation of the traits of traditionalism. For instance, some religious officials advise parties to create the instrument of *nuzriah* (vow) that will allow a surviving non-Muslim spouse to inherit the property of the deceased Muslim to avoid potential disputes. It is important to note that not long ago, the High Court had heard and determined a dispute pertaining to the validity of the *nuzriah* created by a testator. Justice MPH Ruben who presided over the case declared that the *nuzriah* in that case was void as it transgressed restrictions imposed by the Muslim law of inheritance.[20] Though the decision was passed by a court of competent jurisdiction in Singapore, recourse to the use of the instrument continues to be sanctioned. Consistent with the traits of traditionalism that adheres uncritically to selective religious authorities, this approach not only ignores reasoning that forms the basis of judgement in rejecting *nuzriah*, it also reveals the lack of significance accorded to the legal judgement on this issue. This can give rise to misleading advice with implications on rights of parties involved.

Yet another manifestation of traditionalism lies in the measures adopted by MUIS to deal with Muslims who decide to enter into civil marriages. It is the general practice for MUIS to accord itself the obligation of calling on the Muslim party for counselling once notice of civil marriage involving a Muslim party is posted at the registry of marriages.[21] Feedback from religious officials from the Office of Mufti reveals that the overriding objective is not to police these Muslims as assumed by some quarters, since counselling is purely voluntary. The aim is to provide guidance and advice to parties based on the assumption that they are unaware of the implications of a civil marriage in the eyes of Muslim law and its repercussions on their rights as well as those of the children. This paternalistic approach reveals the traits of traditionalism which provides little scope, if any, for individual judgement and decision. Traditionalism is also manifested in the persistence of the policy despite limited response and no shows by parties affected. The usefulness of its purpose is doubtful and can be achieved in other perhaps more effective ways.

ISSUES FOR CONSIDERATION

While there have been reforms in the personal law of Muslims to some extent, traditionalism continues to operate in the manner in which these laws are understood, interpreted, and applied. The struggle in battling the ill effects of traditionalism on the development of Muslim personal law, in particular the issue of marriage to non-Muslims, has engaged much debate amongst Muslim thinkers. Some have advocated systematic legal methodology, based on guiding principles infused with moral assessments and rationality. Others, taking the position that historical syariah on non-Muslims is no longer justified in the light of contemporary conditions, propose an alternative foundation within the Islamic tradition and the context of contemporary realities.[22] These contributions, though not specific to the context of Singapore, provide highly useful and relevant insights that can serve as principles for law making and reform to Muslim law as applied here. Nevertheless more specific proposals for legal amendment on the issues in point can assist in curtailing some of the unwarranted effects of traditionalism.

One possible measure is to synchronize marriage law under the WC affecting Muslims with the law governing inheritance. The above discussion reveals that a Muslim who marries a non-Muslim continues to be bound to the Muslim law governing inheritance by virtue of his identity as a Muslim. This gives rise to a gamut of problems involving the rights of the surviving non-Muslim kin, including spouse and children, to his/her estate. Thus far, the community has not been confronted with legal conflicts arising from this arrangement. Problems that have occurred have been resolved in largely non-contentious ways outside the scope of the judicial system. However, legal inconsistency in this area has given room for the force of traditionalism with all its attendant ramifications. While problems have been resolved behind closed doors, so to speak, exempting the Muslim of a civil marriage from the operation of the Muslim personal law in the matter of inheritance would go a long way to avoid potential disputes and conflicts, apart from ensuring greater transparency and certainty in the law. This change is to be seriously considered since inheritance is indivisibly linked to rights of children and surviving spouse. Both the Wills Act as well as the AMLA should be amended to achieve this effect. The AMLA can be modified to provide Muslims married under the WC the option to use Islamic law or otherwise. The Wills Act should be inclusive, so as to allow a Muslim to dispose of his property as he wishes, including having recourse to the Muslim law of inheritance (*faraid*). This was, in fact, the legal position until the coming into force of the Muslim Ordinance 1957 (Ahmad Ibrahim 1976, p. 32). Should a Muslim wish to exercise the right to will away his/her entire estate according to the *faraid*, the arrangement ought to be recognized as valid. This will allow Muslims the choice of law without being inevitably bound by Muslim law *per se*.

Alternatively, law-makers may consider reinstating a proviso within the AMLA similar to the one found in the Muhammedan Amendment Ordinance (No. 26 of 1923), which allowed for the operation of Muslim law on inheritance on a Muslim dying intestate, while simultaneously including the proviso to the effect that any next of kin, not a Muslim, shall be entitled to share in the distribution of the estate as though he were a Muslim. This provision prevailed until it was removed in the Muslim Amendment Ordinance 1960. The change was initiated by a number of Muslims in Singapore through the Muslim Advisory Board. While some members of the Select Committee hesitated to abolish the proviso as they perceived the urgings as an interpretation of a particular school of Muslim law, the amended ordinance gave effect to the proposal.

Law-makers can also consider the possibility of allowing disputes pertaining to the status of marriage, as well as those ancillary to divorce, such as custody, and division and disposition of property currently heard and determined by the Syariah Court, to be heard in the civil court in cases where they involve conversion or apostasy of any party to the marriage or allegations of these. This proposal should be seriously considered to provide a neutral ground in which the best interests of the parties and their offspring can be considered. Undoubtedly, the welfare of the child is paramount and is the overriding consideration in both Muslim and civil law. Under the AMLA, the High Court's jurisdiction to hear matters of custody and property upon divorce affecting Muslim parties or parties married under the Muslim law, is not completely ousted, which implies acknowledgement of commonality of principles in the matter. The jurisdiction of the High Court, however, is not automatic, subjected as it is to certain preconditions stipulated in section 35A of the AMLA.

In cases involving apostasy, the Syariah Court's jurisdiction to hear and determine disputes over custody can mean that overriding consideration is given to the factor of religious affiliation of the parents in light of the principle of welfare of the child.[23] It is generally recognized within the Shafie school that while the mother has the right to custody of her children, her preferential right is lost in the event of her abjuration of Islam. The essence of this principle is also embodied in a *fatwa* of MUIS published in MUIS's newsletter *Warita* (March–May 1977). While the principle of giving overriding importance to the interest and welfare of the child is no doubt supreme in Muslim law, this guiding principle may give way to fixed determination of rules within traditionalism. Hence, the civil court may provide a more neutral forum in determining the rights of the parties without compromising the guiding principle, namely, the best interest of the child. As Wee in elaborating the principle underlying custody maintains, "Customary practices and religious tenets of the various communities are regarded as relevant but they must give way if the welfare of the child so demands. It is also clear that the welfare of the infant is not simply the first among a list of considerations — it is the overriding criterion, which, after every other relevant interest has been considered, must be satisfied." (Wee Kim-Seng 1976, p. 44).[24]

Yet another consideration in curtailing the influence of traditionalism is by allowing Muslims the option of registering their marriage under the WC should they choose to. Currently, this right is extended to cases in which one of the parties is a Muslim. The WC should be extended to include cases where both parties to the marriage are Muslims. This position will give the Muslims as citizens of the state the right of being subjected to legislation of their choice for reasons best known to themselves. This does not mean that the Muslim law is no longer applicable or that it should be subsumed in a very minimum way into secular law. It is reiterated that the effect of providing the option does not eradicate Muslim law, it merely gives Muslims the right of choice of law.

Further support for this view is found in the argument that, to a large extent, Muslim personal law in Singapore has dynamically assimilated and interacted with the civil law and judicial system. The assimilation of civil law principles and procedures in the application of the Muslim law reinforces the argument that congruence exists in respect of values and guiding principles. It cannot be doubted, for instance, that laws pertaining to custody of children do abide by similar consideration, namely the welfare of the child. In the case of the division of property upon divorce, the amendment to the relevant provisions of the AMLA in 2000 has largely assimilated factors stipulated in the WC. Furthermore, Muslims divorced by mutual consent have long resorted to the civil court for settlement of their ancillary claims, as the Syariah Court until the recent amendment in 2000 did not have the power or jurisdiction to hear and determine disputes on matters ancillary to divorce by mutual consent. Furthermore, the Syariah Court has all along permitted applications to have ancillary matters heard in the High Court, either because of the limited power of the Court, including its power to enforce its orders, or because the Court found no objection to the legal forum which parties chose. Furthermore, maintenance of wives during the subsistence of marriage and that of children have thus far been heard and enforced by the civil court. It is also inevitable that judges appointed to the Board of Appeal, many of whom are trained in civil law, have incorporated guiding principles, mode of reasoning, and sources from their experience and expertise in the practice of the civil law. Given the extent of influence, assimilation, and interdependence between the two legal systems, members within the community who wish to avail themselves of the civil law governing marriage, divorce, and family issues, should not be impeded if they so wish.

It is needless to say that such a development may find opposition. The secular basis of the state may give rise to disapproval against what is perceived as interference in the religious affairs of the community. However the State must also ensure and facilitate the right of the individual to his choice of law. This exercise of the individual right of judgement is a fundamental principle in Islamic teachings. Each and every person is solely responsible for his or her own actions and beliefs. Because accountability is individual, no one is expected to shoulder the decisions and judgement of another. It is this emphasis on individual judgement that has contributed to the rich jurisprudential diversity in Muslim legal heritage.

Notes

1. See for instance the writings of G.W. Bartholomew (1964), R.H. Hickling (1979), Balasubramaniam Reddy (1977), Ahmad Ibrahim (1965), Daw (1972).
2. Though the introduction of the Charters of Justice made English law the only applicable law, the British gradually recognized and applied the Muslim law in areas pertaining to marriages and divorces. Muslim property law was recognized via s27 of the Muhammedan Marriage Ordinance 1880. In 1923, Muslim law on inheritance was introduced by virtue of ordinance 26. Similarly although wills made by Muslims were initially construed according to the principles of English law, these were gradually replaced by the Muslim law. Ahmad Ibrahim MLJ (1965, pp. 3–11). British colonial acknowledgement of religious laws governing family and succession matters was preceded by the Indian experience. For a discussion on the rationale for this policy in India, refer to Tahir Mahmood (1977, pp. 6–10).
3. Select Committee Proceedings, AMLA 1966.
4. AMLA, section 89.
5. AMLA, section 32(7).
6. For a discussion on this theme, refer to Mannheim, "Conservative Thought", in *Essays on Sociology and Social Psychology* (London: Routledge, 1966).
7. The concept of traditionalism in the domain of religion is discussed in Towler (1984, pp. 80–93).
8. As Maaruf (1998, p. 89) observed, "The development of humanism did not take the same path as the West. There was no revolt in SEA against the shackle of religion or the church in the name of liberating and emancipating man. There was no development of philosophy with a clear idea of the centrality of man in the universe. There was also no major phase marked by humanistic optimism or the ideal of progress. Strictly speaking, there was no development of rationalism

in the philosophic sense on the historical plane. In terms of intellectual and scientific tradition, SEA cannot claim to have much. Though humanistic philosophy was not totally non-existent in SEA, its nature and development is different from the western experience. Social philosophy or ethics was never fully secularised as there was no philosophy that makes man the centre and point of reference. In this regard, Southeast Asian humanism remains within the fold and mould of religion and theology with all its ramifications."

9. Even the declared faith has to be recognized by MUIS as Islam. In the case of the Ahmadiyah sect, which is not recognized by MUIS as within the fold of Islam, marriage involving a member of the sect cannot be solemnized by ROMM.

10. The idea of consensus itself is not sanctioned by any institution or legislative body. Rather, it refers to ideas of dominant scholars.

11. Interview was conducted in September 2006 at MUIS.

12. Tahir Mahmood (1978, p. 47).

13. These arguments are reflected in Tahir Mahmood (1978, pp. 42–61).

14. This unreported Syariah Court judgement was referred to in Ahmad Ibrahim, "Marriage of Muslims with non-Muslims", *Malayan Law Journal*, March 1965, p. xvi.

15. Qardawi's prohibition was aimed at achieving certain social ends which, in his opinion, benefit the Muslims. Yet his views are presented as theological injunction which has the effect of denying the right of the individual to marriage with a *kitabiyah*.

16. Refer to Singapore Parliament, Select Committee Proceedings on the AMLA, 18 April 1966, pp. 69–70.

17. Interview conducted in September 2006 at MUIS.

18. These examples were highlighted in an interview I conducted with officials from the Office of the Mufti in September 2006 at MUIS.

19. To the best of my knowledge, there has not been any contested case of this nature heard by the High Court.

20. Mohamed Ismail bin Ibrahim and Another v Mohammad Taha bin Ibrahim (2004), <http://lwbl.lawnet.com.sg>. The practice was also

confined to isolated Muslim communities and lacked robust reasoning.

21. Section 18 of the WC allows any person who objects to the issue of a certificate for marriage to lodge a caveat with the Registrar after notice of marriage is posted up in the Registry of Marriage.

22. See for instance the work by Fyzee (1963, pp. 84–115); El Fadl (2001, pp. 170–88); Engineer (1999); An-Naim (1998, pp. 222–38).

23. Refer for instance to the dicta expressed in the Syariah Appeal Case of Jamaludin bin Mohd Ibrahim (SYC No. 11/1993) where the judge maintains that on the basis of established principles of Islamic law, a mother is disqualified from custody of her child if she has apostatized. The Board however did not make a judgement on this ground of preferential right of custody as the issue for determination in this case was on the Syariah Court's powers to vary a consent order agreement within the meaning of section 52(3)(c) of the AMLA as it existed then.

24. One cannot change traditionalists' view of the law but the law should allow parties to be free from dominant views if they so choose.

References

Abdur Rahim. *The Principles of Muhammedan Jurisprudence According to Hanafi, Maliki, Shafie and Hanbali Schools*. Lahore: All Pakistan Legal Decisions, 1963.

Administration of Muslim Law Act (Chapter 3). Singapore: Singapore Government Printer, 1999.

Ahmad Ibrahim. "Marriages of Muslims with Non-Muslims". *Malayan Law Journal* (March 1965): xvi–xvii.

———. "The Distribution of Estates According to Shafii Law". *Malayan Law Journal*, 1976.

An-Naim, Abdullahi A. "Sharia and Basic Human Rights". In *Liberal Islam: A Source Book*, edited by Charles Kurzman. New York: Oxford University Press, 1998.

———, ed. *Interreligious Marriages Among Muslims: Negotiating Religious and Social Identity in Family and Community.* New Delhi: Global Media Publications, 2005.

Balasundram, Reddy. "Marriage of the Muslim Women and the Women's Charter". *Law Times* (1977): 17–20.

Bartholomew, G.W. "The Application of Shariah in Singapore". *The American Journal of Comparative Law* 13, no. 3 (1964): 384–413.

Daw, Rowena. "Some Problems in Conflict of Law in West Malaysia and Singapore's Family Law". *Malaya Law Review* 14, no. 2 (1972): 179–208.

El Fadl, Khaled Abou. *Speaking in God's Name: Islamic Law, Authority and Women.* Oxford: One World, 2001.

Engineer, Ali Asghar. *The Quran, Women and Modern Society.* New Delhi: Sterling Publishers, 1999.

Fyzee, Asaf. *A Modern Approach to Islam.* Asia Publishing House, 1963.

Hickling, R.H. "Conversion and the Kitabia in Malaysia". *Jernal Undang-Undang* (1979): 55–70.

<http://lwbl.lawnet.com.sg>.

Mannheim, Karl. *Ideology and Utopia.* London: Kegan Paul, 1946.

———. "Conservative Thought". In *Essays on Sociology and Social Psychology.* London: Routledge, 1966.

"Mixed Marriages in Israel". *Journal of Palestinian Studies* 1, no. 4 (Summer 1972): 966.

Muslim Religious Council of Singapore (MUIS). *Warita*, March–May. Singapore: MUIS, 1977.

———. *Kumpulan Fatwa.* Singapore: MUIS, 1991.

Noor Aisha Abdul Rahman. "Traditionalism and its Impact on the Administration of Justice: The Case of the Syariah Court of Singapore". *Inter-Asia Cultural Studies* 3, no. 3 (2004): 415–32.

———. "Changing Roles, Unchanging Institutions: Traditionalism and Its Impact on Women and Globalization in Muslim Societies in Asia". *The Muslim World* 97, no. 3 (2007): 479–508.

Qardhawi, Yusuf. *Halal dan Haram Dalam Islam.* Singapore: Himpunan Belia Islam Singapura (Muslim Youth Assembly), 1980.

Ramadan, Said. *Islamic Law: Its Scope and Equity.* London: Macmillan, 1970.

Shaharuddin Maaruf. "Some Theoretical Problems Concerning Tradition and Modernization among the Malays of SEA". In *Asian Traditions and Modernization*, edited by Yong Mun Cheong. Singapore: Times Academic Press, 1992.

———. "The Social Sciences in SEA: Sociology of Anti-Sociology and Alienated Social Sciences". In *Reflections on Alternative Discourse in SEA*, edited by Syed Farid Alatas. Singapore: ISA Regional Conference, 1998.

Singapore Parliament. Select Committee of the Administration of Muslim Law Act, 1966.

Tahir Mahmood. *Muslim Personal Law: Role of the State in the Subcontinent*. New Delhi: Vikas Publishing, 1977.

———. *Civil Marriage Law: Perspectives and Prospects*. Bombay: N.M. Tripathi Pte Ltd, 1978.

Towler, Robert. *The Need for Certainty: A Sociological Study of Conventional Religion*. London: Routledge, 1984.

Tyabji, Faiz Badruddin. *Principles of Muhammedan Law*. London: Law Publishers, 1919.

Wee Kim-Seng, Kenneth. "Family Law". *Malaya Law Review*. Singapore: University of Singapore, 1976.

INDEX

A

Abdullah Badawi, 63, 225
Ayah Pin, of sky kingdom, 72, 90

C

Cairo Declaration on Human
    Rights in Islam, 9, 14–15
Central Islamic Committee of
    Thailand, 195
Centre for Strategic and
    International Studies (CSIS),
    152–53
Chinese converts, 24, 221
Christianization programme,
    110, 150–52
Compilation of Islamic Law
    (CIL), 8–9, 122–23, 130,
    146–47, 154–55, 255–57,
    264, 279
Counter Legal Draft (CLD), 155,
    256–57, 279

D

Dutch Civil Code, 103–05

F

Federation of Malaya, 6

G

Golongan Karya (GOLKAR), 153

H

Hertogh, Maria, 2, 92

I

India
    Special Marriage Act 1954, 12–
    13, 294
Indonesia
    Civil Registration Office (KCS),
    39–40, 42, 44, 107, 118
    differences in government
    bureaucracy, 39–40
    interfaith marriage, 34–43,
    121–29, 148–56
    marriage and conversion, 10–
    11
    separation of marriage
    registries, 106

Indonesia Ulama Council (MUI),
8, 20, 22, 122, 140, 143,
147, 264, 271, 273
decree on interfaith marriage,
144–46
formation, 280n
Interethnic marriage, 220–23,
226–36
coping mechanisms, 241–43
integration strategies, 233–41,
244
Inter-Faith Council (IFC), 89–91
Islam, as humane religion, 259–60
Islam, as religion of Malaysia
Federation, 64, 86, 88, 92
Islam Hadhari, 226
Islamic family law, 6, 17, 86
Islamic Law reforms, 65–66
Islamic Party of Malaysia (PAS),
62, 89, 223–26, 229–30
Islamic Religious Council, 66
Islamic tradition on interfaith
marriage 140–43
Islamic University of
Paramadina, 3, 124
Islamization movement, 60–64
Islamization, spread through the
rule of law, 67–72, 94
Islam, view on interreligious
marriage, 260–69

K
Kaum Muda, 5
Kitabiyah, definition, 296–301

M
Mahathir Mohamad, 63, 224–25
Majelis Ulama Indonesia (MUI),
see Indonesia Ulama Council
Majlis Ugama Islam Singapura
(MUIS), 25, 286, 302, 307
Malay-Islam identity, 69–70, 220
Malay nationalist movement, 2
Malaysia
marriage and conversion, 10–
11, 221, 227–36, 245
post-independence
developments, 5–7
prohibition of cross-religious
marriage, 72–74
Malay special privileges, 16
Marriage Law, of Indonesia, 108–
20
differences in government
bureaucracy, 39–40
discontinuation of civil
marriages, 119–20, 131
interpretation of mixed
marriages, 170, 182
legal vacuum on interfaith
marriage, 47–52, 118
marriage contract, 41
multiple marriage laws, 104–06
position on interfaith
marriage, 43
segregation of religious groups,
42
under colonial heritage, 103–
05

Melaka Laws, 6
Minangkabau identity, 163, 179–
    82
  Christianization, 168–69, 176
  integration of Islamic law,
    166–67, 177–79
  interreligious marriage, 170
  leaving Islam, 179–80
  matrilineal aspect, 164–66,
    173, 176
  mixed marriage, 171–81
Mixed Marriage Regulation, 105,
    107–08, 114–17
Muhammadiyah, 22, 122, 140, 143
  decree on interfaith marriage,
    145–46
  paramilitary wing, 149

N
Nahdlatul Ulama (NU), 22
  fatwa on interreligious
    marriage, 122, 140, 143–44
  formation, 143
New Economic Policy (NEP), 61,
    220
New Order, 36, 149, 153–54

O
Office of Religious Affairs (KUA),
    39–40, 42, 44, 106–07, 118,
    124, 127, 130

P
Pancasila, 15, 271

Paramadina University, see
    Islamic University of
    Paramadina
People of the Book, see Kitabiyah
Philippines, 9–10

R
Rukunegara, 15–16

S
Singapore
  laws governing Muslim
    marriage, 283–87
  provisions for interreligious
    marriages, 13, 25, 288
  rights to inheritance, 302–03
Southeast Asia
  historical perspective, 4–5
  Islam as practised in, 16
  Islamic reform movement, 4
  under colonial regime, 4–5
Syariah Court, of Malaysia
  as sole judicial institution on
    Islam, 76, 79–80, 82, 84
  jurisdiction to dissolve cross-
    religious marriage, 86, 88
  matters on apostasy, 75–77, 80
Syariah Islamists, 66–67, 89–92

T
Thailand, 9–10
  interfaith marriage in south,
    24, 191, 193–97, 203–04,
    206–11

Khaek, broad reference to
    foreigners, 198–200, 205–
    06, 210
Khao Khaek, conversion to
    Muslim, 200–01, 205–06
marriage and conversion, 10–
    11, 191, 193–96, 198,
    201–09
marriage with westerners, 209–
    10
Muslim marriage ceremony,
    204
population by faith, 191–92

Traditionalism, as style of
    thought, 287–92, 306–07
on interreligious marriage,
    292–94, 298, 301, 304–05
Turkey
    New Turkish Civil Code, 13

U
United Malays National
    Organisation (UMNO), 61–
    62, 223, 226
Universal Declaration on Human
    Rights, 9, 14, 38, 79, 128

www.ingramcontent.com/pod-product-compliance
Lightning Source LLC
Chambersburg PA
CBHW021543260326
41914CB00001B/147